THE COMPLETE IDIOT'S GUIDE® TO

WITHDRAWN

Evangelical Christianity

by David Cobia

D1200970

ALPHA

A member of Penguin Group (USA) Inc.

ALPHA BOOKS

Published by the Penguin Group

Penguin Group (USA) Inc., 375 Hudson Street, New York, New York 10014, U.S.A.

Penguin Group (Canada), 10 Alcorn Avenue, Toronto, Ontario, Canada M4V 3B2 (a division of Pearson Penguin Canada Inc.)

Penguin Books Ltd, 80 Strand, London WC2R 0RL, England

Penguin Ireland, 25 St Stephen's Green, Dublin 2, Ireland (a division of Penguin Books Ltd)

Penguin Group (Australia), 250 Camberwell Road, Camberwell, Victoria 3124, Australia (a division of Pearson Australia Group Pty Ltd)

Penguin Books India Pvt Ltd, 11 Community Centre, Panchsheel Park, New Delhi—110 017, India

Penguin Group (NZ), cnr Airborne and Rosedale Roads, Albany, Auckland 1310, New Zealand (a division of Pearson New Zealand Ltd)

Penguin Books (South Africa) (Pty) Ltd, 24 Sturdee Avenue, Rosebank, Johannesburg 2196, South Africa

Penguin Books Ltd, Registered Offices: 80 Strand, London WC2R 0RL, England

Copyright © 2007 by David Cobia

International Standard Book Number: 978-1-59-257586-2
Library of Congress Catalog Card Number: 2006936693

09 08 07   8 7 6 5 4 3 2 1

Interpretation of the printing code: The rightmost number of the first series of numbers is the year of the book's printing; the rightmost number of the second series of numbers is the number of the book's printing. For example, a printing code of 07-1 shows that the first printing occurred in 2007.

Printed in the United States of America

Publisher: *Marie Butler-Knight*
Editorial Director: *Mike Sanders*
Managing Editor: *Billy Fields*
Senior Acquisitions Editor: *Paul Dinas*
Development Editor: *Michael Thomas*
Senior Production Editor: *Janette Lynn*
Copy Editor: *Jennifer Connolly*

Cartoonist: *Richard King*
Cover Designer: *Bill Thomas*
Book Designer: *Trina Wurst*
Indexer: *Tonya Heard*
Layout: *Brian Massey*
Proofreader: *Aaron Black*

This book is dedicated to my wife Dee, in appreciation for her constant friendship and loving support; and to my children, Josh, Lindsey, and Brendan—who I pray and believe will carry the light to the next generation.

Contents at a Glance

Contents

Appendixes

Introduction

"Do you *really* believe that a loving God would send people to hell?"

I must have heard that question a thousand times. Along with it, I've been in conversations where people (sometimes quite animatedly!) vehemently disagreed with the "standard" evangelical positions on everything from pre-marital sex to euthanasia. And every time I have a conversation like that, it changes me.

Over the years, I've come to have a great respect for people who are asking good questions and won't settle for pat answers. I've seen people express deep, soul-wrenching, heartfelt desires for a connection with God that makes sense—of their worlds and of their lives. And I've heard lots of questions, such as ...

- If God is good, why do people suffer?

- Aren't all religions basically the same?

- Is the Bible really reliable?

- Doesn't Christianity conflict with science?

- Is God a prude?

- What about unanswered prayer?

- Don't Christians think women and gays are inferior?

- Do we really need religion to be spiritual?

- Why do Christians think everyone has to think and vote like they do?

- Is Jesus the *only* way?

These are good questions, and they deserve honest and thoughtful dialogue. Often, we evangelicals are the reason that doesn't happen. In our desire to persuade, we often short-change the conversation process. In our passion to help people see some beautiful things that we have discovered, we reduce those things to sound-bites (ironically, so that people can get the "whole gospel") or are so passionate about what we share that people feel like they're trying to take a drink from a fire hose. We need to be more respectful. (Not to mention empathetic.)

In the conversations I've had around these and a myriad of other issues, I've also seen that most people who are not evangelicals really don't understand the evangelical Christian point of view—*although they think they do*. They have accepted the sound-bites. They have let unfortunate experiences with over-zealous individuals stop them from continuing to seek. They go to a movie or read a book (fiction, no less!) that calls into question the validity of the Bible, and they believe it. They need to ask more questions.

Evangelicals are very, very guilty of tunnel-vision about their own beliefs, but so are those who are not evangelicals. It's time for a good, thoughtful, honest conversation. That is what this book is about.

Full Disclosure

If I am to guide this conversation, it's important that you understand who you're talking to. So in the interest of giving you the context from which I write (so that you can keep in mind the biases that come with it), here's my story.

I became a Christian when I was about 12 years old. When I say, "became a Christian," I mean that when I was twelve, I had an experience of personal conversion. I made a volitional commitment to follow Jesus. It happened through my sister, who was in college at the time, and had experienced a conversion herself. When I saw her life, and especially when I saw the quality of her relationships with her Christian friends, it was something I wanted, too.

Since that time, I have tried to continue to follow Jesus. Sometimes I've done better in that, and often done worse. At this point in my life, having gone to college, graduate school, gotten married, had children, and pursued a first career in communications, I am now in a second career as a pastor. (I've been in church work now nearly 15 years.)

Since I was twelve, I've been more or less immersed in evangelical culture, but have always felt more like an observer than a participant in much of it. Perhaps it comes from growing up in a nonevangelical household (except for my sister, who was already living away at college); perhaps it comes from being a natural skeptic. I don't know. But at age 45, I've matured enough to have a great appreciation for my evangelical heritage, even in my skepticism about some of it (particularly the way it often gets expressed in our current culture). So that is one of my biases.

Another bias comes from being a pastor at a unique evangelical church. The church where I now serve is more postmodern than modern in its sensibilities (see Chapters 19–20 to understand that statement fully), though much of my background in church work has been more "modern." As a matter of fact, I was in at the forefront of the "seeker church" movement in Evangelicalism, serving in several very innovative churches in that pinnacle of the "modern" church expression. Now, however, I am "seeking" a bit of a different path, still fully evangelical in my beliefs, but looking for a new way to express that in the postmodern world. So, as a postmodern (some would say post-evangelical) evangelical, by definition I carry a second bias that is important for you to understand in reading this book.

Although I have many other biases as well, I'm not sure we have the space (or you have the inclination) to have them all explained here. Just remember as you read that you have biases, too.

How to Get the Most from This Book

This book is broken into five parts, and the way you read it should depend on your own needs.

Part 1, "Keeping the Faith: The Story of Evangelicalism," traces the history of Evangelicalism. You may be skeptical of this next statement, but believe me: the history is quite fascinating. If you want to see how Evangelicalism got to where it is today, or if you enjoy a good story, you'll want to read this section. Knowing the history of the movement sets us up for Part 2 …

Part 2, "Believe It or Not: A Survey of Evangelical Theology," looks into the basic theological beliefs of evangelical Christianity. Here is where you'll find the answers to many of the questions I've listed previously, from "Is the Bible really trustworthy?" to "Is Jesus the *only* way?" This is a great section for you if you have questions, and want to see how what you think lines up with what evangelical Christians believe. It's also a good "theology 101" primer for those of you seeking to understand what C. S. Lewis called *Mere Christianity*—the basic core of Christian belief. As you read this part, I encourage you to stop and reflect often. What do you really believe?

Part 3, "What Would Jesus Do? Evangelical Hot Buttons," looks at the "hot buttons" of evangelical practices in the modern world, and the beliefs behind them. This is great for those of you seeking to understand why an evangelical friend or relative acts like they do, or for those of you seeking to understand the basic evangelical point of view on these issues where evangelicals seem very different from the world around them.

Part 4, "Mission Possible: The Cultural Impact of Evangelicalism," traces the cultural impact of evangelicals. From the rise of the Christian right, to the rise of "Christian rock," to the story of several highly influential megachurches and organizations, this part will help those of you who want to understand more fully the importance of Evangelicalism in today's culture.

Part 5, "The Future of Evangelicalism: The 'Emergent' Church," looks at the future of the movement. Nothing less than a seismic shift is taking place in Evangelicalism today, as the postmodern generation begins to put its stamp on the movement. If you've been hearing about the "emerging" church, and want a quick primer on it, this part is for you.

Extras

Along the way, you'll find sidebars sprinkled throughout the text to add even more interest and info to your journey.

> ### The Gospel Truth
>
> Little-known facts that clear up misconceptions with regard to Evangelicalism.

> ### def•i•ni•tion
>
> Definitions of theological or evangelical cultural terminology.

> ### In Their Own Words
>
> Quotes from evangelicals (or others) that add depth and color to the issue being discussed.

> ### Culture Clash!
>
> Often tongue-in-cheek, these are tips on how to deal with potentially sensitive subjects or issues in Evangelicalism, or how to spark good conversations between evangelicals and non-evangelicals.

Don't Forget the Appendixes!

In particular, the "In Their Own Words" appendix is a key part of this book. There is possibly no better way to understand Evangelicalism than through the stories of those who are living it. As a matter of fact, you may even want to read them first if you need more context from which to engage in the rest of the book.

Also, the "For Further Study" appendix not only includes a listing of resources, but I've included comments on each of the works listed to help you choose how to continue your journey of exploration.

A Word on Language and Scope

In writing about two very broad subjects—Evangelicalism (very broad) and God (very, very, very broad)—one ends up having to make choices about language that do not always portray the preciseness of actuality. For instance, I do not believe that God has a gender in the way we understand male and female. However, I do see that the Bible uses a male pronoun to refer to God, so I have chosen to do so as well.

Also, it is important to note that in this book I have focused in almost exclusively on American Evangelicalism. This does not mean that American Evangelicalism is the only kind—in fact, from a global perspective, most scholars believe that the "center of gravity" of Evangelicalism is clearly shifting from the United States to the Southern Hemisphere. However, the history of the movement has had much to do with the United States up to this point, and that is the focus of this book.

Further, American Evangelicalism (as you will see) is extremely diverse. In speaking for American evangelicals as a whole, I have often had to generalize in order to explain what is the most prevalent belief or practice defining the movement. I recognize that there are many evangelicals who do not believe some of the specifics in any given arena (especially the social issues) that I've written about. However, I do feel confident that where I've generalized, the generalization holds true for the majority of the movement. Further, I have not written as much about charismatic evangelical theology as I have about theology that covers all of Evangelicalism, charismatic or not. Again, this was a studied choice made in order to keep the scope of the book consistent with an overview of the entire movement.

A Note on Bible Resources

Unless otherwise noted, all scriptures are taken from the New International Version of the Bible (NIV).

Scriptures taken from the Holy Bible, New International Version © (NIV) are used by permission. Copyright © 1973, 1978, 1984 International Bible Society. All rights reserved throughout the world. Used by permission of International Bible Society.

Scripture quotations taken from the New American Standard Bible © (NASB), copyright © 1960, 1962, 1963, 1968, 1971, 1972, 1973, 1975, 1977, 1995 by The Lockman Foundation, are used by permission. (www.Lockman.org)

Scriptures taken from the New King James Version (NKJV), copyright © 1982 by Thomas Nelson, Inc., are used by permission. All rights reserved.

Scripture quotations taken from the Holy Bible, New Living Translation (NLT), copyright 1996, are used by permission of Tyndale House Publishers, Inc., Wheaton, Illinois 60189. All rights reserved.

Scriptures taken from *The Message*. Copyright © 1993, 1994, 1995, 1996, 2000, 2001, 2002, are used by permission of NavPress Publishing Group.

Quotation from *Inside the Mind of Unchurched Harry and Mary*, copyright © 1993. Used by permission of Zondervan, Grand Rapids, Michigan. All rights reserved.

You Can't Have a One-Way Conversation

Since the whole purpose of this book is not just to inform and inspire, but also to spark conversation, my final suggestion to you is that as you read it, you engage in conversation with someone about it. Preferably, someone with a different point of view than your own. And if you want to converse with a 45-year-old sort-of-post-modern-pastor-who-used-to-not-be-a-pastor, you can always e-mail me through my church's website: www.baymarin.org.

Let the conversation begin!

Acknowledgments

My thanks to Paul Dinas of Alpha Books, whose vision was responsible for this project coming about, and whose patient and thoughtful advice along the way have been essential to the final product. Also to Judy Mikalonis and Andrea Hurst, who suggested I do this, have been my cheerleaders along the way, and have given me a great gift in the process.

Michael Thomas and Jennifer Connolly gently guided me to much better expression than I could ever have come up with in many cases; my thanks go out to them for their superb editing skills.

Most importantly, I want to thank my family for the lost hours when I was in my "cave" writing. I am especially grateful and indebted to my wife Dee, who took up the slack for me so many times and in too many ways to count (*how did you fix that screen door, anyway?*). You are more gracious than you'll ever know. It is a joy to live with you.

Trademarks

All terms mentioned in this book that are known to be or are suspected of being trademarks or service marks have been appropriately capitalized. Alpha Books and Penguin Group (USA) Inc. cannot attest to the accuracy of this information. Use of a term in this book should not be regarded as affecting the validity of any trademark or service mark.

Part 1

Keeping the Faith: The Story of Evangelicalism

The best starting point for understanding modern Evangelicalism is understanding the rich story of how it came to be. The story of the evangelical movement in the United States is surprisingly diverse and engrossing—a unique reflection of the American spirit, and the picture of an entrepreneurial social force.

This section also traces the human foibles and in-fighting of a movement that has no defined authoritative structure. Its cross-denominational structure and numerical power create a high-stakes atmosphere as various ideologies vie for dominance in the movement at various points in its history.

Most importantly, in this section you'll meet some of the leaders who define this movement. Through their extraordinary commitment to their mission you'll see the steadfast personal devotion that lies beneath their ultimate personal call: keeping the faith.

Chapter 1

What Is Evangelicalism?

In This Chapter

- ◆ What is an evangelical?
- ◆ How many people are evangelicals?
- ◆ Where do the beliefs of evangelicals come from?
- ◆ Are evangelicals fundamentalists?

On February 2, 2006, U2 front man and international celebrity Bono showed up in a very unusual place: he was the featured speaker at the annual National Prayer Breakfast in Washington, D.C.

Bono—the ultimate rock and roll "god"—sitting at the same podium as George W. Bush—the president whose relationship with God has created more controversy than an evangelical at a Marilyn Manson concert. Strange bedfellows. It was a surreal moment. Bono began his remarks by saying, "Please join me in praying that I don't say something we'll all regret."

It was quintessential Evangelicalism.

The reach and diversity of this movement is astounding. Its co-opting of popular culture is consistent. Its ability to provide common ground to quite different lifestyles is surprising. And as a result, it is notoriously difficult to define succinctly. In this chapter, you will find an overview of this incredibly influential movement that brings together conservative presidents with bohemian iconoclasts.

From Bono to Bush

Estimates vary, but there are somewhere around two billion Christians in the world (out of six billion people on the planet), about half a billion of whom have been identified as "evangelicals." (Which explains how all those car fish-sticker guys stay in business.) Thus, about one in every ten people subscribes to some of the beliefs, lifestyles, and culture that this book describes.

From the fictional Ned Flanders (Homer Simpson's evangelical cartoon neighbor), whose goofy behavior reflects much that is real, to Britney Spears, whose claim of religiously motivated virginity proved to be—well, ... let's just say, "suspect,"—the reputation of evangelicals or supposed evangelicals is not stellar. One recent survey showed that evangelicals are disliked more than any other population sector with the exception of prostitutes. The very public fall of televangelists in recent years, and the number of "God hates fags" pictures in the newspapers, point to the unfortunate truth of some of the stereotypes.

> ## In Their Own Words
>
> "We've been away at Christian camp. We're learning how to be more judgmental."
> —Ned Flanders, the fictional evangelical neighbor of Homer Simpson on *The Simpsons*

However, as with all stereotypes, the reality is much more complex and much less dramatic. For every evangelical holding up a poster of hate speech, there are those who abhor it. For every evangelical misogynist, there are those who champion the rights of women. For every judgmental comment, there are evangelicals sacrificially opening their wallets and emptying their pockets to give graciously to those in need. For every evangelical campaigning to take certain books out of the schools, there is another one fighting for free speech and artistic expression. In other words, evangelicals are just like the rest of our culture—a mixture of the good and bad that is common to all of humanity. Perhaps one difference is that evangelicals are a bit more aware of that mixture—especially within themselves.

According to pollster George Barna, 96 percent of evangelicals in America describe themselves as "deeply spiritual" as compared to the national average of 61 percent.

Barna reports that they are more likely than any other "faith segment" (including other Christians, adherents of other faiths, and atheists/agnostics) to …

- ♦ Discuss spiritual matters with other people.

- ♦ Volunteer at a church or nonprofit organization.

- ♦ Discuss political matters with other people.

- ♦ Discuss moral issues and conditions with others.

- ♦ Stop watching a television program because of its values or viewpoints.

- ♦ Go out of their way to encourage or compliment someone.

Estimates of the number of evangelicals in the United States vary. A 2005 Gallup poll reported that up to 42 percent of the population of Americans self-identify as evangelical. However, if the same people are asked specific questions that would define them as evangelical by their beliefs, the number drops dramatically according to Gallup, to about 22 percent. Evangelical pollster George Barna qualifies the number even further, believing that based on actual beliefs and practices, about 7 percent of the population can be considered evangelical. Of that approximately 14–16 million American evangelicals, Barna reports that 31 percent are college graduates (the national average is about 21 percent), 77 percent are married, 85 percent are white, 84 percent are registered to vote, and 58 percent live outside of the South.

Most evangelicals attend church (spread across nearly every denomination, including Catholics), many of them attend the "megachurches" that have weekly attendances of up to 30,000 (see Chapter 18). Evangelicals have gained an important measure of cultural power in the past few years, as evidenced by everything from presidential elections to the vast success of movies, television shows, and books that are in sync with evangelical values. In 2003, megachurch Pastor Rick Warren's book, *The Purpose Driven Life*, sold more copies in a single year than any previous nonfiction book in history.

All of this adds up to a vast subculture, but not a monolithic one. Evangelicals come from all walks of life—white collar and blue collar, male and female, all races, and all ages. There are hundreds of different evangelical denominations. There are supporters of war, and committed pacifists; there are Democrats, Republicans, and Independents.

Evangelical scholar Mark Noll's research shows that over ⅓ of evangelicals are not militantly pro-life, and favor increased rights for homosexuals. Half of all evangelicals favor aggressive government policies on environmentalism and the fight against

In Their Own Words

"God's politics reminds us of the people our politics always neglects—the poor, the vulnerable, the left behind. God's politics challenges narrow national, ethnic, economic, or cultural self-interest ..."

—Evangelical author and activist Jim Wallis, in his 2005 book, *God's Politics*

poverty. About the same number support the idea of national health insurance. Indeed, there is a growing "liberal" political presence among the evangelical movement, developing under the radar much like the conservative presence that moved Evangelicalism from being primarily Democrat to primarily Republican in the last generation.

Further, a brand new generation of evangelicals are coming of age with very different agendas from the baby boomers who preceded them. They are starting culturally postmodern churches (often called "emerging" churches), and are questioning not only the cultural and political practices of their forbearers, but are (perhaps more importantly) blazing new theological trails. As you will see in the later chapters of this book, these new leaders are charting a course for modern Evangelicalism that is strikingly similar in its history to the emergence of modern Evangelicalism out of Fundamentalism after World War II.

Theological Streams of Evangelicalism

Even though there is surprising diversity in Evangelicalism, it is the similarities that define the movement. And for the most part, these similarities, whether they are personal, cultural, or political, arise from a common set of beliefs that distinguish evangelicals from the culture at large. These theological distinctives, which form the ethos of modern Evangelicalism, have primarily evolved from three major theological "streams." Understanding those historical streams is an important part of understanding the modern evangelical mind-set.

Puritanism

The first stream of beliefs from which modern Evangelicalism emerged is Puritanism. Puritanism was a reform movement originating during the English Reformation of the 16th century, when the church of England split from the Catholic church. The Puritans sought to reform the Church of England even further—to "purify" it not only from the abuses of Catholicism, but also from the secularistic tendencies of its connection to the English monarchy. This desire for an overall purity within the English church's leadership structure and practices eventually expanded into an impulse toward radical individual purity on the part of church members, and the purification of the rest of society as well.

Historically, the Puritans achieved some measure of political success in England, but eventually fell from power. During the early 1600s, two Puritan groups grew frustrated to the point of separating from England entirely, and founded two colonies in America as "pilgrims" (the Plymouth Colony, and the Massachusetts Bay Colony). Their influence as founders in America went beyond the political and cultural to their spiritual beliefs. Thus, long after the first Puritan settlements were gone, their spiritual influence was still prospering.

Puritanism can be summarized by four major beliefs, all of which can still be seen in evangelical theology today.

First of all, Puritans believed in a personal salvation that comes entirely from God. They believed in the Augustinian doctrine of *original sin*—or the idea that fallen humans are not only unwilling, but unable on their own to relate righteously to a perfectly holy God. According to the Puritans, God alone—not human effort—is able to give humans both the desire and ability to turn to Him for forgiveness. God calls; humans answer.

def•i•ni•tion

Original sin refers to the doctrine, held by many evangelicals, that human beings are born into the "curse" of sin (passed down through Adam and Eve's disobedience in the Garden of Eden), and are thus bound to sin. The capacity to overcome sin is only given by God's grace, and only actualized in part in this life.

Secondly, Puritans held the Bible in extremely high regard. So high, in fact, that they came to believe that Christians should do *only* what the Bible commanded, particularly in public worship services. Anglicans (those in the Church of England), on the other hand, believed that Christians were free in worship, as long as they *not* doing something the Bible *prohibited*. While linguistically subtle, this was a quite profound difference on an everyday, practical level. It led the Puritans to important distinctions in their lifestyles and worship practices, much of which gained them their reputation for being, well, puritanical.

Third, the Puritans believed that the church should be organized according to scriptural principles, and that no other organizing principles, no matter how pragmatically helpful, should be utilized. These beliefs (and theological arguments they produced) were an important part of the development of congregational polity that is key to evangelical churches today.

And fourth, the Puritans believed that the Bible sanctioned a form of social, political, and theological government that was to be under the auspices of a single set of authorities. In other words, they believed that all of society should be "Christian"— and "Christian" on their terms. Although the dangers of this point of view are obvious to the modern observer, it provided a comprehensive, socially conscious vision at the beginning of America that has proven foundational to much of the ultimately charitable character of the country.

It's easy to see the strains of modern Evangelicalism—for good and for bad—in the Puritan mindset. Perhaps the most important and lasting contribution it made was a certain kind of theological emphasis and method, often known as "Reformation theology," which became the doctrinal foundation for most of the modern evangelical church. The "Westminster Confession and Catechisms," precise reformation theology statements of faith based on the Bible, grew out of the Puritan reformation and was produced in 1647–1648. These documents are even today the basis of the majority of formal evangelical church "creeds" (statements of theological belief)—particularly the Presbyterian and Baptist churches of today. But Puritanism is only one of the primary streams that formed into the modern evangelical river.

Pietism

As opposed to the Puritans, who focused on the propositional (i.e., precise, Bible-based theology) to develop their spiritual lives, Pietists emphasized the experiential as key. They were less concerned about the structures and scholastic doctrines of Christian living, and more focused on the individual's personal experiences with Christ.

Pietism was founded in Germany, primarily by two men, Philipp Jakob Spencer, and August Hermann Francke. It was born in the late 1600s, and came out of the frustration produced by the political and cultural climate of a region plagued by rancor and the Thirty Years War (1618–1648). As with Puritanism, Pietism can be summarized by four basic tenants.

First of all, Pietism focused more on the individual experience of Christian living than the cognitive emphasis of Reformation-style theology. At their heart, Pietists were people whose primary concern was spiritual devotion and a resulting warm-hearted lifestyle.

This lifestyle represents the second, and perhaps most unique, Pietistic distinctive. Pietists tend toward a perfectionism in moral behavior. This is a good impulse in that it is evidenced by a very strong commitment to holy living, serving those in need, and spreading the gospel. It has proven to be a bad influence when Pietistically influenced evangelical movements through history have tried to convince people that they can live so close to Christ that they can be (and thus should strive to be) virtually without sin.

Third, Pietists shared with the Puritans a reverence for the Bible. Their standards of holy living, and their missionary zeal to help others and spread the gospel, comes directly from the pages of scripture. This emphasis on individual, devotional commitment to scripture is clearly seen in modern Evangelicalism.

> **In Their Own Words**
>
> "When the inner spirit is liberated from all that weighs it down, it can hardly be described as dull drudgery. Singing, dancing, even shouting characterize the Disciplines of the spiritual life."
>
> —Modern-day Quaker Richard Foster in *Celebration of Discipline*, explaining the experience of engaging in spiritual disciplines, and displaying the modern Pietistic leanings in Evangelicalism

Fourth, the Pietists had a propensity to adaptation. They would oppose cold and formal religious expression in favor of contemporized, culturally relevant forms that they would often produce in response to the needs around them. John Wesley's emphasis on spiritual growth through small groups of people meeting regularly to hold one another accountable (see Chapter 2) is a good example of this kind of cultural innovation.

Pietism, through its adaptable, experiential focus, is the primary theological progenitor of several strains of modern Evangelicalism. The Pentecostal/charismatic movement, with its emphasis on experiential worship (and its use of "speaking in tongues," healings, and other experiential signs of God's presence), can trace its roots back to here. So can churches of the Wesleyan bent (including modern Methodist and Nazarene churches).

The spiritual vitality of Pietism provided fertile ground for the Great Awakenings in the late 1700s and early 1800s (see Chapter 2), both of which were absolutely primary in the development of modern Evangelicalism. Even today, the influence of Pietistic thought is a major contributor to the "spiritual formation" emphasis of many evangelicals, especially many of those in the "emerging church" movement (see Chapter 19).

Fundamentalism

Fundamentalism is often confused with Evangelicalism in current culture. They are not the same. Arriving on the scene much later than Puritanism and Pietism,

Fundamentalism has perhaps had the most influence of all three on modern evangelical belief.

def•i•ni•tion

Modernism is a multifaceted term that is often used in fundamentalist circles to point to a theological tendency toward liberalism (often defined as a lack of respect for the authority of the Bible), and a cultural tendency that moves away from traditional values and toward a more secular mindset.

Born in the early 1900s, Fundamentalism grew out of a reaction to a theological and cultural *modernism* that was taking America by storm at the time. Fundamentalism shares many of the primary theological beliefs of modern Evangelicalism, and was responsible for articulating them in a way that is still characteristic of some circles in Evangelicalism. Fundamentalism and Evangelicalism, in general, share the following tenants:

◆ An emphasis on Jesus' death as the "substitutionary atonement"—the payment for the sin of all humankind.

◆ The need for definite personal conversion on the part of each person.

◆ A strong commitment to the Bible as authoritative.

◆ A social activism born of religious conviction.

However, Fundamentalism is distinguished from Evangelicalism by several important characteristics.

Culture Clash!

If an evangelical friend gets in your car, make sure to have a CD of Amy Grant or Michael W. Smith ready to play. If they're really hip, you can go with U2. If they're really *really* hip, play them some Bruce Cockburn. If a fundamentalist friend gets in the car, don't turn on the radio.

The first difference is the fundamentalist characteristic of separatism. The fundamentalist disposition is to move away from culture, in response to the biblical command to "come out ... and be separate" (II Corinthians 6:17). The evangelical impulse is to interact with culture in a redemptive manner—seeking a critical engagement (i.e., involvement with things that do not cross moral boundaries) that enables them to help cause change for the better. This difference is seen clearly, for instance, in the evangelical willingness to co-opt the form of rock music for Christian purposes—something to which fundamentalists have been very opposed.

The second (and closely related) difference is a more generous attitude in Evangelicalism toward minor theological differences, resulting in a movement with a wider spectrum of beliefs. For instance, evangelicals are more willing to live with scripture as authoritative, but not necessarily "infallible" (i.e., absolutely perfect and without contradiction or error). Thus, questions about whether the book of Genesis teaches that creation occurred in a span of six twenty-four hour days or presents a picture of theistic evolution are more open for evangelicals than for fundamentalists. And whereas fundamentalists often advocate what is sometimes called "second degree separation" (separating themselves from both those who disagree with them and also from those who *work with* those who disagree with them), evangelicals have shown themselves willing to cooperate with a wide spectrum of people and organizations working toward a common goal. (A good example would be when Billy Graham invited Martin Luther King, Jr. to give an invocation at one of his crusades during the height of the American Civil Rights Movement—which fundamentalists fumed about.)

A third point of separation between fundamentalism and Evangelicalism is the higher value evangelicals place on intellectual achievement. While early fundamentalists evidenced a high degree of academic prowess, as the movement progressed its separatism and dogmatism tended to keep it closed-minded. Evangelicals, on the other hand, are more keen to use modern scholarship in pursuit of their supernatural beliefs.

And fourth, evangelicals tend toward a more holistic approach to Christianity. They are more socially conscious, more supportive of the creative arts in modern culture, and in general are more likely to hold to a gospel that is concerned with *being* good news, not just *telling* good news.

As you'll see in Chapters 3 and 4, much of the modern personality of Evangelicalism came out of its struggle to separate itself from Fundamentalism. So in its original tenants and even in its separation, Fundamentalism has had a profound effect on the modern evangelical movement, at least equal to the influences of Puritanism and Pietism.

> ### In Their Own Words
>
> "The church exists to minister to people ... [T]o all kinds of needs: spiritual, emotional, relational, and physical. Jesus said that even a cup of cold water given in his name was considered as ministry ..."
>
> —Rick Warren in *The Purpose Driven Church*

Remixing the Faith

Overall, evangelical theology is a mixture of all three of the traditions of Puritanism, Pietism, and Fundamentalism. Evangelical churches and denominations are a wide spectrum of the mixture of various amounts of one, two, or all three of the traditions—often with a few other things thrown in. The leadership and the people involved in a particular evangelical enterprise are more often the arbiters of the theology than an authoritative creed or body that is "over" them. All of this creates the notorious difficulty of a definitive definition of the term "evangelical."

Interesting (and ironic) is the fact that evangelicals, while having a richly pluralistic background, are not historically affirming of theological pluralism within individual churches or evangelical enterprises. The many different flavors of Evangelicalism we have today have often resulted from splits in the name of maintaining doctrinal integrity or theological balance.

Defining Evangelicalism

So how, then, does one "define" Evangelicalism?

The diversity of the movement has caused many serious scholars to throw in the towel. For example, one tongue-in-cheek definition by an exasperated scholar is that an evangelical is "anyone who admires Billy Graham." Another favorite is "a fundamentalist with better manners." But as is obvious by now, the first is way too broad, and the second way too narrow.

As opposed to succinct definitions, most scholars agree on somewhere around five characteristics that frame Evangelicalism today:

- A focus on the centrality of Jesus' death on the cross as the substitutionary payment for the sins of humankind, and on his bodily resurrection as the confirmation of God's plan in human redemption.

- A belief in the necessity of personal conversion, based on an understanding of the above.

- An emphasis on a transformed life based on personal conversion.

- A passion for social activism based on personal conversion, particularly a high priority on sharing their faith with others.

- A confidence in the authority of the Bible in all of the above.

Some scholars add other things to these distinctives, including specific beliefs about the Trinity, human nature, the church, and the perspectives on the end of time and divine judgment. For the most part, however, the above five characteristics form the beliefs that identify Evangelicalism uniquely (as opposed to other forms of Protestant or Catholic Christianity). Of course, the caveat must always be thrown in (because of the diversity of the movement) that this is a *general* definition—many evangelical enterprises carry specific beliefs or emphases that define them that are not on the previous list (although those specific beliefs are most likely in addition to what is listed previously).

It is important to remember that Evangelicalism is a very loosely connected movement, not a coordinated and specifically structured organization. It has no defined central authority making decisions, and in fact is quite populist in the operations of its various ministries. Indeed, even to speak of it as a "movement" gives a perception of structure that is somewhat misleading. Evangelicalism is a strong coalition at best, a fractured family at worst.

It is also important to recognize the incredible propensity for adaptation that has characterized Evangelicalism from its very foundations. As in their theology, evangelicals consistently mix tradition and innovation in their culture and practices.

You Might Be an Evangelical if ...

Participation in the evangelical world is voluntary and self-selected; some participate in the movement without even affirming all five of its basic characteristics. I like to use the metaphor of a "family resemblance" when describing evangelicals—which is another way of saying that even if they are hard to describe, evangelicals are not so hard to recognize. For instance, you yourself might be an evangelical if ...

- ◆ You love *The Sopranos*, but are afraid to tell anyone.
- ◆ You know what to do when someone shares an "unspoken" prayer request.
- ◆ You're on your third copy of Led Zeppelin's *Houses of the Holy* after burning and then repurchasing the first two.
- ◆ You've ever marched against abortion.
- ◆ You've ever marched for civil rights.
- ◆ You've marched against civil rights.
- ◆ You've ever, *ever* bought a pack of "Testamints."

The Best Definition

In all seriousness, perhaps the best way to describe evangelicals is to go to the very name itself. The word evangelical comes from the Greek word *euangelion*, which is literally translated as "gospel" or "message of good news." Mark 1:15 records Jesus at the beginning of His public ministry saying these words: "The time has come … the kingdom of God is at hand. Repent and believe the good news (*euangelion*)!"

For all their foibles, evangelicals are those who actually believe this. They believe that Jesus came to inaugurate a new in-breaking of God into the world of humans. They believe that the life we all long for at our deepest levels is really possible. They believe that people can change. And they believe that all of this is good news. From presidents to rock stars to everyday people, this "kingdom" is available to all who will respond to the invitation to follow Jesus.

Evangelicals are those who seek to spread that kingdom.

The Least You Need to Know

- Evangelicalism is a large and definite subculture, but not a monolithic one.

- Evangelicalism grew primarily out of three separate theological streams: Puritanism, Pietism, and Fundamentalism.

- In general, evangelicals are more liberal in their lifestyles and open in their theologies than fundamentalists.

- Scholars differ on their precise definition of Evangelicalism, due to the diversity of the movement.

2

Rocking the Ages: The Origins of a Movement

In This Chapter

- ◆ Evangelicalism's roots in pre-revolutionary America
- ◆ The birth of some of the techniques of modern evangelistic crusades (such as those used by modern leaders like Billy Graham)
- ◆ Some fascinating early evangelical leaders
- ◆ The beginnings of the social and political emphasis in Evangelicalism

Evangelicalism as we know it today did not arise out of a vacuum. In fact, events associated with its beginnings became some of the most important events in the cultural history of the United States. Evangelicals throughout the eighteenth and nineteenth centuries were on the forefront of the burgeoning growth of the country. Scholars believe that the "Awakenings" during the eighteenth century, for example, played a strong role in strengthening the lines of communication between the colonies that enabled the cause of American independence.

In the early years of the nation there were many believers, and yet no definable "evangelical" movement. As a result of some of the events and people described in this chapter, however, a movement emerged that had strikingly similar characteristics to what is happening today—over 250 years later—in Evangelicalism.

A look at the start of this movement reveals some of the characteristics, quirks, and heroes that became the seedbed of a modern cultural juggernaut.

The First Great Awakening

The modern evangelical movement in the United States had its beginnings in a unique and unusual moment in history (or in a unique and unusual movement of God, depending on your persuasion). Historians call it "The First Great Awakening." Emerging during the early to mid 1700s, the Awakening was an interconnected series of events that effected a new sense of religious identity among groups that had previously been unconnected. In 1730, there was no evangelical "movement" in America; by 1750 (largely as a result of the ongoing First Great Awakening), there was.

Powered by a spontaneous and fresh sense of the message of the "new birth," the Great Awakening was centered primarily in the work of three men. Their unique leadership capabilities combined with their particular time in history to form the heart, the head, and the feet of Evangelicalism in the United States. Their stories point out an enduring legacy that anticipates much of the current evangelical impact on the contemporary world.

George Whitfield

When George Whitfield was brought before a group of five Anglican clergymen in Boston in September of 1740, he was already a quite famous, innovative, and consequently controversial figure. It was the eve of one of his most powerful public crusades—a new form of evangelism that had raised the eyebrows of quite a few of the religious traditionalists of the day.

In defending himself and his methods to his contemporaries, Whitfield said, "It was best to preach the new birth, and the power of godliness, and not to insist so much on the form: for people would never be brought to one mind as to that; nor did Jesus Christ ever intend it."

In that one statement, Whitfield laid out two very important characteristics of Evangelicalism that still hold true today: an emphasis on personal conversion, and a willingness to innovate. Pioneering new forms of religious expression has been a hallmark (for better and for worse) of Evangelicalism ever since.

Whitfield's part in the Great Awakening had its impetus in 1733, when he joined with four of his fellow students at Oxford in England, in what was maligned by other students as "The Holy Club." The founder of the club, a young man by the name of John Wesley, had suggested some reading material to Whitfield, who through it became convinced of his need for a "new birth" experience. Whitfield's conversion set him off on a mission that would change the face of American religion.

Whitfield began to preach. Beginning in the Church of England, but soon becoming a traveling evangelist, his unique personal style and innovative methods soon propelled him to fame throughout Great Britain. From 1739–1770 he made seven trips to America, during which he stoked the fires of evangelism that were being stirred through the efforts of men like Jonathan Edwards and John Wesley (whose stories you'll read later in this chapter). On each of his American ventures, Whitfield fanned the sparks of revival in the United States through his powerful charisma and ecumenical reach, both of which were far beyond the ability of local church pastors, who joined with him in his efforts. Those who saw and heard Whitfield were floored by his abilities—he was by all accounts the most amazing orator of his day.

Whitfield's style combined incredible personal spiritual intensity, a straightforward message of repentance, and an absolutely urgent call for individual response from his hearers. His amazing ability to draw people into his messages through his theatrics earned him the nickname "The Divine Dramatist." But it wasn't just his personal style that made him a forerunner of modern evangelists, it was also his pioneering methods.

> **In Their Own Words**
>
> "I have seen upwards of a thousand people hang on his words with breathless silence, broken only by an occasional half-suppressed sob … He speaks from a heart all aglow with love, and pours out a torrent of love which is almost irresistible."
>
> —Sarah Edwards, the wife of Jonathan Edwards, describing the experience of seeing Whitfield speak

Denied access to most traditional churches because of what they perceived of as a sensationalistic approach, Whitfield simply bypassed them all and began to preach out of doors. No one had ever done that before, and in addition to being innovative, the move provided Whitfield with a virtually unlimited stage wherever he went. That was a good thing, because as Charles Wesley (John's brother) once said, "The churches will not contain the multitudes that throng to hear him." In 1739 alone, estimates of the numbers of people in attendance when Whitfield preached on one of his first trips to America reached as high as 50,000. These crowds were likely the largest crowds that had ever gathered for anything in the young history of the United States.

Whitfield was also the first evangelical media magnate. He sold more publications than anyone else in America between 1739 and 1745. He also made use of extensive mass advertising in newspapers, and took full advantage of press coverage at his events—often writing the copy himself! His savvy foreshadowed the evangelical marketing prowess seen today.

In his lifetime, it is estimated that Whitfield preached 7,500 messages to crowds that frequently numbered in the tens of thousands. Many believe that he was used by God to provide the passion that fired much of the Great Awakening as it spread across pre-revolutionary America.

Jonathan Edwards

If Whitfield was the heart of the Great Awakening, Jonathan Edwards was the head.

Edwards has been called "the single most important evangelical in America" of his time, and the "theological genius of the Awakening."

Edwards studied Latin at six, and read Greek and Hebrew before he was thirteen. In 1716, he was admitted to Yale (at the age of twelve), and graduated in 1720 at the top of his class. In 1721, while studying for a Master's degree at Yale, he experienced a conversion that changed his life.

In Their Own Words

"As I read the words, there came into my soul, and was as it were diffused through it, a sense of the glory of the Divine Being; a new sense, different than any thing I had ever experienced before ... I thought with myself, how excellent a Being that was, and how happy I should be, if I might enjoy that God ... and be as it were swallowed up in him forever!"

—Jonathan Edwards, describing his own "new birth" experience while reading the Bible

As a result of his "new birth," Edwards prepared for pastoral ministry, and at age 24 he went to work at a very influential church in Northampton, Massachusetts, becoming its pastor in 1729.

From 1735–1736 (just prior to one of Whitfield's first trips to America), Edwards began to preach a series of messages on the baseline protestant doctrine of justification by faith. This was the idea (that became foundational for evangelicals) that a person comes into a relationship with God not on the basis of their good works, but on the basis of their faith in God's forgiveness through Christ. The result of Edward's messages was astounding, as person after person in his church began to experience their own new birth conversions.

Convinced that this was important, in 1737 Edwards published an account of this revival in his church, called *A Faithful Narrative of the Surprising Work of God*. The book became an immediate sensation, and was widely printed (even internationally). It not only described the revival experience that was emerging throughout New England through leaders like Edwards and Whitfield, but perhaps more importantly, it gave this experience intellectual credence. Even today, Edwards' book is an essential text for evangelicals studying the phenomenon of "revival."

As the revival grew in New England, Edwards found that his own perspective about it was in between the sometimes excessive emotionalism of the traveling revivalist-types and the more conservative nature of the traditional church around him. As a result, he saw the need to help fellow Christians distinguish between authentic spiritual revival and simple emotional manipulation.

Between 1741 and 1746, he published three books, *Distinguishing Marks of a Work of the Spirit of God* (1741), *Some Thoughts Concerning Revival* (1742), and *Concerning Religious Affections* (1746). In particular, *Concerning Religious Affections* was a balanced, brilliant response to the traditionalists, who tended to be skeptical of the revival. Its deeply devotional yet pristinely logical nature has ensured that it continues to be widely read, even today.

> ### In Their Own Words
>
> "A person who has a knowledge of doctrine and theology only—without religious affection—has never engaged in true religion."
>
> —Jonathan Edwards in *Concerning Religious Affections*

Through his books and sermons (which were often published), Edwards had an enormous influence both in bringing about revival and in interpreting it to his culture. His ability to interpret theological experiences into culturally relevant language prefigured the same characteristic that is so essential to Evangelicalism in contemporary culture. Further, through his combination of experiential piety and unmatched intellectual depth, Edwards produced a legacy of immediate followers of his brand of theology that paved the way for the Second Great Awakening in the early 1800s.

John Wesley

If Whitfield was the heart of the Awakening, and Edwards was its head, John Wesley represented its feet. During his lifetime, it is estimated that he traveled over 250,000 miles on horseback as an itinerant evangelist in Europe and America, preaching 42,000 sermons in the process. And although the time Wesley spent in America was very short (1735–1737), his methods (the foundation for what was later called "Methodism") provided for an ongoing reproduction of what was happening in the Great Awakening that enabled its spread.

Wesley came to America in 1735 as a missionary to the native peoples of Georgia, a newly established debtor's colony. After experiencing limited success and multiple problems, Wesley returned to England in 1737. His own explanation shows one major cause of his difficulties: "I left my native country in order to teach the Georgian Indians the nature of Christianity. But what have I learned myself in the meantime? Why … that I who went to America to convert others was never myself converted to God."

Through his contact with the strong personal faith of a group of Moravian immigrants to Georgia, Wesley had discovered a deep need for authentic faith in his own life. After returning to England, he experienced his real conversion during a meeting of a Moravian society in London. His description of this conversion experience is now classic in evangelical history:

> About a quarter before nine, while [the speaker] was describing the change which God works in the heart through faith in Christ, I felt my heart strangely warmed. I felt I did trust in Christ for my salvation, and an assurance was given me that he had taken away *my* sins, even *mine*, and saved *me* from the law of sin and death.

Wesley's organizational genius had a huge impact on American evangelicals. His "methods" included detailed instructions for itinerant evangelists—down to how they should structure their sermons. His example of "circuit-riding" (traveling evangelists who moved from town to town on horseback) became a staple of American evangelism well into the following century. Perhaps most importantly, his detailed organization of small, lay-led cell groups and their leaders enabled the multiplication of the evangelical movement. It was also the precursor to much of the "small group" life that figures so heavily into American Evangelicalism today.

Wesley's theology has also proven to be a key influencing factor in the development of American Evangelicalism. The openness and pietistic tendencies of his theology became a key strain of modern charismatic and Pentecostal theologies—movements which today are the largest in world-wide Evangelicalism. Further, his focus on personal holiness heavily influenced developing evangelical thought. Perhaps most obviously, all of the various types of Methodist denominations that are a part of Evangelicalism today trace their direct lineage to Wesley.

In his own day, Wesley's effectiveness is shown in the numbers. In 1734, there were about 50 people who had joined in Wesley's small groups, using his highly organized "methods." By the time of his death in 1791, there were 71,668 in England and 43,265 in America.

> **The Gospel Truth**
>
> Who converted who?
>
> The Moravian meeting in London where John Wesley experienced conversion probably originated as a result of George Whitfield's preaching in the area the year before. George Whitfield preached there because of his own conversion in John Wesley's Holy Club—which Wesley invited *him* to prior to Wesley's *own* conversion. So Whitfield was converted because of Wesley, who was later converted because of Whitfield!

The Second Great Awakening

The first Great Awakening had been known as "a surprising work of God." In contrast, following the American Revolutionary War the can-do American spirit spawned a new revival that was encouraged much more intentionally. From about 1795 to the late 1840s, what historians generally call "The Second Great Awakening" took the country by storm, characterized by some different qualities than what had happened a little over a half century before:

- ◆ It was more wide-spread geographically.

- ◆ It lasted longer.

- ◆ It was more intentionally orchestrated (or encouraged—depending on your point of view).

- ◆ It foresaw the beginnings of institutionalism in Evangelicalism, anticipating the massive evangelical subculture of today.

Not only was the revival much longer, it was more diverse. It took place in three main "theaters" across the United States

New England

In New England, the followers of Jonathan Edwards had solidified his legacy both theologically and methodologically following the First Great Awakening. His followers organized churches and trained church leaders in specific practices emanating from Edwards' theology.

Although this contributed to a sense of stability in the fledgling evangelical movement, by the turn of the century times were tough. It had been about 60 years since the dramatic growth created by the first Awakening, and evangelical leaders were worried. Was all of this just a flash-in-the-pan?

During what has been called the "lowest ebbtide of vitality in the history of American Christianity," several key leaders arose who became the captains of a new surge of spiritual energy in New England.

Timothy Dwight

Timothy Dwight was the grandson of Jonathan Edwards, and he shared his famous grandfather's genetic intellect. Among his other accomplishments, while he was a student at Yale studying the classics he helped to found a group called "The Connecticut Wits"—thought to be the first American school of literary criticism. After serving as a chaplain in the Revolutionary War and as a pastor following the war, he became president of Yale in 1795.

One of the first things Dwight did was launch a campaign against what he saw as a creeping theological liberalism (and a resulting immorality) among the students. He did this by focusing formal campus debates on questions relating to the trustworthiness of the Bible.

Culture Clash!

The trustworthiness of the Bible is (and always has been) a huge and defining issue for evangelicals. However, contrary to popular conceptions, evangelicals do not necessarily take the Bible "literally." A more accurate way to describe their point of view is that they take the Bible *seriously*—although even this can get a little weird at times. For example, there were those in the 1970s who interpreted parts of Revelation as symbolically pointing to Henry Kissinger as the anti-Christ. (Really—I'm not making that up.)

Additionally, he created a four-year cycle of sermons designed to communicate the essentials of the faith. These sermons were highly influential, and later published as *Theology Explained and Defended.* They were subsequently used as foundational texts in theological schools until the mid-nineteenth century.

Dwight's fervor, combined with his considerable intellectual capabilities, had an impact. In 1802, there was a revival at Yale, in which it is reported that about one-third of the student body was converted. Many historians point to this revival, and the influence it had because of Yale's standing and widespread reach, as the spark that began the Second Great Awakening in New England.

Lyman Beecher

Meanwhile, another New England pastor, Lyman Beecher (who had been a student of Dwight's at Yale), was stirring up revival fires in other parts of the area. At first from East Hampton Presbyterian Church in Long Island, and later from the very influential Hanover Street Congregational Church in Boston, Beecher called for a new commitment from his congregants as he preached a strong message of individual conversion. Uniquely for his time, he combined his strong evangelistic message with a call for social reform. People responded in droves.

As time went on, Beecher became well known for involvement in social issues. He became involved in the temperance movement, the antidueling movement, and the antislavery movement. As such, Beecher is a clear example of a key emphasis of the Second Great Awakening—its social conscience.

This legacy was played out in Beecher's own family. In addition to having a son who also became a famous preacher (Henry Ward Beecher), he had a daughter (Harriet Beecher Stowe) who became a social force in her own right through authoring the classic abolitionist novel, *Uncle Tom's Cabin.*

The efforts of Dwight, Beecher, and other leaders like them led to the reality that by the 1830s nearly every church in New England was following an Edwardsian-style theology. The resulting impact was that both the number of personal conversions and the beginnings of social reform entered into a new phase of growth.

The American West

While New Englanders were hearing from people like the erudite Timothy Dwight and the socially minded Beecher, the wild and wooly westerners in the U.S. experienced a simultaneous movement of the Spirit that was uniquely connected to their own cultural realities.

As Americans moved westward in the wake of the Louisiana purchase, there was a great concern on the part of early evangelicals that the rigors and lawlessness of frontier life would spawn a generation with no concern for God. So, in characteristically evangelical fashion, they innovated. The pioneer lifestyle resulted in one of the most uniquely American forms of religious expression ever invented: the *camp meeting*.

Camp Meetings

Camp meetings were a mixture of food, fun, socialization, and (quite controversially) a big dose of religious emotionalism. But for those living in the new west, life was lonely and hard, and camp meetings were tailor-made to meet their cultural needs while serving up an energetic call to holiness.

def•i•ni•tion

A frontier **camp meeting** was a several-day-long camp-out, typically with hundreds of other people, where multiple experiences of singing and preaching were designed to convert unbelievers and encourage new holiness in those who already believed.

A typical camp meeting would consist of a large number of people (usually hundreds or even thousands) gathered at a campsite. Tents and wagons would form the perimeter, while wooden platforms were set up at multiple sites in the camp for singing and preaching. People would camp, socialize, sing, and listen to preaching together for around four days. The meetings usually began in mid-week and lasted through Sunday, ending with a special service of communion.

The First Woodstock

Although many camp meetings were attended by large numbers of people during this time, no one was expecting what happened in the Cumberland River Valley in central Kentucky in August of 1801. Known as the "Cane Ridge Revival," it began when Barton W. Stone, a Presbyterian pastor working near Lexington, Kentucky, decided to hold a camp meeting for his area. After traveling to see one in nearby Logan County, Stone became convinced that a camp meeting would be helpful for the people of his area as well.

Perhaps because of the success of the Logan County camp meeting, people came from as far away as Ohio and Tennessee. The numbers swelled to somewhere between 10,000–25,000 (historians differ on the exact count). In an area where the largest town (Lexington) had a population of 1,795, this was quite overwhelming. The descriptions of wagons, carriages, horses, and people leaving their wagons to move on foot toward the camp are evocative of the pictures of people leaving their cars by the side of the road and walking into Max Yasgur's farm in 1969. Indeed, this was a nineteenth-century Woodstock, complete with a similar social impact for the people of that generation.

The activities at the meeting, however, were decidedly different from sex, drugs, and rock and roll. The Cane Ridge Revival was an extraordinary example of frontier-style enthusiastic religion. Presbyterian, Baptist, and Methodist pastors came from all around to preach and counsel with the attendees. Thousands were moved by the Spirit, some quite visibly. The Cane Ridge camp meeting was full of reports of people who fell under the sway of the Spirit with convulsions (called "jerking"), hysterical laughter, dancing, shouting, and even barking like dogs. (Maybe in some ways it wasn't so different from Woodstock after all ...)

In Their Own Words

"No matter whether they were saints or sinners, they would be taken under a warm song or sermon, and seized with a convulsive jerking all over, which they could not by any possibility avoid, and the more they resisted, the more they jerked ... I have seen more than five hundred persons jerking at one time ..."

—Peter Cartwright, a noted Methodist leader in the 1800s, describes the phenomenon known as "jerking."

These unusual experiences were so prevalent that Cane Ridge came to be called "America's Pentecost"—after the New Testament story in Acts 2, where on the day of Pentecost (a Jewish holiday) the Holy Spirit fell on the early church with unusual physical results, causing the believers to speak in languages that were not known to them for the benefit of an international crowd gathered in Jerusalem at the time.

More genteel Eastern evangelicals such as Timothy Dwight were appalled at the quite animated activities at Cane Ridge (which anticipated similar kinds of activities in modern-day Pentecostal revivals). However, historians agree that probably no other single initiative of the era had a more practical effect on the faith of the region than the Cane Ridge camp meeting. Large numbers of people were converted, and the Second Great Awakening's influence spread well beyond New England.

Upstate New York (Charles Finney)

The most influential of all of the revivals of the Second Great Awakening happened in upstate New York in the late 1820s and 1830s. The key figure was a man named Charles Grandison Finney.

Finney was a former lawyer who had undergone a dramatic personal conversion experience in 1821 at the age of 29. He immediately left his law practice to spend his time spreading the gospel. With a style that was informal and directly personal, a majestic voice, and a lawyerly command of logic, Finney was extremely effective as a preacher. But as with other pioneering evangelicals, his legacy lay as much in his methods as his style.

In Their Own Words

"I have a retainer from the Lord Jesus Christ to plead his cause, and I cannot plead yours."

—Charles Finney, explaining to a client why he would not be in court on the day after his conversion

Controversially, Finney taught that "religion is the work of man" and that revival is not necessarily a solely miraculous occurrence but "the result of the right use of appropriate means." This was scandalous to many of the church leaders of the day, who placed a high theological value on the idea that the initiation of revival came solely from God. But to Finney, the "appropriate means" were the spring board for innovations that came to be called the "New Measures."

Finney's New Measures were a veritable preview of twentieth-century evangelism. In addition to mass advertising, Finney made extensive use of lay leadership in promoting his campaigns, intentionally pulling together coalitions of various denominations to lead and support the effort (very similar to what Billy Graham would do nearly 150 years later).

Additionally, Finney targeted civic and social leaders, strategizing that their influence would spread the message to others—anticipating another primary strategy of many of today's evangelical organizations. Finney's meetings also featured public praying by men and (notoriously) women alike, and even included praying from the pulpit for sinners—by name—to be converted. He also pioneered calling people to "come forward" at his meetings to experience conversion—a standard evangelical practice to this day. He developed a philosophy of protracted revival meetings—both in terms of the number of meetings and their length—lasting as long as "the Spirit led." This too is another common practice of evangelicals today.

Perhaps his most controversial practice of all, and the one that came to represent to Finney's critics all of the excesses they saw in his methods, was something called "the anxious bench." Set in the very front of the room, the anxious bench was a pew where "anxious" people sat during the revival meetings. There they were showered with special attention (especially from the pastor as he spoke). Many saw this as emotional manipulation; always the pragmatist, Finney saw it as a good way to focus his attention on those who self-identified as needing it the most.

After holding revival meetings in the backwoods of New York state, in 1825 Finney began a series of meetings in the towns of upstate New York that stretched into seven years of some of the most intense evangelistic activity America has ever seen. They reached their peak in the fall of 1830, when he began a series of meetings in Rochester that continued until March of 1831. These meetings reached thousands, and brought Finney international fame. They are often referred to by historians as the greatest revival in American history.

Beyond the large number of individual conversions, the social results of this revival were quite measurable. Rochester taverns closed. The local theater became a livery stable. The District Attorney stated that crime in Rochester dropped by two-thirds. All of these effects were indicative not only of the Rochester meetings, but of the massive social changes in the United States that are directly tied to the Second Great Awakening (see "The Righteous Empire" below).

Because of his efforts, Finney is generally known as the father of modern urban evangelism. But in addition to his fame as a preacher and innovator of evangelical methods, Finney has had a wide and lasting influence through his writings. His *Lectures on Revival* (1835) and his *Memoirs* (published posthumously in 1876) remain influential among evangelicals to this day. With his *Views on Sanctification* (1840), Finney became a major theologian of the emerging holiness movement, following in the lineage of Wesley. The Rochester awakening in 1831 is credited by many as being the spark for a nationwide awakening that same year that stretched beyond the borders of the United States to Europe in its influence. Under the leadership of men like Finney, everywhere the evangelical spark was being fanned into flame.

The Righteous Empire

The combined impact of the New England revivals, the camp meetings, and the waves of revival that Finney's efforts spawned resulted in an important character change for American society as a whole as a result of the Second Great Awakening. Indeed, historians often refer to the first half of the nineteenth century in America as "the righteous empire." Springing from the soil of real individual conversions was a social impetus that left an indelible mark of *Protestantism* on the United States.

def•i•ni•tion

Prostestantism is most easily (and generally) defined as Christianity that is neither Catholic nor Eastern Orthodox. Much of evangelicalism is Protestant in its origins and contemporary expression.

Evangelicals joined forces during this period to birth new educational institutions, prison reform movements, child labor laws, and the women's rights movement. They founded special needs asylums for the mentally and physically ill, numerous anti-slavery societies, ministries to new immigrant groups in the United States, and even led the fight to end dueling after Vice President Aaron Burr killed a political rival in a highly publicized duel. Through their work in the temperance movement, between 1830 and 1845 the rate of alcohol consumption (which was a full four times higher per capita than it is today) was cut in half. This era also saw the rise of the global missions movement, which eventually became a hallmark of modern Evangelicalism.

> **The Gospel Truth**
>
> In addition to social movements, six of the nine colonial colleges in America were born as a result of the Awakenings. Yale, Harvard, and Princeton were all originally founded for the specific purpose of training ministers.

In short, the Second Great Awakening saw the embryonic emergence of what would become evangelical social politics. Finney, in particular, with his social reform focus and ability to organize large urban campaigns, represented a new form of Evangelicalism. Indeed, as America entered a more industrial and urban era, Evangelicalism was moving with it.

Leading into the Twentieth Century—D. L. Moody

By 1870, a quarter of the American population lived in urban areas, and the trend was growing. And as urban life began to take hold, so did new lifestyles. How Evangelicalism adapted to the Industrial Revolution and urbanization of the country is a story that can be seen in the life of one of its most important pioneers: Dwight Lyman Moody.

At age 17, D. L. Moody struck out from his family home and birthplace in Northampton, Massachusetts. He headed for Boston, where he became a Christian while working in his Uncle's shoe store. By 18, he had made his way to Chicago, where his prodigious personal qualities were already evident, as he became phenomenally successful as a simple shoe salesman. Ever the "man on a mission," however, in 1861 he gave up his career and began to work full time in social and evangelistic efforts through a local YMCA.

During the next three years, he started a Sunday school outreach that later became a church, which by 1867 had an average Sunday attendance of over 1,700. This church, known as Moody Memorial Church, still exists today. It is home to some 2,500 people, and is one of the most influential evangelical pulpits in America.

Through his church and YMCA work, Moody was unusually effective. But his key contributions to the evangelical movement eventually came from his decision to leave local church and YMCA work to become a full-time evangelist.

The Entrepreneurial Evangelist

In 1873, Moody set out for England to implement a series of crusades that resulted in his returning to America several years later as an international sensation. From 1875 to 1878, Moody conducted a series of American campaigns in which he pioneered techniques like door-to-door canvassing of homes prior to crusades, the rental of large public buildings for crusades, and developing the philanthropic and nondenominational financial support of the business community for crusades. Further, Moody created unique entertainment value in his crusades by showcasing a gospel musician who was also a phenomenally popular song writer. His name was Ira Sankey, and not only did he become known as Moody's partner in the crusades, he eventually wrote over 1,200 songs, many of which are still standards in modern evangelical hymn books.

By combining the tried-and-true methods of his forbearers with the sophistication and even technical prowess of an increasingly modern society, Moody was instrumental in moving the cause of Evangelicalism to the next step in its evolution.

In addition to his evangelistic crusades, Moody founded three schools (even though he himself had only the equivalent of a 5th grade education). One of them, now called The Moody Bible Institute, has figured prominently in the history of Evangelicalism all the way through modern times. Seeing the need for evangelical institutions of higher learning as the sophistication of society increased, Moody foresaw the modern evangelical educational impulse.

> **The Gospel Truth**
>
> Since its founding in 1837, Moody Bible Institute has seen steady growth. Today, the graduates and staff of the school (that now boasts a $90 million budget) read like a who's who of the evangelical movement.

It is estimated that D. L. Moody communicated the evangelical message of salvation, through voice or pen, to an astounding 100 million people during his lifetime. His message was simple, delivered in homespun and sentimental terms that reflected both his working-class heritage and his buoyant personality. He taught the "three R's"—Ruin by sin, Redemption by Christ, and Regeneration by the Holy Spirit. But although his message was simple, his methods were innovative and amazingly effective. So effective that many of the methods he pioneered go unchanged in a typical evangelistic rally today.

The Personable Evangelist

Moody's effervescence and popular appeal can be seen in some of the pithy sayings he coined. To his children, he declared, "Don't wait for something to turn up. Go and turn up something." Explaining his compulsion for evangelistic work, he said, "I look upon this world as a wrecked vessel. God has given me a lifeboat and said, 'Moody, save all you can!'"

Such was the ideology of evangelicalism as it passed from the nineteenth century and into the twentieth, as Moody died in December of 1899—nine days before the turn of the century.

The Least You Need to Know

- The First Great Awakening represented the beginning of a definable, connected evangelical movement in the United States

- The Second Great Awakening solidified the movement through its organizational advances, and added a social action dimension that anticipated the modern evangelical social and political impulse.

- Evangelist D. L. Moody led Evangelicalism into the twentieth century, communicating the gospel through his speaking and writing to an estimated 100 million people.

- Many of the practices of modern evangelists (e.g., Billy Graham) were pioneered during this period in history.

Modernity and Monkey Business

In This Chapter

- ◆ Evangelicalism goes urban
- ◆ The historic split between Protestant liberals and evangelicals
- ◆ How fundamentalists got their name
- ◆ The Scopes trial and the loss of evangelical cultural power

Less than a generation had passed since Moody's heyday when evangelicals found themselves in the position of a severe loss of influence over the cultural ethos in the U.S. In particular, the rising influence of Darwinism on the scientific front, modern industrialization and immigration on the social front, and a new form of scholarly biblical criticism on the theological front created a world in which religious conservatives found themselves uncharacteristically out of the mainstream. A new, modern era was dawning, and with it came a concurrent fall in religious credibility.

Generally, Protestants tended to tone down the offenses to modern ears of a strong Bible-believing faith by adjusting their theology and practices. The rise of the "social gospel" movement, along with a generally more liberal slant, was the order of the day among many Christians. All of this, however, did not sit well with those of a more conservative stripe, who saw some of their foundational beliefs and practices being systematically chipped away.

The first few decades of the 1900s saw some of the most important defining moments for Evangelicalism. Indeed, by the end of World War II, the evangelical movement had seen internal changes that were proportionate to the paradigm-shifting post-war changes in the world at large.

The Fundamentals

Responding to an increasingly secular culture and an increasingly liberal theological direction in scholarly circles, conservative religious leaders sought to protect what they saw as their orthodox heritage. One of the clearest examples of this came in 1910, in the publication of a group of books that have proven to stand the test of time as some of the defining documents of Evangelicalism. Called *The Fundamentals*, the publication was a series of 12 books containing around 90 articles that articulated what the authors considered to be the foundational tenants of orthodox faith.

The authors were scholarly luminaries of the evangelical world—even today scholars of all stripes praise the high level of argument and theological reflection in the books. People like B. B. Warfield of Princeton Seminary, R. A. Torrey (educated at Yale; later the Superintendent of Moody's Bible Institute), and A. C. Dixon (who pastored several highly influential churches in America and Europe) wrote articles of high caliber designed to counteract the drift of theological modernism. About one-third of the articles dealt with the issue of biblical inspiration (and the challenges to it by the school of "higher criticism"), and the others dealt with issues such as the authenticity of Jesus' virgin birth and bodily resurrection, the Genesis account of creation, and the presuppositions of modern scholars to discount the miraculous in scripture.

> **In Their Own Words**
>
> "[T]he work of the Higher Critic has not always been pursued in a reverent spirit nor in the spirit of scientific and Christian scholarship."
>
> —From "The History of Higher Criticism" by Canon Hague, the first article in the first volume of *The Fundamentals*

Two wealthy oilmen (Lyman Steward, President of Union Oil, and his brother Milton) who were also active Presbyterian laymen financed having the books sent out to over 3 million pastors, seminary professors, and church leaders. The irenic, brainy, and ecumenical tone of *The Fundamentals* was much more open and thoughtful than the theological movement which eventually took its name. The publication had quite an impact, setting out the boundaries of Evangelicalism for decades to come. *The Fundamentals* are still in print today, although for the most part they are widely read only among scholars, pastors, and other evangelical "professionals."

What's In a Name?

Nowadays, calling someone a "fundamentalist" conjures up notions of all kinds of extremism. However, the term (which is now used to describe a broad spectrum of religious and social movements) originally arose as a way of identifying a specific stream of Christian theological conviction. Much like we use the terms "liberal theologian" and "conservative theologian" today, it was a way of identifying those who held to the principles contained in the twelve volumes discussed above.

The term "Fundamentalism" was first coined in 1920 as a badge of honor by Curtis Lee, writing in a Baptist newspaper called *The Watchman Examiner*. As such, it was more of a media creation than a self-appointed title for the loose federation of people involved in the conservative movement of the time. Lee pointed to these people as those "who still cling to the great fundamentals and mean to do battle royal for the faith." Within that statement, both the positive and negative sides of what was to come of this new, more focused form of Evangelicalism are clear.

On the positive side, the fundamentalists were seeking to retain the historical orthodoxy of the faith that had stood the test of nearly 2,000 years of church history. The subtitle of *The Fundamentals, A Testimony to the Truth*, displays an ambition for theological integrity that was the driving force at the beginning of the movement. The impetus, however, wasn't theological integrity alone. This was a counter-cultural movement. Importantly (and unique up until that time in U.S. history) Fundamentalism was about orthodoxy *in confrontation with modernity*. The key tenants of the movement were primarily shaped by what it was reacting against.

This confrontational foundation is the seed from which many of the negative characteristics associated with Fundamentalism today grew. The separatism, the cultural alienation, and the anti-intellectualism that came to define the movement in the public eye had their roots in its initial contrary

> **Culture Clash!**
>
> Underneath the fundamentalist's desire to be "separated" is an impulse to remain pure. Showing respect for that impulse is key to having a productive dialogue around issues where you may disagree. Or you can invite them to a local bar to continue the conversation over a drink.

posture toward society at large. Beginning with a historically Christian reaction of being "holy" or literally "set apart," Fundamentalism eventually took on more and more of an embattled mind-set. The "battle royal" motif identified by Curtis Lee would eventually become the popularly defining characteristic of fundamentalists.

Eventually, this militant mentality would be the reason evangelicals separated from fundamentalists. But for now, they were one and the same. And the culture wars were on.

The Culture Wars Begin

Whereas in the nineteenth century evangelicals had generally been centrists culturally, the twentieth century saw increasing marginalization with the rise of Fundamentalism. This fissure began in theological circles, and grew as the culture at large became increasingly more secular.

As Fundamentalism grew, it solidified around some distinguishing theological characteristics. In addition to a commitment to the absolute authority of scripture, a movement toward an absolutely literal interpretation of scripture developed. In addition, a specific theological interpretive system became popular, known as *dispensational premillennialism*. This complex classification of chronological eras that explained God's work in the world provided a systematic approach to scripture that was a rationalistic counter to liberal theology. In other words, it provided an intellectual foundation for conservative theology that was equally as "scientific" (actually rationalistic) as the liberal approach, which tended to disbelieve the supernatural claims of the Bible based on its own rational values.

def•i•ni•tion

Premillennial dispensationalism is a specific, systematic way of interpreting the Bible. Using a chronology drawn from scripture, it divides human history into five different ages, or "dispensations," in which God has worked with humanity in different ways. "Premillennial" refers to a specific belief about the order of events at the end of the age of human history, and is the theological basis of the popular *Left Behind* book series.

During the first two decades of the 1900s, the split between conservatives and liberals slowly became more and more undeniable—especially when the two points of view coexisted in the leadership bodies of various churches, seminaries, and institutions.

All of this came to a head in an important episode around 1922 that many religious historians point to as perhaps *the* defining moment in the separation of conservatives and liberals in U.S. mainline denominational churches. It is also pointed to by many as the impetus of the downward numerical spiral of liberal mainline churches that characterized the second half of the twentieth century. In other words, the liberals won the academic "fight," but ultimately lost the participation "war." While they gained respect from modernist intellectuals, in the second half of the twentieth century liberal churches generally lost members in droves, while conservative churches grew at an astounding rate.

Fodsick and the Protestant Split

The opening shot in the battle was fired in 1922. Reflecting what was happening in denominations all over the United States, the issues of liberal/conservative theology that had been simmering for some time came to a boiling point in the influential Presbyterian Church in the United States (PCUSA). Pastor and writer Henry Emerson Fodsick threw down the gauntlet by preaching a sermon titled, "Shall the Fundamentalists Win?" from the pulpit of New York's First Presbyterian Church on May 21, 1922; 130,000 copies of the sermon were printed and distributed, rewritten by a skilled PR person, and financed by John D. Rockefeller. (Rockefeller would later, as a result of the controversy, build Fodsick a new church—Riverside Church in New York City—which is still today a leading force in American protestant liberalism).

> **In Their Own Words**
>
> "The new knowledge and the old faith cannot be left antagonistic or even disparate ... We must be able to think our modern life clear through in Christian terms, and to do that we also must be able to think our Christian life clear through in modern terms."
>
> —From "Shall the Fundamentalists Win?" by Harry Emerson Fodsick

Reaction to Fodsick's sermon was strong and swift. Clarence E. Macartney of Philadelphia's influential Arch Street Presbyterian Church countered with a message called "Shall Unbelief Win?"—and the battle lines were drawn. Presbyterians in the pews were forced to either side with the "unbelieving liberals" or the "reactionary fundamentalists." There were some middle-ground voices, but they were mostly drowned out. The result was an eventual separation of the conservatives from the PCUSA, some starting independent churches, and others starting a new denomination called the Presbyterian Church of America.

> ### In Their Own Words
>
> "The [liberal] movement is slowly secularizing the Church, and if permitted to go unchecked and unchallenged, will ere long produce in our churches a new kind of Christianity, a Christianity without worship, without God, and without Jesus Christ."
>
> —From "Shall Unbelief Win?" by Richard Macartney

Characteristic of the ongoing separatist impulse in Fundamentalism, the Presbyterian Church of America soon split as well, with the quick succession of a group that became yet another denomination—the Bible Presbyterian Church. This whole story is symptomatic of what was happening all over the ecclesiastical world. In denomination after denomination during this time period, when fundamentalists recognized that they would not be able to reform existing institutions from within, they created their own. Yet again, the entrepreneurial roots of Evangelicalism are seen.

Princeton Seminary

Another key episode that illustrates the growing split happened at Princeton Seminary around the same time. Princeton (started as an evangelical school during the Second Great Awakening) had historically been a bastion of conservative theology—some of its key faculty members had even been contributors to *The Fundamentals*. However, as theological modernism began gaining ground, Princeton began to allow more diversity of belief in its faculty.

In 1929, in what proved to be a historically decisive move, four members of the faculty of Princeton resigned to start a new seminary more in line with their theological convictions. They founded Westminster Seminary. They also took with them some of the school's most promising students, two of whom (Carl McIntyre and Harold J. Ockenga) later proved to be key in Evangelicalism's rise out of Fundamentalism.

Even today, people talk about the "Old Princeton" and the "New Princeton"—and the difference between the two is a key watershed for evangelical theology. The Old Princeton had a fundamental commitment to teaching and maintaining "biblical inerrancy"—the literalist approach to the absolute authority of Scripture that was characteristic of the fundamentalists. The New Princeton moved more to the theological left, away from the historic creedalism of its past and toward a complete embracing of modernism as its primary approach. Again, the story of Princeton (uniquely important because of both the influence of the school and its historic moorings) more or less began to be repeated throughout the ecclesiastical world.

It was obvious that the theologies of the left and the right were becoming more and more incompatible. But the theological differences were simply the harbinger of changes across the greater culture. No single event marked the watershed of the conservative/liberal ethos throughout the United States on the level of overall culture more than a unique, often historically misunderstood moment in history known popularly as the "Scopes Monkey Trial."

Monkey Business: The Scopes Trial

A hot and humid Tennessee courtroom in 1925 was the scene for what became a huge moment in cultural history.

Fresh from the political victory of prohibition (which took effect in 1920), conservatives in the early 1920s in a handful of states passed laws prohibiting the teaching of evolution in public schools. The state of Tennessee passed an anti-evolution statute in 1925, and the fledgling American Civil Liberties Union offered to finance the defense of any teacher who wanted to challenge the law. John Scopes, a first-year science teacher in Dayton, Tennessee, agreed to be the test case, setting the stage for an epic confrontation.

> **The Gospel Truth**
>
> John Scopes, the defendant in the "Trial of the Century," never testified at his own trial.

The conservative side of the case was organized by the World's Christian Fundamentals Association (founded in 1919, it was the first ever organization specifically for fundamentalists). William Jennings Bryan, a three-time presidential candidate, the Secretary of State under Woodrow Wilson, and perhaps the era's most prominent fundamentalist, became the prosecutor seeking to uphold the Tennessee law. The other side, organized by the ACLU, featured Clarence Darrow as the defense attorney. Darrow was the most celebrated defense lawyer of the time; he was also an avowed agnostic and an outspoken opponent of organized religion. He took the case for free, calling the trial "the first case of its kind since we stopped trying people for witchcraft."

The "Media Circus" Is Born

In an unprecedented moment in U.S. history (similar to the O. J. Simpson trial of recent years), hundreds of media representatives descended on Dayton, Tennessee. (The Dayton Chamber of Commerce, seeing an opportunity, had actively worked to get the trial there.) Movie cameras, newspaper journalists, radio journalists, and telegraphers created a unique "media-circus" atmosphere that is now all-too familiar to Americans. Peddlers hawked souvenirs. A fundamentalist preacher set up a tent and preached to the crowds. The Scopes trial was the first in American history to be broadcast nationwide via the relatively new medium of radio.

Even the courtroom itself was a bit of a circus, as the fully packed, airless room was decorated by a banner over the judge's bench that read "Read Your Bible Daily." Darrow succeeded in having it removed, but not without difficulty.

The Courtroom Drama

The highlight of the trial came when Bryan (who hadn't tried a case in 28 years) was brought to the stand as a "witness" to biblical authority. On the stand, he was grilled by Darrow about alleged inconsistencies in the Bible. Normally a powerful orator, Bryan fumbled, as shown in one illustrative passage from the court record:

> Darrow: "What do you think?"
>
> Bryan: "I do not think about things I don't think about."
>
> Darrow: "Do you think about things you do think about?"
>
> Bryan: "Well, sometimes."

Darrow showed Bryan to have no knowledge of the geology involved in evolutionary arguments, no knowledge of ancient civilizations, and in addition, he seemed to be very naïve in his own religious views. Realizing that he had floundered, Bryan stayed up all night preparing a response to his witness stand performance, but the next day the judge ended the arguments and sent the case to the jury.

Bryan won the case. Scopes was found guilty and fined $100, although he never paid a dime; his verdict was later reversed on a technicality. But in the court of public opinion—the real target of those on both sides—Fundamentalism lost, badly. Bryan, exhausted and embarrassed, died in Dayton five days after the trial.

The Lasting Effects of the Trial

Bryan's passing can be seen as a historical metaphor for the passing of an era in which conservative religious beliefs represented the undisputed cultural mainstream. The Scopes trial has been called the "biggest PR disaster in history for fundamentalists" by religious historians. Its outcome highlights some important ongoing characteristics that have existed ever since in the conversation between fundamentalists, evangelicals, and the popular culture at large.

First of all, the Scopes trial represented the beginning of an ongoing attitude toward religious conservatism in popular media. Journalist H. L. Mencken—a literary critic and journalist for the *Baltimore Evening Sun* (to whom author Sinclair Lewis later dedicated *Elmer Gantry*)—exemplified this trend through his very influential coverage of the event, which is generally considered by historians today to have been obviously biased. Throughout the trial, Mencken painted a blanket picture in the mind of the country at large of religious conservatives as anti-intellectual, intolerant, backwards, and even as bigots. As with all stereotypes, there is some truth in this portrayal; but ever since, it has tended to unfairly put all evangelicals in the same box.

Culture Clash!

Evangelicals today continue to be frustrated by the stereotypical view of them often portrayed by the media. Only a few *actually* marry their cousins. When you're not sure about an evangelical's position on something—simply ask about it. They're usually happy to talk.

The Scopes trial also raised issues about religion in public life and public education that are still being debated today. It exposed a growing fissure in American life between the pursuit of new knowledge and a desire to hold on to traditional religious beliefs. The two have often been seen as at odds with one another, with the loudest and most raucous voices on both sides making the best story from a media perspective. The Scopes trial, and especially the popular play and subsequent movie about it that cemented the trial into public consciousness (*Inherit The Wind*), showed that the extremes of a position usually get the most press. This is a trend that continues today—although the extreme points of view usually do not accurately portray the majority.

Perhaps the most important effect of the Scopes trial was that it was the final straw that drove Fundamentalism out of the cultural mainstream. The convergence of a myriad of forces within American culture coalesced with the confrontation between Jennings and Bryan on the witness stand. But although it went into retreat, the fundamentalist movement was hardly inactive.

Retreating to Regather

As they became more separatist in the 1930s and beyond, fundamentalists began to build their own churches and institutions. Bible Schools, in the genre developed and now led by Moody Institute, increased dramatically in enrollment. Communications networks such as independent, nondenominational newspapers sprang up and were eagerly consumed, mostly under the radar of mainstream popular culture. Evidence of the growth in Fundamentalism's popularity in this period is seen in the fact that the Southern Baptist Convention, the Assemblies of God, the Christian and Missionary Alliance, and the Nazarene Church (all key evangelical denominations today) grew at a faster rate than did the population of the country as a whole.

Overall, during this time period fundamentalists set about building alternatives to the mainstream religious institutions of the day. Over time, these alternative groups grew to form a loose network of like-minded people. Not only did this strengthen the movement, eventually this network would form the framework for the emergence of a new kind of Evangelicalism in the years to follow.

The National Association of Evangelicals

The "new Evangelicalism" as it came to be known, was birthed out of a struggle within Fundamentalism itself.

As fundamentalists grew stronger through the creation of separate institutions, many within Fundamentalism became uncomfortable. Along with the growth of the movement, there was a corresponding growth of a more and more separatist, and even militant, mentality. Old-guard fundamentalist leaders who had fought for doctrinal integrity against creeping modernism tended to be very suspicious, and increasingly negative, toward the culture at large. Yet newer leaders, many of whom were younger and more naturally in touch with the culture around them, grew increasingly uncomfortable with the negativism. They wanted to move beyond the battles of the previous generation, and look to the future—a vastly different cultural landscape as the post–World War II years approached.

These rumblings went on for some time within Fundamentalism, creating more and more dissonance within the ranks. A definitive break finally came in 1943, when, sensing an unorganized camaraderie and the need to develop a voice that more effectively spoke to the prevailing culture, a group of leaders from across the country gathered together and founded the National Association of Evangelicals (NAE).

Originally led by Harold John Ockenga (Pastor of the influential Park Street Church in Boston, and later the first President of Fuller Seminary and the first Board Chair of *Christianity Today*), this group

The Gospel Truth
In President Harold John Ockenga's address to the first assembly of the NAE, he told the group that they would be "the vanguard of a new movement," bringing together the "unvoiced multitudes" of Evangelicalism.

shared very similar theology with their fundamentalist siblings, but differed with them in three important ways:

- **A willingness to tolerate minor theological differences within their organization and fellowship.** For example, the NAE's statement of faith contained seven general precepts which could be written out in less than a page. In contrast, *The Fundamentals* stretched to twelve volumes.

- **A desire to set forth evangelical faith with a rigorous intellectualism often missing in the more dogmatic approach of fundamentalists.** The founders of Fuller Seminary, for example, referred to their dream of a seminary (located near the famed California Institute of Technology) that would be "a Cal-Tech of the evangelical world."

- **A more holistic focus toward the needs of humanity beyond individual conversion.** "No evangelicalism which ignores the totality of man's condition dares respond in the name of Christianity," stated Carl F. H. Henry in *The Uneasy Conscience of Modern Fundamentalism*, a work that became a virtual manifesto of the new movement of conservatives out of Fundamentalism.

The formation of the NAE was a seminal step for the future of Evangelicalism. Historically, this is the closest thing we have to the "birth" of the modern evangelical movement that we know today. The formation of the NAE created a definitive distinction between Fundamentalism and Evangelicalism, while setting in place a new personality for Evangelicalism that was key to its development as a movement. The NAE was a clear sign that evangelicals no longer wanted to be seen as separatist and anti-intellectual. Emerging out of Fundamentalism, Evangelicalism began to move in new directions, engaging culture in new ways, and creating a wider tent for the involvement of a much greater constituency. In the years to follow, Evangelicalism would see explosive growth.

At its founding, the NAE drew together what had been a huge but quieter constituency in the evangelical world. The popularity of its grass-roots support is seen in how quickly it grew and multiplied. It wrote a constitution in 1943, founded a public affairs office the same year, founded what would become *the* major evangelical media association (the National Association of Religious Broadcasters) in 1944, and founded a missions agency in 1944, and helped to launch what would later prove to be a world-leading humanitarian relief agency (World Vision—see Chapter 17) in 1945.

The NAE has gone on to found (among other organizations) the Evangelical Press Association, the Evangelical Fellowship of Mission Agencies, and commissions on social issues, higher education, philanthropy, and the special needs of minority groups within Evangelicalism. Today, it boasts millions of members, including over 450,000 congregations from over 50 denominations, and 250 parachurch organizations (see Chapters 4 and 17 for more on parachurch organizations). It is currently by far the largest clearinghouse for cross-denominational evangelical outreach in the United States.

Fuller Seminary

At about the same time as the formation of the NAE, another key institution formed that would be prominent in the shaping of modern Evangelicalism: Fuller Seminary in Pasadena, California.

The seminary was founded by Charles Fuller, an early pioneer of religious radio broadcasting who had built up an astounding base of 20 million listeners to his prime-time "Old Fashioned Revival Hour" in the 1930s. Indeed, during its heyday, it was virtually the most popular radio program of any kind of its time, outstripping Amos 'n' Andy, Charlie McCarthy, and even Bob Hope.

> ### In Their Own Words
>
> "Listen, my friend, out in radio land tonight. You have tried a thousand ways to find peace and comfort … there is only One throughout eternity that you can trust … Jesus. He's the one."
>
> —Charles Fuller, on "The Old-Fashioned Revival Hour," 1935

Fuller's radio popularity provided the funding for another of his dreams—a training institute for evangelists. He recruited Harold Ockenga, who desired to build a new, scholarly, evangelical Princeton. Ockenga recruited the best and the brightest of the evangelical scholars of the day. With money, strong leaders, and the huge advertising advantage of Charles Fuller's radio audience, Fuller Seminary began in 1947.

As perhaps the first modern evangelical graduate school, Fuller became a center of the "new Evangelicalism" that was becoming characteristic of those who had split off from the fundamentalist movement. Its influence has been felt in much greater proportion than even its numbers (which consistently rank it among the top three theological schools in the United States in terms of enrollment) suggest. From its founding with a constellation of influential evangelical theologians, it has remained both a thought leader and a center of evangelical cultural influence.

Its close association with Billy Graham (and thus the many evangelical institutions he had a hand in founding) in its early years put it at the center of the evangelical orbit.

In more recent years, when Fuller reformed its stand on the Bible in 1976 (see Chapter 5), it was a shot heard round the evangelical world. In 1982, it started a course called "The Miraculous and Church Growth" that, although controversial, was extremely influential in bringing a charismatic influence into the mainstream of Evangelicalism. And its courses on church growth, taught by C. Peter Wagner through the 1980s and 1990s, provided the seminal research and codification of principles that fueled much of the modern megachurch and "church growth" movement.

Fuller's founding in 1947 represented a new turn in Evangelicalism. On the heels of the founding of the NAE, and on the eve of the rise of explosive expansion for Evangelicalism after World War II, Fuller's "new Evangelicalism" soon simply became "Evangelicalism." And as the evangelical movement gained identity, no one was more important to its developing personality than the rising star who would become the most important evangelical of the twentieth century: William Franklin Graham, Jr.—known to the world as Billy Graham. We'll look at his story in our next chapter.

The Least You Need to Know

- *The Fundamentals*, published in 1910, represented a definitive conservative religious response to theological modernism and its influence in the culture.

- The 1920s saw the definitive split between American Protestant conservatives and liberals.

- The trial of John Scopes is a historical marker for the movement of Fundamentalism out of the American cultural mainstream.

- The formation of the National Association of Evangelicals in 1943 was a seminal moment for the emergence of modern Evangelicalism out of Fundamentalism.

- The founding of Fuller Seminary in 1947 reflected a new moment in evangelical history, providing an important intellectual base for the emerging evangelical movement.

Chapter 4

Modern Evangelicalism Arrives

In This Chapter

- The influence of Billy Graham on Evangelicalism
- The Rise of the "Jesus Movement" counterculture in the 1960s and 1970s
- TV evangelists
- The megachurch phenomenon

After World War II, things looked very different for everyone. In the United States, a new sense of hope and prosperity arose, as the post-war boom got underway. The economy was growing, as were families—evidenced by the baby boom. Breathing the air of peace, Americans buckled down and built lives and suburbs.

As the country came into a new era, so did Evangelicalism. In the second half of the twentieth century the movement would grow to an influence unimagined by its early founders. By the end of the 1990s evangelicals had grown the largest churches in the history of Christendom, become instrumental in the politics of the most important leaders in the world, and reached out in an unprecedented way to the entire globe with the message of Christ.

Chapter 3 ended with two important events that set the stage for all of this in Evangelicalism: the founding of the National Association of Evangelicals in 1943—both reflecting and developing a new personality for the movement out of Fundamentalism— and the founding of Fuller Seminary in 1947, representative of a new academic prowess in the movement. A third incident during this remarkably short time of convergence for evangelicals happened in 1949, when a young evangelist by the name of Billy Graham burst onto the scene.

The Rise of Billy Graham

William Franklin Graham, Jr. was born in 1918 to an upper-middle class dairy farming family near Charlotte, North Carolina. His family was a strongly committed church-going family, and young Billy was raised in an environment that revered the Bible and held Christian values in high esteem.

When Graham was sixteen years old, an itinerant fundamentalist evangelist by the name of Mordecai Ham began holding revival meetings where Billy lived. Moved by Ham's preaching, and convinced that it was time to make his own decision for Christ, Billy was converted.

After his graduation from high school several years later, Graham enrolled in the fundamentalist Bob Jones University. Uncomfortable with the tone of the school, however, he moved after one semester to Florida Bible Institute. After graduating from there, he continued his education at Wheaton College, where he graduated with a BA in Anthropology in 1943. It was during his time in Florida and at Wheaton that Billy began to speak publicly and engage in the activities that would eventually become his calling.

Upon his graduation from Wheaton and his marriage to Ruth Bell in 1943 (whom he met at Wheaton), Graham took on the pastorate of First Baptist Church in Western Springs, Illinois. Two years was enough to convince him that he was not designed to work in a local church, and he left in 1945 to help start Youth for Christ, an evangelistic organization that, among other things, used modern culture and communication methods to help students convert to Christianity. Graham was the organization's first full-time evangelist.

From Obscurity to World-Wide Fame

Learning through the following years how to organize a successful series of revival meetings, in 1949, Graham preached a crusade (for adults) in Los Angeles that became the launching pad of his career. His homespun, yet direct and intelligent, presentations of the gospel showed his maturing ability to reach all kinds of people. The Los Angeles crusade was successful beyond all measure. It was originally planned to last three weeks; the crowds that kept coming resulted in its extension to two months. Total attendance during that time was over 350,000. Celebrities and mob figures were among the 3,000 reported conversions. Perhaps most importantly for Graham's blossoming career, the crusade caught the attention of media magnate William Randolph Hearst, who instructed his reporters to "puff" Graham. The resultant mass media exposure made Graham a national, and ultimately international, figure.

In 1950, Graham called together his closest associates and formed the Billy Graham Evangelistic Association (the BGEA), whose by-laws gave Graham the task to "spread the gospel by any and all means." This proved to be exactly what he did, utilizing his speaking and organizing abilities, and a gift for mass media, to share Christ with probably more people than any other person in history.

> **In Their Own Words**
>
> "Blond, trumpet-lunged North Carolinian William Franklin Graham, Jr. ... dominates his huge audience from the moment he strides on stage ... rising to his toes to drive home a point, clenching his fists, stabbing a finger at the sky, and straining to get his words to the furthermost corners of the tent."
>
> —From *Time Magazine*, November 14, 1949, covering Graham's Los Angeles crusade

Through the BGEA, Graham has conducted crusades all over the world, including places where other evangelists—or even Americans—were unable to go. During the Cold War, for example, he took the message of Jesus into Soviet bloc countries, and even China. Further, the BGEA continued to expand throughout Graham's career, until today it encompasses a family of organizations that all told have a total budget of nearly $100 million.

The BGEA oversees a weekly radio program called "The Hour of Decision" that is heard around the world. It also publishes *Decision Magazine*—with a circulation of about 1.75 million in over 150 countries. Further, it has created World Wide Pictures, which has produced over 140 films. Graham has written 18 books, many of them best-sellers, and founded a book-publishing division through BGEA. His organization also trains evangelists and pastors through its international schools of evangelism, and the Billy Graham training center near Charlotte. In 1974, Graham spearheaded the Lausanne Congress on World Evangelization. Among its other accomplishments, the conference pulled together a wide variety of evangelical organizations from across the world to produce a document known as the "Lausanne Covenant," which has served as a near manifesto for the entire evangelical world ever since in its call to mission.

Graham founded *Christianity Today*, the flagship evangelical publication. His commitment to financial integrity led to the founding of the Evangelical Council for Financial Accountability in 1979, an organization that set strong professional standards for evangelical fund-raising and financial accountability. Graham has been a personal advisor to every President from Truman to George W. Bush. His son Franklin was named CEO of the BGEA in 2000, and also heads Samaritan's Purse, an international relief agency serving in countries across the globe by providing emergency relief, community development, HIV/AIDS resources and education, a medical mission program, and various programs to serve disadvantaged children throughout the world.

Graham's Influence

Graham's influence on Evangelicalism in the twentieth century is nearly impossible to overstate. His steadfast integrity has earned him the respect of even his detractors. His willingness to cooperate across theological, racial, and national lines has created partnerships both within and outside of Evangelicalism that has carried the movement forward countless times. The impact of his pollinization and involvement in a myriad of evangelical organization start-ups is likely incalculable.

> **In Their Own Words**
>
> "The world is changing, and with it the methods of evangelism will change also. But the message will *not* change, for it is timeless, meant for every generation."
>
> —Billy Graham, in his autobiography, *Just As I Am*

So great has Graham's influence on Evangelicalism been that one prominent historian and scholar wryly states that the very definition of evangelicals is "anyone who likes Billy Graham" (as was mentioned in Chapter 1). He has even been called the "Protestant Pope." In short, Billy Graham *was* the face of Evangelicalism for the twentieth century.

Although it is impossible to estimate how many people he has spoken to, one estimate is that he has personally spoken to 200 million people. In just one event in his 1995 Global Mission Crusade, Graham and his organization used satellite technology to reach over 1 billion people.

Historians will no doubt count Graham's future passing as marking the end of an era for Evangelicalism. But it all began in the tent crusade outside of Los Angeles in 1949, where Graham did what he did best: share the simple message of Christianity. At the time, no one could have imagined his eventual impact.

Christianity Today

As a result of the 1949 Los Angeles crusade, Graham began to have contact with evangelical leaders across the country. As he did, he saw that although evangelicals shared much of the same values, they were separated by both geography and denominationalism. There was no voice that could speak for all of Evangelicalism—no voice to communicate the new values of a movement that was more orthodox than mainline liberalism, yet eschewed the separatism, negativism, and extreme cultural conservatism of Fundamentalism. In order to both bring the new Evangelicalism to a larger public and provide a rallying point for evangelicals who had few, if any, formal connection points, Graham founded the magazine *Christianity Today* in 1956.

The magazine quickly became a focal point of the evangelical world. The combination of the intuitive cultural awareness of its leadership and an editorial staff filled with evangelical scholars soon made it the most widely read religious magazine in the nation. In its first-issue editorial, the magazine declared, "*Christianity Today* has its origin in a deepfelt desire to express historical Christianity to the present generation." Today it enjoys a paid circulation of well over 200,000, and its parent company, CTi, has spun off nearly a dozen other magazines with even more specific targets, such as *Leadership* journal (for pastors), *Today's Christian Woman*, *Christian Parenting*, *Campus Life*, and even *Computing Today*. CTi also maintains a popular website (www. christianitytoday.com) that offers much of its content online.

Christianity Today's arrival in 1956 signaled an important shift for the fledgling evangelical movement. Separated from Fundamentalism, yet staying true to its more conservative theological moorings, the movement had become clearly identifiable in its own right in American (and international) religious and cultural life. It was that clear identification, along with the new cultural movements that America as a whole was soon to experience, that opened the way for a whole new stage of growth.

The '60s and the Rise of the "Jesus People"

The 1960s saw massive cultural changes across America. As the younger generation explored, experimented, tuned in, turned on, and dropped out, younger people who were attracted to the message of Christianity began seeking newer, more culturally connected ways to express their faith. All of this found a synthesis in what is now generally called "the Jesus Movement."

Centered in California, the Jesus Movement spawned a plethora of coffee houses, communes, new music, new Bible translations, new congregations, and eventually even new denominations across the country. This was the Woodstock generation's expression of Christianity, and Evangelicalism was at the perfect point in its own development to encourage and be expanded by such expression. Committed to both cultural relevance and orthodoxy, the evangelical movement for the most part opened its arms to the next generation, having prepared the way for them with structures and organizations that enabled the rapid spread of the new expressions. By 1971, Billy Graham recognized the orthodoxy beneath the counter-cultural expression of this younger set, and placed his seal of approval on it in a book called *The Jesus Generation*. In June of 1971, the movement was recognized as a national phenomenon with *Time* magazine's cover story on "The Jesus Revolution."

The impact of this movement was as important for an Evangelicalism coming out of adolescence as the counter-cultural movements of the sixties and early seventies were for the rest of America as the baby boomers came of age. "Jesus music" was born, launching the multi-million dollar Christian music industry of today. In southern California, Pastor Chuck Smith welcomed the counter-cultures into his Calvary Chapel church, creating a paradigm for "culturally-relevant" churches and eventually launching a denomination in the process.

Parachurch organizations such as Campus Crusade for Christ, begun in the late 1950s, began to come into their own. In 1972, over 200,000 students from across the country attended Explo '72 in Dallas, a week long event organized by Campus Crusade that included Bible teaching, evangelism training, and a Jesus music festival that included people such as the long-haired hippie-looking Larry Norman (generally considered the father of "Christian Rock") and

> ### In Their Own Words
>
> "Why should the devil have all the good music?"
>
> —A lyric from Larry Norman's groundbreaking Christian rock album, "Only Visiting This Planet," released in 1972, voted the best Christian album of all time by Contemporary Christian Music Magazine

country singer Johnny Cash. Even today, echoes of the music birthed by the Jesus Movement can be heard every week in the praise choruses of nearly every evangelical church.

In short, the Jesus Movement provided the cultural spark that popularized Evangelicalism for the rising generation. That spark, combined with the organizational structures that had been built by the early pioneers of Evangelicalism, resulted in the phenomenal growth that characterized the decades to come.

The "Battle for the Bible"

However, not everyone was happy with the changes taking place within Evangelicalism. In particular, the new, less fundamentalist approach to understanding the Bible that was growing in the early 1970s was ruffling the feathers of the old-guard fundamentalists.

In 1972, crystallizing what was happening across the board in Evangelicalism, Fuller Seminary revised its statement of faith. The seminary removed the idea of the "inerrancy" of the Bible, and replaced it with more moderate terminology, calling the Bible "the only infallible rule of faith and practice." Although this was certainly conservative when compared to most mainline Protestant theology of the day, it was quite controversial, as many with more fundamentalist leanings saw it as an acquiescence to liberalism. (See Chapter 6 for a more complete treatment of the specific theological differences between "inerrancy" and "infallibility.") In recognizing on paper what had essentially been in practice in the seminary's faculty for some time, the seminary formalized a position that was becoming increasingly popular across Evangelicalism. It also set itself up to be a lightning rod for the criticism of those who disagreed.

The debate was brought out into the open with the publishing of *The Battle for the Bible* in 1976. Harold Lindsell, its author, had been on the original faculty of Fuller Seminary, and was the editor of *Christianity Today* when *The Battle for the Bible* was published. Convinced that the evangelical movement was drifting away from its center as it moved away from strict inerrancy, he produced a work that included examples of denominations, publishing houses, and in particular Fuller Seminary moving away from the idea that scripture was absolutely without error or contradiction.

Coming in the midst of a decade in which Evangelicalism was enjoying enormous popularity and a rising profile, the book created quite a controversy within the movement. It sparked a wide array of debate throughout the evangelical world, including

> ### The Gospel Truth
>
> Southern Baptists are not all conservatives. Many Southern Baptists support positions like the ordination of women and a less conservative viewpoint on the Bible, as evidenced by the over 1,800 churches who are "dually aligned" with both the Southern Baptist Convention and the more moderate Cooperative Baptist Fellowship.

several book-length responses. The disagreements that the book identified became the center of some important breaks in Evangelicalism, not the least of which was a controversy within the Southern Baptist Convention (by far the largest evangelical denomination) which eventually resulted in effectively splitting the denomination.

However, Lindsell's book and the controversy surrounding it signaled something else that was very important: a further diversification of Evangelicalism. Although a few reverted to calling themselves "fundamentalist" in the midst of the "battle for the Bible," the evangelical movement as a whole continued to hold together even as it wrestled internally—displaying a growing ability to enfold diverse beliefs while maintaining subgroupings around certain distinctions. In addition to perspectives on the Bible, other theological perspectives, in particular the "charismatic" or Pentecostal perspective, gained influence in overall Evangelicalism during this time period. Chuck Smith's Calvary Chapel, for example, practiced speaking in tongues—something that never would have occurred in the earlier stages of Evangelicalism.

Jimmy Carter and the "Year of the Evangelical"—1976

All of this set the stage for a remarkable moment when, in 1976, *Newsweek* magazine and the Gallup organization both declared "the year of the evangelical."

Even in the midst of some internal controversy, the growing influence of Evangelicalism was being felt in all corridors of society, from pop culture to academia. Evangelical churches were growing. Evangelicals had become major forces in the media industry, selling millions of books and records, and propelling Christian broadcasting to unprecedented heights.

But all of that paled in comparison to the rise of a south Georgia peanut farmer—and self-proclaimed evangelical—to the highest office in the land. When Jimmy Carter was elected President in 1976, a Gallup poll showed that fully half of all Protestants, and up to a third of all Americans, considered themselves to be "born again"—as did Carter himself. The October 25, 1976 *Newsweek* article (preceding Carter's election) explained:

Carter's dramatic capture of the Presidential nomination has already focused national attention on the most significant—and overlooked—religious phenomenon of the 70's: the emergence of evangelical Christianity into a position of respect and power.

Coming on the heels of Watergate, the country was hungry for moral values such as the honesty and integrity Carter exuded. His high level of academic achievement (in addition to other things, Carter had done graduate work in nuclear physics), combined with his Baptist upbringing, obvious personal commitment to Christ, and his long-term tenure as a Sunday School teacher at his hometown church in Plains, Georgia, made him the poster boy for an Evangelicalism that was sophisticated, yet solidly grounded. Evangelicalism had gone mainstream.

Finally recovering from the backward reputation its fundamentalist progenitors had gained after the Scopes trial in 1925, Evangelicalism had come into its own. And as America entered the high-flying 1980s, so did its most unique religious expression.

The Prime of the Parachurch—1980s

One clear indicator of the success of Evangelicalism during this time was the maturation of a plethora of *parachurch* organizations that were evangelical in mission. "Para" is a Greek preposition meaning "alongside," and the phenomenal growth of these organizations in Evangelicalism had developed into quite a cottage industry by the 1980s. In addition to Billy Graham's multifaceted organization, there were thousands of others (experts say there may be as many as 50,000 today—see Chapter 17) running the gamut of the needs and the interests of American culture.

def•i•ni•tion

A **parachurch** organization is a Christian group whose mission is directly related to the Christian cause, but is not a church. The word "para" comes from a Greek preposition meaning "to come alongside."

Student organizations such as Campus Crusade for Christ and Young Life were growing fast, counting hundreds of thousands as participants. Campus Crusade, for example, was spinning off other organizations left and right. These included a "Family Life Ministry" focusing on marriage and parenting, and the "Jesus Film" organization, which spread out world-wide in a ministry that focused on showing a film version of the life of Jesus to everyone from world leaders to displaced refugees in third world camps.

Evangelical political organizations were sprouting up and growing incredibly fast, as the stories of the Moral Majority and the Christian Coalition (see Chapter 15) point out. Evangelical relief organizations were providing help in unprecedented ways across the world. But none of these organizations captured the ethos of America in the conspicuous consumption 1980s quite as strongly as the televangelists, whose rise and fall exposed the dangers of religious power as it once again brought definitive damage to the evangelical reputation in the culture at large.

Televangelism: "I Was Wrong"

In Jim Bakker's appropriately titled 1996 memoir, *I Was Wrong*, the televangelist displayed a rare moment of understatement in saying, "What I learned in prison (was) that my previous philosophy of ministry and life was fundamentally flawed." What it took Bakker years behind bars to recognize was painfully obvious much earlier to the rest of the watching world.

At its height in the mid-1980s, Bakker's organization took in as much as $170 million a year through its TV program (PTL, which stood for "Praise the Lord"), its Heritage USA theme park (which drew as many as six million visitors a year—second only to the Disney theme parks), and other ancillary publications and ministries.

On screen, Jim and Tammy Faye were the perfect couple, but their 13 million–plus viewers got a dose of reality when it was revealed in 1987 that Bakker had an affair with a young secretary named Jessica Hahn, and then used PTL funds to pay her to remain silent about it. This prompted further investigation, ultimately resulting in Bakker being convicted of 24 counts of mail fraud, wire fraud, and conspiracy to commit fraud, in connection with multiple fundraising schemes and financial felonies.

The revelations of Jim and Tammy Bakker's lavish lifestyle both fascinated and revolted the country. The couple had six luxury homes, multiple luxury cars, jewelry, clothes, and an overall lifestyle that was more suggestive of sultans than ascetics. Their famously air-conditioned dog-house was the stuff of a late-night comedian's dreams. And their larger-than-life personalities—Jim with his boyish, likeable goofiness, and Tammy Faye with her mascara eternally running from her tears—would never have been believed if a Hollywood writer had made them up.

Further, the investigation and intense media focus on the Bakkers shone a light on the overall practices of televangelists throughout the nation who were raking in millions of dollars by decidedly unchristian means. During the same general time period as the Bakkers' rise and fall, Oklahoma Pentecostal televangelist Oral Roberts claimed to have had a vision of a 900-foot-tall Jesus telling him about the need for more funds. Roberts publicly stated that Jesus told him that God would end his life if the money the ministry needed did not come in soon.

In 1988, televangelist Jimmy Swaggart, who had built a $140 million empire of his own, was caught having had a tryst with a prostitute. After a tearful public confession, and a restarting of a new ministry, he was caught again in 1991. Also in 1991 Dallas evangelist Robert Tilton was the subject of an ABC *Primetime Live* broadcast, in which the show raised significant questions about the ministry integrity and fund-raising tactics of a man whose lavish lifestyle perhaps outstripped even the Bakker's.

Needless to say, all of these revelations and allegations gave Evangelicalism a black eye. Despite the general conspicuous consumption environment of the 1980s, the obvious disconnect between what these "leaders" said, and what they did, reinforced the doubts of many about both the believability of Christianity and the gullibility of those who followed it. The skepticism that developed toward Evangelicalism in general has yet to subside.

The Church Growth Movement

While the televangelist scandals were titillating the country, the vast majority of evangelical churches were faithfully doing their work. One result of this was the explosion of the *megachurch* phenomenon that was taking place by the 1980s.

The megachurch phenomenon was undergirded by a specific kind of thinking about church by evangelical leaders that combined the insights of modern management theory with the ancient theology of the church. This specific school of thought, which had become very influential and nearly universal in Evangelicalism by the 1980s, was known as the "church growth movement."

def•i•ni•tion

A **megachurch** is defined by church scholars as a church that has a weekly attendance of over 2,000 people.

Church growth teaching had actually begun to take root a generation earlier, when a missionary named Donald McGavran wrote several books (in the late 1950s) combining the insights of social sciences with his own experience as a cross-cultural missionary. Perhaps most famously, McGavran advocated the growth of churches through targeting what he called "homogeneous units"—or populations of people who were similar in culture. McGavran's principles were carried forward even further by the enfolding of his Institute of Church Growth into Fuller Seminary in 1965.

Over the next 20 to 30 years, countless numbers of church leaders were affected by church growth thought. Modern marketing techniques began to be used even more intensively in evangelical churches, and "target marketing" was particularly successful in white, suburban areas, where most of the early megachurches grew up. Further, the need-based programming that characterized the church growth emphasis was very attractive to the "me generation" baby boomers, particularly as their children reached the age of needing religious instruction.

C. Peter Wagner, a student of McGavran's, was instrumental in mainstreaming the church growth movement as he became Vice President of Fuller's Institute of Church Growth in 1971. Through the Institute's seminars, books written by a variety of evangelical leaders, and denominational training that began to emphasize church growth methods, evangelical pastors became quite adept at the pragmatic management techniques that could be added to the theology of the church to help its growth. By the 1980s any evangelical leader who was not familiar with these methods would have seemed neglectfully out of touch with the latest techniques for moving forward the mission of Christ.

Although the church growth movement, when seen from a historical perspective, was simply another example of the cultural improvisation and entrepreneurship that has always characterized Evangelicalism, it was and still is quite controversial. The pragmatism and even the "worldliness" of some of its techniques have been criticized by many both inside and outside of Evangelicalism. Many believe that the "homogeneous unit" principle, in particular, was not consistent with the biblical ethos of Jesus, who was conspicuously interested in diversity. However, the criticism was muted by the incredible success of the church growth methods. As America entered the 1990s, a new, unprecedented phenomenon was at full maturity within Evangelicalism, and as a result within the culture at large: the megachurch.

The Megachurch '90s

In the 1950s there were only a handful of churches that exceeded 2,000 in weekly attendance (the generally accepted scholarly definition of a "megachurch"). With the church growth movement in full swing, and the phenomenon of baby boomers growing into parents and looking for ways to ground the values of their kids, by the 1980s and into the 1990s there were hundreds of churches cresting the 2,000 or more mark.

In 2005, experts estimated that there were over 1,200 megachurches in the United States. Overall, the average weekly attendance in these churches was nearly 3,600 people, with at least one church drawing as many as 30,000 to its weekly services. Well over 4.2 million people (nearly a third of evangelicals overall) are a part of a megachurch. This does not include the thousands of other churches that are 1,000 or more in attendance. Increasingly, the large church experience is becoming the norm for evangelicals.

> **The Gospel Truth**
>
> At this writing, the largest megachurch in America is Houston's Lakewood Church, a nondenominational church that reportedly draws an average of 30,000 people a week to its home—the former CompaqCenter in Houston, formerly home to the NBA's Houston Rockets.

Importantly, megachurches often have a profound influence beyond their own membership. Through the dissemination of materials, training programs, and the high profiles of their leaders, the megachurch influence is felt all the way to the smallest churches in Evangelicalism. Indeed, many contemporary megachurches fulfill the role traditionally filled by denominations to smaller churches—providing curriculum for Sunday school and small groups, training for pastors and lay leaders, and even gathering churches together to cooperate in international missions efforts.

The megachurch, and even the large church experience, is important because of how it influences the overall evangelical culture. The niche-marketing of programs has created evangelicals who are quite sophisticated "consumers" of religious goods and services. Megachurches provide specifically targeted worship service styles—with a more contemporary soft-rock style for baby boomers, more traditional services for older generations, and more experiential and even liturgical services for gen-Xers—sometimes all within the same church.

Further, a standard strategy of megachurches is to provide smaller-group activities that are even more specifically targeted to various audiences and their needs. Sunday school classes for single adults, small groups for divorce recovery, parenting seminars for young families, large middle and high school programs whose schedules rival the activities calendars of the local YMCA—all of this and more is normal for the megachurch. Nearly all of the megachurches employ an overall "small groups" strategy to develop community among their members—creating weekly or semi-monthly gatherings of ongoing groups whose members share their lives and study the Bible together in homes throughout the community in addition to their Sunday worship attendance.

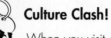

Culture Clash! _____

When you visit a megachurch, make sure to let them know you're a "first time visitor." That way they'll show you to their preferred parking, and you won't have to remember later whether you parked in the "Peter" or "Paul" section of the parking lot (sort of like the "Mickey" or "Minnie" sections at Disneyland).

Although many of the perceptions of the mega-church reflect real characteristics that have resulted in their general reputation (they are large, they do offer a plethora of programs, they are intensive in their focus on reaching out to others, and they do often feel much like a religious shopping mall), many characteristics are surprising. For example, only about 16 percent of megachurches are politically involved, according to a 2005 independent study. Further, they are frequently multiethnic, and often make a concerted effort to be so. Additionally (and surprisingly), according to pollsters, fund-raising is a fairly low priority for most megachurches, and the majority intentionally choose to engage in extensive community relief efforts, giving significant amounts of their budget away each year. And perhaps most importantly, megachurches are not low-commitment organizations. Most have high spiritual expectations of their members, and are quite vigilant about the orthodoxy of the beliefs taught in the church.

Into the Future ...

There has been much speculation about the decreased interest in megachurches by the upcoming generation of evangelicals (currently in their 20s to mid 30s). However, the statistics show that the phenomenon of megachurches continues to grow. From 2000–2005, the number of megachurches in the United States nearly doubled, and the trend is expected to continue.

On the horizon is a brand new movement that will likely change the face of Evangelicalism for the twenty-first century (see Chapters 19–20 on the "emerging church" phenomenon). But in the meantime, the megachurch may just be the apex of the modern evangelical movement. Their sophistication, impact, and sheer numbers show the influence of Evangelicalism as the movement moves into the twenty-first century.

The Least You Need to Know

♦ Billy Graham has played perhaps the most important role of any single individual in mobilizing and legitimizing evangelicals and evangelical institutions in the twentieth century.

♦ The Jesus Movement of the 1960s and early 1970s provided the cultural spark that combined with established organizational structures to create explosive growth for Evangelicalism in the years that followed.

♦ With Jimmy Carter's presidential run and the overall growth of Evangelicalism, 1976 was named by *Time* magazine, "The Year of the Evangelical."

♦ The 1980s saw the spectacular fall of several prominent TV evangelists, bringing Evangelicalism once again into disrepute.

♦ The 1990s saw the maturation of the megachurch phenomenon in Evangelicalism; some of the largest churches in the history of Christianity became home to thousands of people.

Part 2

Believe It or Not: A Survey of Evangelical Theology

The engine that drives the momentum of Evangelicalism is the basic personal beliefs of the people of the movement. And these beliefs are no side matter—typical evangelicals are not only more educated in their theology than most other Americans, they are also very committed to living their lives by it.

The clichés of the movement (e.g., being "born again"), and what those clichés connote in popular culture, have obscured the reality of a quite intelligent and responsive theology. In this section, you'll get a quick course in "Theology 101" that will not only help you understand Evangelicalism, it will serve as a reflection point for your own beliefs.

Get ready for a thought-provoking tour of basic Christian beliefs that will challenge and encourage you—whether you already believe it or not.

5

God, Are You Out There?

In This Chapter

- ◆ How can anyone know if God actually exists?
- ◆ How are faith and knowledge related?
- ◆ If God does exist, what is He like?
- ◆ Does God actually communicate with us?

In the movie "Signs," Mel Gibson plays a priest who has lost his faith. In the face of the possible impending doom of the planet, Gibson is seen in one scene sitting on the couch with his brother, watching mysterious lights in the sky on TV, and discussing what may be happening.

"People break down into two groups," he says to his questioning brother, who is looking for a spiritual answer to the situation. "When they experience something lucky, group number one sees it as more than luck, more than coincidence. They see it as a sign—evidence that there is someone up there watching out for them. Group number two sees it as just pure luck—a happy turn of chance. Deep down, they feel that whatever happens, they're on their own."

Evangelicals definitely fall into group number one. Why they feel that way is the subject of this chapter, which serves as the doorway to understanding most of the other theological tenants of Evangelicalism. God is definitely "there" for evangelicals—and not just "out there" but even "in *their*": in their daily lives, in their habit patterns, and even in their moment-by-moment decisions.

Leveling the Playing Field

There are essentially three options people have when approaching the idea of faith in God. Option one is *atheism*—the belief that there is no God. Option two is *agnosticism*, the belief that one cannot ever know whether or not there is a God. Option three is *theism*, the belief that God exists, in some form.

def•i•ni•tion

Atheism is a belief in the non-existence of God.

Agnosticism is a belief that it is not possible to know whether or not there is a God.

Theism is a belief that God exists, in some form.

According to evangelicals, each of these approaches—not just theism—takes a bit of faith. Atheism takes faith because one cannot empirically disprove the existence of God any more definitively than one can empirically prove the existence of God. There are simply too many unknowns. Thus, evangelicals would say that atheism is no more "intellectual" or fact-based than theism—it is just a different kind of faith.

Agnosticism, according to Thomas Henry Huxley (1825–1895), who coined the term, is "not properly described as a negative creed, nor indeed as a creed of any kind, except insofar as it expresses *absolute faith* in the validity of a principle, which is as much ethical as intellectual …: that it is wrong for a man to say that he is certain of the objective truth of any proposition unless he can produce evidence which logically justifies that certainty" (italics mine). Thus, Huxley identifies agnosticism as faith in a principle—but faith all the same.

Evangelicals believe that given the choice of the faith of atheism in no God, the faith of agnosticism in the human ability to reason, and the faith of theism that ties together human reason with evidence for God's existence, the weight of the evidence falls toward theism. It is important to recognize here that most evangelicals are highly concerned with intellectual credibility. Most see faith as a "leap into the light," not a "leap into the dark."

The Limits of Reason and the Nature of Faith

Before getting into some of the specifics of the evidence that evangelicals cite regarding the existence of God, it is important to understand the limits of reason and the nature of faith from the standpoint of evangelicals.

Simply put, evangelicals believe that human reason has limitations. For instance, scientific proof is limited by the ability to reproduce and simultaneously observe things. Thus, because the creation of the universe (for example) cannot be reproduced and observed, science is limited in what it can absolutely assert with regard to creation.

Further, evangelicals are suspect with regard to the absolute faith that many in the modern world put in the human ability to parse absolute truth from human experience. Only God is infallible for evangelicals, and thus part of the "fallen" nature of humankind includes a built-in fallibility factor for human logic. That doesn't mean that evangelicals are not logical—on the contrary, many of the "proofs" for theism below are quite complex when presented in their full form. It does mean, however, that evangelicals are careful to maintain a humility with regard to the limitations of human wisdom.

Faith, for evangelicals, is thus the integration of truth, human reason, *and* divine revelation. One way to look at it is to say that evangelical faith involves five factors:

- Truth

- Logic

- Beauty

- Accountability

- Doubt

Truth is that which is objective and revealed by God through "general revelation" (i.e., creation, human reason, etc.) and "special revelation (i.e., the scriptures or individual human interactions with God). Logic is the reasoning of the human mind with regard to the truth. Beauty is found in the response of the human heart to the truth. Accountability involves the responsibility of the human will to act on the truth. Doubt is the humility of humanity toward the truth.

All of these factors combine to create evangelical faith. It is a faith of the head, the heart, and the will. Based on all of this, the rest of this chapter unpacks three beliefs about God that are foundational to Evangelicalism:

- A belief that God exists

- A belief that God is simultaneously transcendent (beyond humanity) and immanent (accessible to humanity)

- A belief that God personally and individually interacts with people

As you read, it is important to understand that evangelicals are monotheists (believing in one God) as distinguished from pantheists (who believe that god is literally in everything) or polytheists (who believe that there are many gods).

A God Who Exists

The first foundational belief of evangelicalism is simply that God exists. Why do evangelicals believe this? Several of the most often cited lines of thought are the following:

- The existence of a universal human idea of right and wrong

- The complexity and order of creation

- The variety of evidence in individual human experiences with God

Each of these arguments carries its own nuances and distinctives, as we shall see below.

Right and Wrong as a Clue

If you've ever been in an argument, you've experienced the first of our "proofs" about the existence of God.

Someone takes something that is yours. Someone tells you a lie that harms you. Someone cuts in line in front of you at the grocery store. "Wait a minute," you say to them, "that's not fair!" The existence of that ingrained sense of fairness—of morality—of universal "rights and wrongs" is proof, evangelicals say, that we are more than just cosmic accidents.

> **In Their Own Words**
>
> "If there was no God, we would all be 'accidents' … There would be no right or wrong, and no hope beyond your brief years here on earth."
>
> —Evangelical Pastor Rick Warren in *The Purpose Driven Life*

C. S. Lewis is a favorite writer of many evangelicals. In his book *Mere Christianity*, he explains this appeal to right and wrong as a clue to God's existence by pointing to the universal nature of people's response, when they are in an argument, to being wronged:

… what interests me about all these remarks [i.e., "That's not fair!"] is that the man who makes them is not merely saying that the other man's behavior does not happen to please him. He is appealing to some kind of standard behavior which he expects the other man to know about. And the other man very seldom replies, "To hell with your standard." Nearly always he tries to make out that what he has been doing does not really go against the standard, or that if it does there is some kind of special excuse.

One response to this argument from unbelievers is that the ideas of "right" and "wrong" are very subjective. Evangelicals counter by saying that while there are indeed specifics that are carried out differently, there are still bottom-line beliefs in fairness that are universal. No one, for example, believes that it is good to hurt innocent children. No one believes that it is right to kill someone else in cold blood, simply for fun. These kinds of foundational human values come from somewhere, and evangelicals say that they come from God.

Another response to the universal right and wrong argument is that it could be the result of instinct. Couldn't this sense of right and wrong simply be a result of a protective evolutionary trait that enabled humans to be the most fit to survive?

Possibly, say evangelicals, but that does not account for the self-*less*-ness that is integral to many of our universal beliefs. For instance, story after story in human history venerates the idea of a person sacrificing themselves on behalf of others. People who lay down their lives for others because of love are lifted up as heroes. An over-riding evolutionary instinct for personal survival would not produce such a sacrificial impulse.

Yet another possible refutation of this idea is that rights and wrongs have been socialized into humans. But evangelicals would ask, "Where did the original idea to socialize these values come from?" They do not arise spontaneously, evangelicals say—they come from Someone outside of human existence.

Creation as a Sign

A second key argument for the existence of God is literally all around us. Evangelicals believe that creation—from the vastness of the universe to the immediacy of our individual bodies—is a sign to those aware enough to see God's hand.

First of all, evangelicals would say that the existence of God makes sense of the universe's origin. Something does not come out of absolutely nothing. Or to put it into a syllogism:

- Whatever begins to exist must have a cause.

- The universe did begin to exist.

- Therefore, the universe must have a cause.

The agent of causation, according to evangelicals, is God. Someone had to start the ball rolling. And although the eternal nature of any being is hard to grasp, evangelicals say that God as the "uncaused cause" makes more sense than existence with no prime mover.

Following from that logic is the sign of the incredible intricacy and complexity of the universe. Evangelicals believe that this is not simply the result of a random, growing sophistication, but of intelligent design. They point to scientific evidence that confirms the incredible—even unbelievable—coincidences that would have had to take place for life as we know it to come into existence.

For example, physicist and author Steven Hawking (not an evangelical) has calculated that if the universe's expansion rate after the Big Bang had been smaller, by even one part in a hundred thousand million, the universe would have been destroyed in a great fireball. It is evidence such as this that convinces evangelicals that creation was (and continues to be) initiated, planned, and held together by an all-powerful, all-knowing God.

> **In Their Own Words**
>
> "… I'll tell you this: the precision [of the universe] is so utterly fantastic, so mathematically breathtaking, that it's just plain silly to think it could have been an accident."
>
> —Dr. William Lane Craig, Ph.D., from an interview in *The Case for Faith* by Lee Strobel

In laymen's terms, think about Michelangelo's "David" sculpture. The intricacy, the beauty, the obvious craftsmanship of the work are stunning. Now imagine that someone told you that it simply naturally occurred in that formation—over billions of years. Would you believe them?

Overall, evangelicals believe that if there is a design, there must be a designer. For them, the burden of proof lies with those who believe in a random creation out of nothing producing the universe that we inhabit. Logically, they believe that it makes more sense to have faith in God than to have faith in a random, uncaused creation.

Human Experience as a Confirmation

Perhaps the most personal argument evangelicals make about the existence of God has to do with the vastness and variety of human experiences that have been attributed to God. Throughout the ages, and even today, evangelicals argue, God can be and is personally experienced by people.

Generally, this argument points to the fact that countless people of different eras and of widely different cultures claim to have experienced God on a personal level. Answered prayers, specific guidance and/or interaction with God, conversion experiences, and even miracles are examples. These intimate interactions with God have had an astounding impact on the lives of the individuals who experience them, and collectively, on the development of cultures. For evangelicals, the vast number of people and the powerful impact of their experiences is strong evidence for the reality of God.

Many would say that these "experiences" with God could be interpreted differently. But evangelicals would say that the vast number of people reporting these experiences in essentially similar terms leaves the burden of proof to those who say the experiences do not exist. The consistency of these claims over vast periods of time, the fact that normal, trustworthy people from all walks of life make these claims, and the positive impact of the experiences all point toward the reality of a God who exists. Beyond logic and argument, evangelicals would say that changed lives through interaction with the divine are the ultimate confirmation of God's existence.

One final "experience" argument often cited by evangelicals has to do with those who have experienced God without even knowing it. As strange as this sounds, it is actually an appeal to the human desire for goodness and meaning that goes beyond our everyday existence. This universal desire for something greater than ourselves, evangelicals say, is the experience of God "calling" individuals—a gentle suitor drawing people to Himself. As C. S. Lewis described it succinctly in *Mere Christianity*: "If I find in myself a desire which no experience in this world can satisfy, the most probable explanation is that I was made for another world."

So—since evangelicals believe that God exists, it naturally raises another question: what is He like?

Here, There, and Everywhere

Popular culture's conceptions of God run the gamut from "God-the-old-man-in-the-sky" who is sort of an absent-minded professor, to "God-the-policeman" who can't wait to bust us. The evangelical understanding of God can be summarized under two main ideas: God as transcendent, and God as immanent. This is the second foundational belief of evangelicalism with regard to the nature of God.

The Transcendent God

One way to understand the idea of the transcendence of God is to simply say that God is "other." This is a good definition of the word "holy" (which literally means to be "set apart"). When evangelicals say that God is "holy" they are referring to much more than His moral purity. They are referring to His utterly-other-than-human nature.

Cornerstones for evangelicals in this regard are the "omni" (or "all") characteristics of God. God is "omnipotent"—all powerful. God is "omniscient"—all-knowing. God is "omnipresent"—having the ability to be everywhere at the same time. God is eternal, unchanging, self-existent, unlimited by space, and beyond time. All of these "holy" aspects of God point to the fact that He is not just quantitatively different than humans, but qualitatively different. He transcends the human condition.

This transcendence also extends to things like God's ability to love, to be just, and to wisely rule. He is not just better at these things than we are; they emanate from His qualitatively different nature. The exciting thing, evangelicals believe, is that He has gifted us as humans with an ability to see these ideals and put them into practice (however imperfectly). This is part of how we are made in His image.

The Immanent God

But God is not only beyond us in transcendence, evangelicals believe that He is simultaneously immediately available. This is known in theological language as the "immanence" of God.

Jesus begins the Lord's Prayer with the words: "Our Father in heaven …" Because of the cultural understanding we have come to develop about heaven, these words seem to separate God from us. But from the standpoint of those who actually heard Jesus say these words, they had the exact opposite effect. In Jesus' day, the "heavens" were often synonymous with what we today would call the atmosphere, or even the air that we breathe. Jesus' followers understood Him to be saying that God is literally as close to us as the air that we breathe. This is not pantheism (the belief that everything is God), but instead a striking example of the fact that God is closer than we think. Evangelicals believe this very strongly; one way it can be clearly seen is in the familiar-styled language that they often use to address God in prayer. Often striking in their informality, evangelicals' prayers reflect their belief that God is indeed a close and personal Father in addition to being the Creator whom they revere.

Additionally, a very important foundation of evangelical theology is the immanence of God actually indwelling a person through the Holy Spirit. This is a part of the Trinitarian belief of evangelicals (the belief that God exists in three persons—the Father, the Son, and the Holy Spirit), and is key to their understanding of the practical nature of living out their faith (see Chapter 9, "A Model for Spiritual Growth"). For our purposes here, it is important to simply recognize that for evangelicals God is *very* immanent—uniquely in-dwelling in followers of Christ through the Holy Spirit, just as He is simultaneously omnipresent (everywhere) and holy (completely other-than-human).

> **Culture Clash!**
>
> The informal tone of evangelical prayers can sometimes be offensive to those of a more formal church background. If this is true for you, recognize that informality in prayer is not a sign of disrespect for an evangelical, it is instead expressive of the personal intimacy they feel with God.

Overall, evangelical theology affirms that God, in His transcendence and immanence, is *personal*. This is important, because it means that God's connection with human beings is more than the connection of an "energy force." Even in His "otherness" God is someone who thinks, responds, and feels in a way that is at some level similar to human characteristics. In other words, He understands us.

A God Who Interacts

This belief in God's understanding leads to a third foundational belief about God that perhaps most clearly distinguishes Evangelicalism from other faith approaches. Evangelicals believe that God not only exists, but that He personally, even individually, interacts with us.

A prevalent belief in popular culture is that God is "out there," but that He has more important fish to fry than to spend His time involving Himself with the affairs of individual human beings. This is often called "the watchmaker theory" of God (theologians often call it "Deism"). This theory works off of the idea that God created the universe, set it in motion according to specific laws (i.e., gravity, thermodynamics, etc.), and now allows it to run according to those laws and in

> **In Their Own Words**
>
> "[God's] greatness is precisely what allows him to plan his day around me or anyone and everyone else as he chooses."
>
> —Dallas Willard, in *Hearing God*

response to the choices made by those inhabiting the universe. In this view, God is out there, but He is not available. Some Eastern religious viewpoints take this a bit further, advocating an understanding of God as not only unavailable, but as impersonal and even non-relational in character. Neither of these are consistent with the evangelical approach.

As opposed to a belief in God as an impersonal being or force, three specific ways in which God interacts with people are characteristically important to evangelicals: prayer, miracles, and individual guidance.

Prayer

Evangelicals pray to a God from whom they expect personal answers. This does not mean that God is a divine "Santa Claus" to them, however. What it does mean is that faithful evangelicals pray regularly, not just in a crisis. And their praying takes many forms.

They pray to enlarge their vision of God by praising Him for His attributes, much like David the Psalmist, who said, "Great is the Lord, and most worthy of praise; his greatness no one can fathom" (Psalm 145:3). They pray to confess their sins to God—again, like David, who wrote, "Create in me a clean heart, O God; and renew a right spirit within me" (Psalm 51:10—KJV). They pray to express thanks to God, recognizing Him as the source of their blessings.

> **The Gospel Truth**
>
> Many evangelicals use the "ACTS" model for their daily prayers: they begin with Adoration of God (praise); they move into Confession of their sin; they offer Thanksgiving for their blessings; and they end with Supplication (asking) for their needs and the needs of others.

And of course, they pray to ask for what they need. "Give us this day our daily bread" is a prayer that is expressed on a quite specific level for evangelicals. They regularly go to God to ask Him for very specific needs in their lives and the lives of others. They take to heart the apostle Paul's guidance in Philippians 4:6 in the New Testament: "[I]n *everything*... make your requests known to God" (NASB, italics mine).

Overall, evangelicals place so much emphasis on prayer because they believe that God interacts on a specific personal basis with them through their practice of it. But how do they keep this faith in God's interaction when it seems that their prayers are *not* answered?

Answering the question of unanswered prayers is often thought of in this way for evangelicals: sometimes God says, "Yes," sometimes He says, "No," and sometimes He says, "Wait." Evangelicals have great faith in the divine wisdom of God, and thus usually interpret "unanswered" prayer as a prayer that has been answered in a way that is different from what they expected or hoped. For more on this idea (which is a close cousin to the idea of God's response to human suffering), see the section in Chapter 9 called "Reality Checks."

Miracles

A second way that evangelicals believe God's interactive personality is seen is through miracles. In this context, a miracle can be defined as an intervention of God in a specific circumstance that occurs outside of "normal" causes. From Jesus turning water into wine in Galilee thousands of years ago, to God miraculously reaching in to arrest the spread of cancer in a hospital patient today, evangelicals believe that God shows His personal involvement by intervening in specific ways in people's lives. The degree and the frequency to which God acts in this way is sometimes debated in evangelical circles, but the belief that God does indeed intervene is a bedrock credo of Evangelicalism.

Logically, a belief in miracles flows from an understanding of a God who exists and interacts. Think of it this way:

◆ If God exists, miracles are possible. (If God can create the universe, He can certainly heal someone, or turn water into wine.)

◆ If God exists and is both personal and relational, miracles are not only possible, but probable. (God's interactive nature would likely lead him to intervene on behalf of those He created.)

Indeed, it would be illogical, based on the claims of evangelicals regarding God, that they would *not* believe in miracles.

An intriguing way of thinking about miracles comes from the teachings of Jesus about the "kingdom of God." Simply understood, the kingdom of God is any place where what God wants done gets done. A big part of Jesus' message was that He came to bring the kingdom—to make it available in a new way to humankind. ("The kingdom of God is at hand!" He says in Mark 1:15.) Evangelicals of today believe that their mission is to continue to facilitate God's work in bringing His kingdom to their worlds, following in the footsteps of Jesus. Since "the kingdom" includes the in-breaking of God's compassion in a fallen world, miracles in today's world can be seen as simply a logical outcome of the arrival of the kingdom. They are the natural result of the kingdom actually being "at hand."

Ask the average evangelical if they believe in miracles, and they will say, "Yes." However, it would be dishonest to imply that they don't have their doubts. By definition, miracles are uncommon. However, affirmation of the miraculous is an important part of the overall belief structure of the evangelical faith in a God who is personally involved in human lives.

Individual Guidance

Beyond prayer and miracles, a third confirmation for evangelicals regarding God's interactive nature comes through specific personal guidance that evangelicals believe people receive from Him. This happens in several ways.

Culture Clash! _____

The idea of "hearing" from God may seem strange at first, but consider comedienne Lily Tomlin's perspective, as quoted in *Hearing God* by Dallas Willard: "Why is it," she asks, "that when we speak to God we are said to be praying, but when God speaks to us we are said to be schizophrenic?"

First of all, evangelicals believe that people receive individual guidance from God through the Bible. This is not, however, the stereotypical idea of someone opening the Bible at random, pointing their finger on a page, and taking what they read as "God's will." Instead, evangelicals take great care in studying the Bible to fully understand its precepts, and then in using those precepts as a grid through which to make decisions.

For example, the evangelical position on abortion (see Chapter 13) is drawn from an understanding that the scriptures teach that life is sacred. An evangelical facing an important life decision that is not as clear-cut morally (i.e., "Should I accept an offer for a new job in a different city?") would typically evaluate the options by sifting them through the filter of general biblical principles. In the case of a new job, for example, an evangelical might ask questions such as, "If I take the new job, am I simply pursuing more money?" "Is it best for other members of my family?" "How is this job likely to affect my ability to share my faith in Christ with others?" Thus, the clear biblical principles (pursuing righteousness before wealth, caring for others, and sharing the Christian faith with others) inform the specifics involved in making the individual decision.

Evangelicals believe that the words of the Bible are quite "alive" in that God uses them to speak His will into their lives on an ongoing basis. Hebrews 4:12 says that "the word of God is living and active. Sharper than any double-edged sword, it penetrates even to dividing soul and spirit, joints and marrow; it judges the thoughts and attitudes of the heart." Thus, evangelicals believe that God Himself is interacting with them on an individual basis through the scriptures.

Beyond the Bible, many evangelicals believe that God "speaks" to them very specifically about individual issues in their lives. This "speaking" of God often comes through conscious impressions as people pray or seek God's guidance, or even from "open doors"—circumstances that seem to indicate God's invitation. Of course, these are very subjective experiences of guidance, and can be misinterpreted. However, just as one learns to recognize the voice of someone on the telephone through experience with hearing the person's voice, evangelicals believe that the unique quality and authority of God's voice can be recognized through experience in "listening" to Him through various subjective means.

The Nature of Mystery

Can anyone conclusively prove the existence of God?

Surprisingly, according to evangelicals, the answer is no. Although they believe the weight of the evidence leads to the logical conclusion of a God who exists, who is both transcendent and immanent, and who is personally involved with His creatures and creation, evangelicals agree with Christians down through the ages who have maintained that ultimately a belief in God comes from faith. God is a mystery, and by definition is greater than human minds can fully comprehend.

However, evangelicals contend that the mystery of God can be *known*. In the same way two people can know love, but not be able to explain it, the God who loves can be experienced with both heart and head. To the skeptic, evangelicals would say along with the Psalmist (Psalm 34:8), "Taste and see that the Lord is good." And to the believer who wrestles with the mysteries of God, evangelicals would affirm the words of the man who said to Jesus (Mark 9:24), "I do believe, help my unbelief."

The Least You Need to Know

- Evangelicals do not believe that the existence of God can be empirically proven. However, they do believe that the weight of the evidence points to God's existence.

- Evangelicals believe that God transcends human existence, and yet is constantly, immediately, and personally available to humankind.

- According to evangelicals, key ways that God interacts with people include prayer, miracles, the messages of the Bible, and specific individual communication that comes in various forms.

- Evangelicals believe that although God cannot be fully understood, He can be intimately known.

Evangelicals and the Bible

In This Chapter

- ◆ Is the Bible we have the Bible as it was originally written?
- ◆ What do evangelicals believe about ancient books that didn't make it into the Bible?
- ◆ Do evangelicals take the Bible literally?
- ◆ How do evangelicals apply the Bible to their everyday lives?

Glen Proechel has a passion for the Bible.

Like many evangelicals, he reads the Bible regularly, and has even studied it extensively (Glen is an ordained pastor, currently working on a Doctoral degree from Trinity Seminary in Indiana). But Glen took his Bible passion a step further than most, deciding to devote his time to *translating* the Bible. And Glen's language of choice—the vernacular into which he felt called to translate—was one that no one else had ever before attempted. Here is a sample of Glen's work, a translation of Matthew 5:14-16:

> qIbDaq puyjaq tlhiH. Muddaq puvtaHbogh chunDab So"eghlaHbe'. puyjaq bojormoHchugh, luSpetDaq boSo 'laHbe' 'ach logh poSDaq 'ang 'egh ngeHbej wovmoHmo'. vaj latlhpu'vaD peboch ta 'meyraj QaQ luleghlu'jaj 'ej QI'tu 'Daq vavra'vaD quv lunobjaj.

If you're wondering exactly where on earth people speak a language like this, stop wondering. It doesn't exist on earth. Glen has spent a year and a half translating various excerpts from the Gospels into … Klingon. That's right—the language of the warrior race from *Star Trek*. As a matter of fact, Glen has written a book about this, which he has aptly titled, *Good News For the Warrior Race*.

"The purpose behind this was to get people talking about it," says Glen, who makes his home in Red Lake Falls, Minnesota, and who is also the Chancellor of the Interstellar Language School. (Don't believe me? Check them out at www.geocities.com/Athens/8853/.) Glen says that he wanted "to get some Trekkies who wouldn't normally be interested in the Bible interested, and to share the gospel with them that way."

According to Proechel, who has also conducted church services and even weddings in Klingon, the Bible translation project has worked "quite well." "We get letters back about how we've gotten people interested in the gospel through this," he says, recognizing that some folks who may never have connected with the Bible in any other way will have found their way to it through this—perhaps the first—interplanetary missionary work.

Why Is the Bible So Important to Evangelicals?

Glen's devotion to the scriptures is obviously quite unique. However, the lengths to which he has gone to make the Bible relevant can be seen as a picture of the high regard all evangelicals have for the Bible. In a country where 9 out of 10 households own a Bible, and where in the typical household there are more copies of the Bible than people, and where an astounding 76 percent of the population believe the Bible to be divinely inspired, evangelicals stand out as those who actually practice what they preach about it. According to pollsters, about 88 percent of evangelicals read their Bible at least once a week, nearly double the readership of the population at large (45 percent).

In addition, evangelical Bible study resources (for both group and individual purposes) are among the highest volume items for evangelical book sellers. The typical evangelical church spends an average of one-half of the time (usually 30–45 minutes) of its weekly services on what is called "expositional preaching"—a highly researched method designed to expose the truth of the Bible through extensive analysis of the biblical languages, cultures, and interpretations of the passage being presented, the ultimate goal of which is the application of the truths of the Bible to everyday life.

All of this Bible-focused energy comes from the central place the Bible has in evangelical life. Evangelicals see the scriptures as a divinely inspired objective source in a relativistic, subjective world. In their view, the Bible has stood the test of time as a repository of truth, a source of doctrine, a devotional guide, and a meta-narrative that explains the very purpose of human kind.

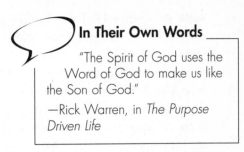

In Their Own Words

"The Spirit of God uses the Word of God to make us like the Son of God."

—Rick Warren, in *The Purpose Driven Life*

Even further, for evangelicals the Bible carries a mystical reality. They believe that God speaks directly to them through the "living and active" word (Hebrews 4:12). How they believe this happens will be discussed later in the chapter, but for now it is important to recognize that the Bible is much, much more than just a book to evangelicals: it is the very word of God.

How Did We Get the Bible We Have?

But where did that word come from? This is an important question for evangelicals, as their veneration of the Bible is based on a bedrock belief in its trustworthiness. Indeed, especially since the early 1900s, an increasing amount of evangelical scholarship has been focused on proving the accuracy and overall reliability of the scriptures we now possess. Like lawyers in a courtroom, evangelicals have sought to provide evidentiary proof beyond a shadow of a doubt that the Bible is not only inspired, but accurate. From many of their perspectives, if the Bible contains errors, it can no longer be regarded as the word of a perfect God. (This quintessentially modern mindset, however, is being increasingly called into question by evangelicals of a more postmodern bent—see Chapters 19 and 20 for more information.) In general, evangelicals believe that the Bible we now have is accurate. How they believe we got this Bible can be described in several steps.

Inspiration

First of all, evangelicals believe that the original writing of the books of the Bible was more than a human affair. Exactly how this happened will be discussed later, but it is important to recognize that the starting point for the evolution of the Bible (okay, so maybe that's a contradiction in terms?) is its inspired conception.

Some evangelicals believe that the Bible was inspired in such a way as to make it "inerrant" in its original documents. The most strident defenders of the doctrine of *inerrancy* believe that every single pen stroke of the authors of the Bible was completely inspired and without error. This doctrine has been quite controversial in evangelical circles (remember the "Battle for the Bible" in Chapter 4?), due to its high dependence on creative interpretations to effect a full harmonization of every single detail of scripture with history, and even with itself. However, those who hold to it see it as a bedrock belief that when strayed from creates a "slippery slope" of interpretative possibilities. If the Bible is incorrect on a small thing, these people argue, it is only logical to believe that it can be in error on other things, including major doctrines. An incredible amount of creative and surprisingly convincing thinking has gone into the interpretation of the Bible along these lines by evangelical biblical scholars.

def•i•ni•tion

Inerrancy is a belief that the Bible is absolutely without error in all its teachings, including those teachings that go beyond theology and have to do with areas like science and history.

Infallibility is the belief that the Bible is accurate in all its teachings with regard to matters of "faith and practice." It is sometimes used as a synonym for inerrancy, but is distinguished by some evangelicals as being a claim for the Bible that is not related to issues of science, history, or minor internal discrepancies in the Bible.

Other evangelicals believe in a doctrine of *infallibility*. This is similar to inerrancy, but is a bit less restrictive in its application. Those who hold to infallibility typically believe that the scriptures are completely true and without error *in all matters of faith and practice*. This means that smaller discrepancies within scripture are allowed to stand without having to be harmonized, because the overall doctrines taught by the Bible stand as completely accurate. As former Fuller Seminary President David Allan Hubbard wrote in a short book on the Fuller statement of faith in 1979 called *What We Evangelicals Believe*, infallible means that "the Scriptures are exactly what God wanted them to be .... The infallible character of the Scriptures means that they will get their message across .... The infallible character of the scriptures also means that they will not deceive us in regards to God's truth."

What's In and What's Out: The Collection of the Canon

Once the scriptures were written, they circulated. Evangelicals believe that those books that were recognized by believers as inspired eventually became part of what is known as the "canon." Some say the Old Testament canon was complete as early as the fifth century B.C., when the prophet Ezra put the texts into a collection. The most certain definitive date for the Old Testament canon is 95 A.D., when the secular historian Josephus identified in one of his documents the 39 books we have now.

The New Testament canon developed in similar fashion, with various writings circulating throughout the first three centuries after Jesus' death. (Most scholars believe they were written within 20–70 years after his death, within the same generation of the eyewitnesses of the events.) At a meeting in 397 called the Council of Carthage, church leaders officially recognized the 27 books of the New Testament that we use today.

It is important to note that the books recognized as canon all had a long history of acceptance in the community of faith as being inspired. Criteria used for acceptance in the canon included factors such as historical accuracy, the consistency of the books with each other and with what people knew to be the character of God, and the authorship of the books. (For instance, only those books written by the apostles of Jesus or a student or associate of an apostle were accepted as a part of the New Testament canon.) The best way to describe it is that evangelicals believe that the books of the canon were "recognized" as inspired, not "chosen" to be in the canon. Indeed, most of the books in the Bible had been recognized as inspired long before various councils made it official.

What About the Other Books?

Lots of noise has been made recently about books that were around during the same time that did not make the cut. Many believe that officials kept them out for reasons of power, or to protect their own theological agendas. However, an honest look into these books generally shows rather quickly why they were not accepted.

The Gospel of Thomas, for example, has received much attention of late. One quotation from the end of the book will serve to show why it was not deemed inspired:

> Simon Peter said, "Let Mary leave us, for women are not worthy of life." Jesus said, "I myself shall lead her in order to make her male so that she too may become a living spirit resembling you males. For every woman who will make herself male will enter the kingdom of heaven."

Evangelicals would say, "Aren't we *all* glad *that* didn't make it into the Bible?"

The Transmission of the Texts

Once the books of the Bible were written and collected, they had to be passed down from generation to generation. This was done through hand copies that were made of the scriptures (no original copies of any of the books of the Bible remain). Evangelicals believe that this process was not only superintended by God, but that it provides for more than ample historical evidence of the essential accuracy of the documents.

For instance, in literary circles, the discipline that is used to test this historic reliability of documents is known as *historiography*. There are three basic tests of historiography, and they are the same whether you are studying the Bible or Shakespeare. The three are ...

- The bibliographical test, which primarily studies the number and dating of the ancient manuscripts of a work.

- The internal evidence test, which looks at factors like the number of eyewitness accounts and the number of internal discrepancies in the text.

- The external evidence test, which seeks corroborating evidence from other writings of the time.

> ### In Their Own Words
>
> "The Bible, compared with other ancient writings, has more manuscript evidence than any ten pieces of classical literature combined."
>
> —Josh McDowell in *Evidence that Demands a Verdict*

In all three of these areas, the Bible is astoundingly well attested to (for more information on this, see Josh McDowell's excellent resource, *Evidence that Demands a Verdict*). To keep this discussion within the scope of this book, let's look in detail at just one of these tests: the bibliographical test.

The idea here is that since virtually no original copies of literature dating this far back are available today, one must test the validity of a work based on the number of copies of the manuscript that are available and the interval of time that passed between the original and the copies.

The second-most well attested piece of literature in antiquity according to this test is Homer's *Iliad*. We have 643 manuscript copies of the *Iliad*, the earliest of which was made about 500 years after the original writing. The first most well attested piece of literature is the New Testament, for which there are 24,000 manuscripts, the earliest of which was written 25 years after the original. Modern scholars accept the textual reliability of other ancient works on far less adequate grounds than are available for the New Testament.

Add to that the absolute obsession of the ancient scribe/copyists as to the accuracy of the text (for instance, counting every single letter of each manuscript, identifying the center letter, and comparing the center letters to insure the accuracy of the copies), and the fact that the essential, overall accuracy of the current texts is not often disputed by the majority of modern scholars, and you can see why evangelicals stand on very solid ground in saying that the Bible we have today is essentially the Bible as it was originally written.

> **The Gospel Truth**
>
> Although there are some textual variants in the oldest New Testament manuscripts available today, scholars Norman Geisler and William Nix (in *A General Introduction to the Bible*) express the overwhelming scholarly consensus in affirming the inconsequence of the variants, saying that "most of them are merely mechanical matters such as spelling or style."

What Is the Nature of the Bible's *Exousia*?

Exousia is a New Testament Greek word that can be translated as "authority" or "power" or—intriguingly in this case—"right." In addition to believing in the overall reliability of the Bible, evangelicals believe that the Bible literally has a "right" to guide us. That's a pretty big claim. What is it based on?

The first answer for most evangelicals is usually some variant of the idea that we have just discussed. The Bible is inspired, accurate, and reliable. Since it is God's word, it is authoritative. But why evangelicals are willing to literally base their lives on the Bible is more nuanced. Three basic ideas describe the nature of the Bible that empowers it in such a dramatic way in evangelicals' lives. The first is the Bible's authoritative quality.

The Bible's Authoritative Quality

The authoritative quality of the Bible for evangelicals goes beyond the rationalistic tests of accuracy and reliability that have often been espoused in the defense of the Bible from modern critique. In a very real way for evangelicals, the authoritative quality of the Bible means that it has an inherent internal witness that authenticates that it stands over and above human experiences in a position to evaluate them. The Bible is Torah, it is the Ten Commandments—it is the authority of healing and renewal that makes it obvious that where the word is, the kingdom of God is at hand. The entire story of the scriptures lays out universal standards in a completely true way, according to evangelicals. Thus, in a subjective world, the Bible becomes a source of objective evaluation. This authoritative quality, they say, is what we feel when we experience the conviction of needing to change our ways based on something the Bible says.

The Bible's Revelatory Nature

Secondly, the Bible's exousia comes from its revelatory nature. Simply put, the Bible tells us things that we would not discover on our own. For instance, we get deep insight into the specific character qualities of God in the Bible. This is an example of what theologians call "special revelation" as opposed to "general revelation" (that which is obvious to us in the world around us). The Bible for evangelicals is not just the record of God acting; it itself is a continuing act of divine self-disclosure—which means that God can speak to us directly through it. This revelatory nature, say evangelicals, is what we experience when we read about something in the scriptures and have an "aha" moment. It is also the revelation we experience when we read about things that no one can know—for example, the creation accounts in Genesis or the descriptions of the beginning of a new era that we get in Revelation.

The Bible's Inspired Character

Third, evangelicals believe that the authority of the Bible comes in its inspired character. The scripture itself claims to be "God-breathed" (2 Timothy 3:16). For evangelicals, the inspiration of scripture means that those who wrote did so through their own personalities and in their own cultures, but carried along in the task by the Spirit of God like a sailboat across the water. 2 Peter 1:21 is often quoted in this regard: "For prophecy never had its origin in the will of man, but men spoke from God [and wrote down what was spoken, evangelicals deduce from the context of this passage] as they were carried along by the Holy Spirit." We experience this inspired character when the sense of the weight of authority we feel from the Bible goes beyond what seems to be normally human, or when the scriptures provide context for something that seems so deep or significant or extraordinary that a merely human account of its origin is unsatisfying.

> **Culture Clash!**
>
> If an evangelical's view of the authority of the Bible causes he or she to quote the Bible to you in a judgmental way, remind them of the words of Jesus in Matthew 7:3: "Why do you look at the speck of sawdust in your brother's eye and pay no attention to the plank in your own eye?"

All of this (and more—indeed we could go on for a long time here) comes together when the exousia of the Bible intersects with the internal witness of the Spirit in the life of a believer. When the word meets the spiritually alive heart, a true miracle of inspiration occurs. In other words, God speaks to us. The authority of the Bible is the authority of God exercised through His word. Evangelicals believe that it is an authority of joy and liberation, not of coercion. It is not author-itarian in our negative sense of the word, it is instead author-ing—generating freedom and life. This, evangelicals say, is what gives the Bible its "right" over us—a right that evangelicals experience as the joy of communion with God.

Interpreting the Bible

Once questions about the origin and authority of the Bible are covered, the next step in understanding the Bible from the evangelical point of view has to do with interpretation.

The first question here is usually, "Why do evangelicals take the Bible literally?" The answer is that they don't. At least not in the way that is usually meant by the question, which generally suggests that evangelicals don't read anything in the Bible symbolically, or allegorically, or from any other of the numerous perspectives that match the literary genres of the Bible.

In Their Own Words

"When Jesus said, 'I am the door,' he didn't mean to imply that he was made of wood or that he swung on hinges."

—Eric Metaxas in *Everything You Always Wanted to Know about God But Were Afraid to Ask*

Evangelicals Interpret the Bible Seriously

A better way to describe the evangelical approach to the Bible is that they interpret it seriously. They take it at face value, and apply the normal rules of interpretive literature. Evangelicals believe that we need to let the Bible speak for itself. Perhaps the best way to describe this attitude is to contrast it with those who tend to interpret the Bible a bit more loosely—often according to their own needs and desires. Evangelical author Lee Strobel does a masterful tongue-in-cheek job of showcasing this attitude in his book *Inside the Mind of Unchurched Harry and Mary*. He uses the example of a parent telling teenagers that they need to be home by 11:00, and he shows how teenagers might interpret this:

They say [to themselves] "What did he really mean when he [my Father] said, '*You* must be home by 11:00?' Did he literally mean us, or was he talking about *you* in a general sense, like people in general? Was he saying in effect, 'As a general rule, people must be home before eleven?' Or was he just making the observation that, 'Generally, people are in their homes before eleven'? I mean, he wasn't very clear, was he?

"And what did he mean by 'You *must* be home by 11:00'? Would a loving father be so adamant and inflexible? He probably means it as a suggestion. I know he loves me, so isn't it implicit that he wants me to have a good time? And if I am having fun, then he wouldn't want me to end the evening so soon.

"And what did he mean by 'You must be *home* by 11:00'? He didn't specify WHOSE home. It could be anybody's home. Maybe he meant it figuratively. Remember the old saying, 'Home is where the heart is'? My heart is still here … so doesn't that mean I'm already home?

"And what did he mean when he said, 'You must be home before *11:00*'? Did he mean that in an exact, literal sense? Besides, he never specified 11:00 PM or 11:00 AM. And he wasn't really clear on whether he was talking about Eastern, Central, or Pacific time. I mean, it's still only quarter to seven in Honolulu. And as a matter of fact, its always before eleven [somewhere] …"

You get the point.

Evangelicals Interpret the Bible Carefully

In addition to trying to take the Bible at face value, evangelicals also interpret the Bible carefully. This means that they make use of key interpretive principles, such as the following:

- ◆ Trying to find the author's intent in each passage, which guards against inappropriate symbolic or allegorical interpretations that sometimes serve to domesticate scripture according to people's own desires.

- ◆ Recognizing that each text has a context, and that authentic interpretation always takes the context into account. This includes taking into account the overall context of all of scripture—the overriding theme of the story of God's redemption of His people and His creation.

- ◆ Letting the clearer parts of scripture interpret parts that are not as clear; and allowing things that are vague in the Scriptures to remain vague, instead of trying to force them into a "system" that meets the rationalistic need for closure.

- ◆ Looking to good scholarship and the ideas of others through the traditions of how the church has interpreted difficult passages.

- ◆ Interpreting according to genre; recognizing that there is history, poetry, biography, allegory, and symbolism (among other things) in the Bible; and that all of these are to be interpreted according to their kind.

Culture Clash!

If your interpretation of a Bible passage is different from the one your evangelical friend believes, challenge him or her to arm-wrestle you. It may not change either of your minds, but at least it will shut you both up for a few minutes.

Evangelicals Interpret the Bible Dependently

Finally (and perhaps most importantly), evangelicals would say that they interpret the Bible dependently. In the belief that the Spirit of God lives and speaks through His word, they actively seek His illumination as they read. This can come in the form of a prayerful attitude that defines their reading and/or study—a recognition that what they are doing is more than academic discovery or even devotional appreciation. For evangelicals, the most important part of interpretation is finding out what the Bible calls them to *do*. As they seek the transformation of their character, they come to the Bible not just to read it, not just to learn from it, but to obey it. This brings us to one last point about evangelicals and the Bible: beyond inspiration and interpretation, they are most interested in application.

Bringing the Scriptures to Life

The application of the Bible to everyday life is a key component of the evangelical ethos. Perhaps the best way to understand this and to get an overall sense of the evangelical outlook on the Bible is to do what evangelicals are so fond of: let the Bible speak for itself. Let's look at several key biblical passages that enlighten us about the applicability of the Bible to everyday life.

2 Tim. 3:16-17 says,

> All Scripture is God-breathed and is useful for teaching, rebuking, correcting and training in righteousness, so that all God's people may be thoroughly equipped for every good work.

Evangelicals bring the scriptures to bear on their lives by trusting them to equip. The Greek word in the verses above means to "thoroughly furnish." Evangelicals consistently and conscientiously lean on the scriptures to provide a grid for decision-making. From looking to specific passages that address specific moral issues (see Chapters 11–14 for examples of this approach), to using the general principles of the Bible as a grid in discerning answers to personal issues not specifically addressed, evangelicals rely on the "furnishings" of biblical principles to help them. They expect their interaction with the Bible to grow them up in their faith, and they come to the Bible with an open attitude for that purpose. They commit themselves to reading and studying the scriptures both publicly and privately, in order to be equipped by them.

Another key verse in scripture where the Bible talks about itself is Hebrews 4:12:

> For the word of God is living and active. Sharper than any double-edged sword, it penetrates even to dividing soul and spirit, joints and marrow; it judges the thoughts and attitudes of the heart.

Evangelicals believe that the scriptures, as they equip, enable honest perspective in our lives. As hard as it might be at times to listen when something is cutting deeply into us, exposing our attitudes and our motivations, evangelicals believe that this kind of hearing is absolutely necessary in a world that so easily lends itself to our self-delusion. Listening to the Bible, enabling it to evaluate our motivations and attitudes, is a key evangelical practice for bringing the scriptures to life.

> **In Their Own Words**
>
> "The truth will set you free, but first it may make you miserable!"
>
> —Rick Warren in *The Purpose Driven Life*

And finally, from the Psalms we see another important perspective:

The law of the Lord is perfect, reviving the soul.

The statutes of the Lord are trustworthy, making wise the simple.

The precepts of the Lord are right, giving joy to the heart.

The commands of the Lord are radiant, giving light to the eyes.

The fear of the Lord is pure, enduring forever.

The ordinances of the Lord are sure and altogether righteous.

They are more precious than gold, than much pure gold;

They are sweeter than honey, than honey from the comb.

By them is your servant warned; in keeping them there is great reward.

The picture that comes out over and over again in this beautiful piece of poetry (Psalm 19:7-11) is the idea of renewal. Evangelicals have truly experienced the scriptures as water to their dry souls. They turn to them in times of need for guidance, in times of sadness for solace, in times of joy for confirmation. Talk to any typical evangelical and they will point you to specific times in their lives where the Bible, just as the Psalm says, has revived them, made them wiser, and through their obedience has brought them great reward. In short, evangelicals believe that the application of the Bible to their everyday lives, as God speaks to them through His word, is an empowering experience of renewal.

The Uniqueness of the Bible

From its origins to its divine inspiration to its practical application, evangelicals believe the Bible to be absolutely unique. Indeed, regardless of what you believe about the Bible, evangelicals would point out that its uniqueness is indisputable. In summary, adapted from what is listed by Josh McDowell in the book *Evidence That Demands a Verdict*, here are just a few of the facts that point to the Bible's absolute uniqueness:

- **It is unique in its *continuity*.** The Bible was written over a 1,500-year time span by 40 different authors from every walk of life, from kings to peasants to poets to scholars and prime ministers, rabbis, tax collectors, doctors, military leaders, and fishermen. It was written on three different continents in three different languages and under every different kind of circumstance that you can imagine, and yet there is a plumbline of continuity and harmony that is amazing as it tells one unfolding story: how God draws people to Himself.

- **It is unique in its *circulation*.** More copies of the Bible have been printed than any other book, and it has been translated more times than any work in human history.

♦ **It is unique in its *survival* through time.** Hundreds of political leaders have tried to destroy it, and yet the Bible lives on while every one of them have died. The Frenchman Voltaire boasted before he died that the Bible would be extinct by the year 1850. Only 50 years after his death, the Geneva Bible Society used his press and his house to produce stacks of Bibles.

♦ **It is unique in its *influence on surrounding literature*.** According to one scholar: "If every bible in any considerable city were destroyed, the book could be restored in all its essential parts from the quotations on the shelves of the city public library."

♦ **It is unique in its *teachings*.** As one man put it: "The Bible is not such a book as a man would write if he could, or could write if he would."

From Glen Proechel and the Klingons to urban evangelists who are now working on hip-hop expressions of the scriptures, perhaps all of this is why so many evangelicals resonate with the words of Isaiah 55:10-13, as God speaks through the prophet:

> As the rain and the snow come down from heaven, and do not return to it without watering the earth and making it bud and flourish, so that it yields seed for the sower and bread for the eater, so is my word that goes out from my mouth: It will not return to me empty, but will accomplish what I desire and achieve the purpose for which I sent it.

The Least You Need to Know

♦ Evangelicals believe the Bible to be more than a human book; they believe it to be the inspired word of God.

♦ Some evangelicals believe the Bible has no errors or discrepancies; others believe that it has no errors or discrepancies of consequence to their faith.

♦ Evangelicals do not take all of the Bible literally; they interpret each scripture according to its intent (history, symbolism, poetry, etc.).

♦ Evangelicals believe that God speaks individually to them through their reading and studying of the Bible.

♦ Evangelicals strive to use the Bible as a guide for their daily lives.

Chapter 7

What's All the Fuss About Jesus?

In This Chapter

- ◆ A very fast overview of the life of Jesus
- ◆ A quick tour of Jesus' most famous teachings
- ◆ What Jesus believed about Himself
- ◆ Why did Jesus have to die?
- ◆ Is the resurrection credible?

I have a friend who has been coming to my church for several years now, and who doesn't identify herself as a Christian. She loves the energy and authenticity she feels in our community, she volunteers regularly, and soaks up the teaching about the Bible she experiences. Overall, she loves our church, but she is hung up by one aspect of it. By her own admission, she just doesn't get the whole "Jesus thing."

She's not alone. Over the years, I've known many people who love the idea of spirituality and/or God, but who simply don't understand the fixation Christians seem to have about Jesus. As a matter of fact, I recently spoke to someone else in my church who told me, "Oh, I just substitute the word

'God' in my mind every time you say 'Jesus.' That way I can listen to you and it doesn't bother me."

When I told my first friend above that I was writing this book, her immediate response was, "Great! Maybe you can write a chapter called 'What's All the Fuss About Jesus?'" I laughed and told her that I thought that was a perfect title. So, dedicated to her, and others like her who think Christianity is nice, but who just don't get the "Jesus thing"—here it is.

Jesus: The Way, or In the Way?

Jesus once said, "I am the way, the truth and the life. No one comes to the Father except through me." (John 14:6) In our culture today, not in small measure due to evangelicals, people often hear this statement as if Jesus had said, "I am *in* the way of the truth and the life." It seems as if many evangelicals see Jesus as the gatekeeper who blocks the entrance into God's kingdom, instead of the gracious host who invites people in. On the other hand, those who are not evangelicals often domesticate, romanticize, or spiritualize Jesus in a way that makes Him seem more like the irresponsible teenager who throws a party and lets everyone in (without His Father's blessing). The irony is that Jesus Himself was much less concerned with who's "in" and who's "out" than He was with who's blessed and who's not (more on that in Chapter 8).

Who was Jesus anyway? A great example? A revolutionary hippie? A magician? A vegetarian? (There actually are complete works on that last idea.) A teacher? A healer? A storyteller? The Messiah? With astonishing regularity, new works appear that seek to reinvent Jesus. It may be of some comfort to know that we in the modern world are not the only ones to wrestle with this. Even in His own day, people called Jesus both a zealot and a compromiser, a drunkard and a prude, a blasphemer and God Himself.

In Their Own Words

"Jesus needs to be saved from Christians who have slimmed him down or fattened him up or otherwise converted him into our own image."

—Brian McLaren in *A Generous Orthodoxy*

For many nonevangelicals, the prevalent evangelical image of Jesus as a "personal savior" has been quite off-putting. Intuitively, they recognize that Jesus is more than the ultimate consumer good (or god), like a personal computer or a personal trainer. They also recognize that the focus on "personal salvation" can (and sometimes does) actually result in making someone a *worse* person—because they can become so focused on life after death that they downplay the importance of life before death. Thus, issues like environmentalism, or justice, or peace, or neighborhood get the short shrift.

Indeed, my personal opinion is that a lot of evangelicals would genuinely dislike the actual Jesus if He really showed up again today. (As would a lot of nonevangelicals.) And to be honest, I might be one of them.

But like all evangelicals, I certainly hope not. Because I hold to the bedrock belief of Evangelicalism that Jesus is more than just a man. Were I to meet Him today, He would likely rattle my cage, disturb me, cause me to wonder, give me great hope, and (hopefully) cause me to worship.

But what else would you expect from God?

The Mystery of the Trinity

Yes, evangelicals believe that Jesus was and is God. And to understand that, you must first understand something about what is called the doctrine of the *trinity*.

Evangelicals believe that the Bible, from the very first chapter, teaches that one God exists in three persons: Father, Son, and Holy Spirit. These three, although distinct, are unified. And although unified, they play different roles. Think of it like different aspects of one person's personality. For instance, in the process of human salvation, the Father "calls" people (wooing them to recognize their need), the Son saves them (fulfilling their need), and the Spirit takes up residence in them (enabling them to live out their new identity in Christ).

def•i•ni•tion

The **trinity** is a doctrine held by Christians that God is one in essence, existing in three persons: the Father, the Son, and the Holy Spirit.

Evangelicals believe that this doctrine is progressively revealed throughout scripture, and is an essential part of God's self-revelation to humans. They also believe that the essence of God's existence as trinity is a mystery. It is not without strong logical formulation, but ultimately it is beyond human logic.

The (Even More Mysterious) Incarnation

As part of His Trinitarian nature, evangelicals believe that God has chosen to reveal Himself most fully to humanity in human form: Jesus, the second person of the trinity. This is what is known in theological circles as "the *incarnation*" (coming from the

def•i•ni•tion

Incarnation (from Latin, "to make flesh") describes the Christian belief that in Jesus, God became a human being.

Latin root "carn-" meaning "flesh"). Simply put, Jesus becomes fully human while retaining all of the attributes of divinity (and thus remaining fully God). John 1:14 describes it this way:

> The Word became flesh and made his dwelling among us. We have seen his glory, the glory of the One and Only, who came from the Father, full of grace and truth.

The Greek word translated here "made his dwelling" literally means "to tent" or to "encamp." In part of the Old Testament, God made His dwelling in the "tent" or "tabernacle" of Israel. The implication here is obvious—that Jesus "tabernacled" among humanity in the same way.

Evangelicals believe that this event—God becoming human—happened at a specific place and time. About 2,000 years ago, in what is now known as the region of Israel and Palestine, Jesus was born. Evangelicals believe that an overview of His life looks something like this:

◆ Born to Mary, a virgin who became pregnant through the miraculous work of God.

◆ Grows up the son of Mary and Joseph (a carpenter).

◆ At about the age of thirty, Jesus begins His public ministry by being baptized by John the Baptist (and thus identifying Himself with a message of redemption).

◆ He embarks on a three-year traveling public ministry, all located within about a 150-mile area. He teaches, heals, and develops a small band of followers (probably around 100 at the time of His death).

◆ He is crucified by the Roman authorities, supposedly for sedition (but more likely to appease the religious leaders of Judaism, whom He had offended).

◆ He rises from the dead, and appears to His followers over about a 40-day period, commissioning them to take His message to all people.

◆ He ascends into heaven, where He now sits at the right hand of God the Father, an advocate for His people.

These familiar facts describe—and sometimes, because of their familiarity, veil—the huge theological concept of the incarnation. The incarnation *is* the life of Christ.

Evangelicals don't believe that Jesus simply lived a good life, they believe that He showed us all how to live. They don't believe that the incarnation is a religious myth designed to set an example for us, they believe that Jesus literally died and rose again, proving Himself to be God. And because of that, they don't believe that you begin with an idea of God, and then fit Jesus into that. Instead, they believe that you look at Jesus and discover the proper conception of God. Simply put, they believe that Jesus was God incarnate.

Again, this is quite a claim. So *why* do evangelicals believe it? Let's take a look at several important reasons. The first of them is the claims of Jesus Himself.

The Claims of Jesus

It would be nice (and much less controversial) to think of Jesus as a great moral teacher, or an unusually gifted healer, or a very effective revolutionary. The problem is, He didn't leave that option open to us. Evangelicals believe that Jesus Himself asserted His divinity in no uncertain terms; that it is not a concept that was made up later by the church.

> **In Their Own Words**
>
> "[L]et us not come with any patronizing nonsense about [Jesus] being a great human teacher. He has not left that option open to us. He did not intend to."
>
> —C. S. Lewis in *Mere Christianity*

Jesus asserts His divinity both indirectly and directly in the scriptures. Indirectly, the gospels show that Jesus claimed divine prerogatives for Himself consistently, such as the authority to forgive sins (Matthew 9:1-8), to bestow life (John 11:25), to teach the truth (John 8:31-32), and to judge the world (Matthew 25:31-46). With regard to His more direct claims, perhaps the best way to get an overview of Jesus' self-understanding is to take a look at seven "I am …" statements that He made that are recorded in the book of John.

Who Did He Think He Was?

Perhaps as a child, when you got "too big for your britches" (as we used to say where I grew up), your parents would look at you and say, "Who do you think you are!" Or maybe as an adult, you've had a run-in with a boss or a co-worker and thought to yourself, "Who do they think they are!" Usually, this question is an expression of a perceived need for humility on the part of the person of whom the question is asked.

Often its complete form is, "Who do you think you are—God?" So imagine if you asked someone you thought was acting a bit high and mighty, "Who do you think you are?"—and they answered you like this:

- ◆ *"I am the bread of life."* (John 6:35) This was Jesus' answer to a crowd of people who were seeking Him out after He had miraculously fed all 5,000 of them. In answer to their cry to be fed like this again and again, He went on to humbly state that if they ate His flesh and drank His blood, they would live forever.

- ◆ *"I am the light of the world."* (John 9:5) This is what Jesus said just before He healed a blind man. He followed it up by saying, "For judgment I have come into this world, so that the blind will see and those who see will become blind." (John 9:39) Further, He used the opportunity to elicit belief in Himself from the man who was healed, and to publicly accuse the religious leaders of the day of hypocrisy when they doubted His motives in the healing.

- ◆ *"I am the door."* (John 10:7) No, Jesus was not channeling Jim Morrison here (even though He would have been the only person there to have known about Jim Morrison). He was instead using this metaphor to contrast Himself to false religious teachers who cannot back up their claims to provide access to the real life for which people search.

- ◆ *"I am the good shepherd. The good shepherd lays down his life for the sheep."* (John 10:11) Not only was Jesus foretelling His own death on behalf of His sheep (us), here, He was also likely consciously comparing Himself to the "shepherd" of Psalm 23—God Himself.

- ◆ *"I am the resurrection and the life."* (John 11:25) This saying was followed up by the small gesture of raising a man from the dead who had been in a tomb four days.

- ◆ *"I am the way, the truth and the life."* (John 14:6) Imagine that someone you know actually said that to you—and that they were serious. Now imagine yourself *outside* of a mental institution.

- ◆ *"I am the true vine."* (John 15:1) Israel's national symbol was the vine—sort of like the American eagle. Claiming this was a sure way to fire up the religious leaders of the day, who would see it as blasphemous, not to mention just flat-out impolite.

Taken together, all of these claims are absolutely arrogant.

Unless, of course, you actually are God.

Two Opposite Responses

Two other incidents from Jesus' life provide even clearer proof of His divine self-understanding. One of them comes in John 8:31-59, where Jesus concludes a particularly rancorous discussion with the religious folk of the day by saying, "I tell you the truth, before Abraham was, I am." (John 8:58) This was blasphemy of the highest order, as "I am" was the Hebrew name for God, not even spoken aloud out of reverence. For those who say that Jesus is just misunderstood by those who read the scriptures today and see in Him a claim to be God, the verse that follows this one is definitive proof that this viewpoint is not a misunderstanding. Not only did Jesus know exactly what He was claiming here, the people around Him knew too, as evidenced by their intention to levy the punishment prescribed in their religious law for blasphemy. John 8:59 says, "At this, they picked up stones to stone him …"

> **Culture Clash!**
>
> If evangelicals' claims about the divinity of Christ are offensive to you, it may help to recognize that these claims are not their own. They are simply being faithful to what the New Testament itself claims. Of course, you can always argue with God about it, but be careful—that is often the first step towards belief.

And finally, in the climactic moment in the book of John, Jesus appears after His resurrection to His disciples and to Thomas (of "doubting Thomas" fame). This is the second time Jesus appears to this group. The first time Thomas was not there, and he has refused to believe that the others are telling the truth about it. So when Jesus appears to Thomas, flesh and blood that rose from the dead, Thomas looks at Him and exclaims, "My Lord and my God!" (John 20:28) This is the literary climax of the entire book—Thomas saying explicitly and out loud what the whole book has been working to prove. And note Jesus' response to Thomas' expression of worship. He doesn't say, "Oh no, I'm not your God!"—He simply accepts the worship of His follower.

Short and sweet: evangelicals believe that Jesus is God, because Jesus believed it Himself.

The Character of Jesus

But it's not only Jesus' claims that convince evangelicals. It is the fact that Jesus' claims were backed up by His character. First and foremost (as regards His divinity) evangelicals believe that Jesus was sinless. As a reflection of His divine nature in this regard, Jesus' responses to His temptation in the wilderness, recorded in Matthew 4:1-11, are instructive. Just after His baptism by John the Baptist, the scriptures say that Jesus was led by the Spirit into the wilderness to be tempted. Most scholars see this as God's quintessential testing of Jesus' character to see if He was actually ready for His mission.

Resisting Temptation

First of all in this passage, Jesus is tempted to become self-serving (4:3-4). After fasting for forty days in the wilderness, He is tempted by the devil to "turn these stones into bread." But Jesus refuses, quoting an Old Testament scripture that references the idea that the will of God always comes before human desires.

Secondly, He is tempted to "put God to the test" (4:5-7). The devil takes Jesus to the pinnacle of the temple, and challenges Him to throw Himself off. The idea here is that Jesus is to test God to respond by saving Him from harm in His leap of faith, thus "proving" His sonship. But Jesus has no need to be a sensationalistic leader. He refuses to ask anything of God that is flippant or to place Himself in the position of a leader who focuses attention on Himself instead of his mission.

Finally, Jesus is tempted to take the easy way out (4:8-10). Satan promises to literally give Him the world if Jesus will simply bow down to Him. For Jesus, this represents a way to Lordship without the cross. He refuses, showing that His character is stronger than even the ultimate temptation could break.

All of the above encapsulates the ongoing character of Christ we see throughout the New Testament. Jesus is consistently faithful to the will of the Father, unwilling to be aggrandized, and always self-sacrificing for His greater mission. (Not to mention loving, gracious, kind, and a host of other qualities that attracted people to Him.) John, who was likely Jesus' best friend, and thus in a position to see Him in even His private moments, says of Him that "grace and truth were realized" in Him (John 1:17, NASB). Can you imagine your best friend—who has seen you in all your unguarded moments—saying that about you? Mine would more likely say something like, "self-centeredness and goofiness were realized in Dave."

But not John with Jesus. The apostle who may have been the closest human of all to Jesus says that "grace and truth were realized" in Him. In other words Jesus was the embodiment of both love and justice, forgiveness and penetrating honesty, mercy and judgment. His perfect ability to live out the picture of God's desire for all humanity is clear evidence to evangelicals of His divinity.

The Wise Teacher

Jesus' character is also shown in His teachings. Even those who are not Christians universally acknowledge the superlative nature of the wisdom of Jesus. Perhaps the place where this can be seen the best is in Jesus' definitive statement about what it means to live life in "the kingdom of God"—the primary theme of all of His teachings (again, defined in simple terms as "where what God wants done gets done"). Known popularly as the "Sermon on the Mount," this teaching comprises three full chapters of the book of Matthew (Matthew 5-7). A sample of just a few of the well-known lines of this message shows the incredible creativity and power of the character of Jesus' teachings:

> **The Gospel Truth**
>
> The beatitudes (" ... blessed are the ...") are not the Sermon on the Mount, they are simply the introduction to the Sermon on the Mount.

- Matthew 5:3-5: Blessed are the poor in spirit, for theirs is the kingdom of heaven. Blessed are those who mourn, for they will be comforted. Blessed are the meek, for they will inherit the earth.

- Matthew 5:14-16: You are the light of the world. A city on a hill cannot be hidden. Neither do people light a lamp and put it under a bowl. Instead they put it on its stand, and it gives light to everyone in the house. In the same way, let your light shine before men, that they may see your good deeds and praise your Father in heaven.

- Matthew 5:38-41: You have heard that it was said, "Eye for eye, and tooth for tooth." But I tell you, Do not resist an evil person. If someone strikes you on the right cheek, turn to him the other also. And if someone wants to sue you and take your tunic, let him have your cloak as well. If someone forces you to go one mile, go with him two miles.

- Matthew 5:43-45: You have heard that it was said, "Love your neighbor and hate your enemy." But I tell you: Love your enemies and pray for those who persecute you, that you may be sons of your Father in heaven. He causes his sun to rise on the evil and the good, and sends rain on the righteous and the unrighteous.

- Matthew 6:3-4: But when you give to the needy, do not let your left hand know what your right hand is doing, so that your giving may be in secret. Then your Father, who sees what is done in secret, will reward you.

- Matthew 6:24: No one can serve two masters. Either he will hate the one and love the other, or he will be devoted to the one and despise the other. You cannot serve both God and Money.

- Matthew 6:31-33: So do not worry, saying, "What shall we eat?" or "What shall we drink?" or "What shall we wear?" For the pagans run after all these things, and your heavenly Father knows that you need them. But seek first his kingdom and his righteousness, and all these things will be given to you as well.

- Matthew 7:1: Do not judge, or you too will be judged.

- Matthew 7:7: Ask and it will be given to you; seek and you will find; knock and the door will be opened to you.

- Matthew 7:12: So in everything, do to others what you would have them do to you, for this sums up the Law and the Prophets.

In addition to magnificent direct teaching such as this, Jesus also taught through remembrable parables—stories that got behind the defenses of the people (especially the religious ones) of the day, and then went off like little time bombs in their heads. The prodigal son, the story of the lost sheep and the shepherd who goes out to find it, and the tale of the good Samaritan (among others) have all woven themselves into the fabric of our world-wide culture because of their timeless universal power. For evangelicals, this is further proof that the one who taught them was no mere man.

The Generous Miracle Worker

Finally, and maybe the clearest evidence of His divinity, is the fact that Jesus' character came through in His miracles. They were not simply displays of power, they were evidence that in Jesus, the kingdom of God really was at hand. Healing the sick, feeding the hungry, and even raising the dead—Jesus' miracles were all expressions of His goodness and mercy, never simply for show, or to gain power for Himself. As a matter of fact, Jesus often asked the recipients of His power *not* to tell others. He wasn't interested in gaining followers who were looking for the "next big thing."

Thus, the claims of Jesus and the character of Jesus are clear evidence to evangelicals that He was more than human. However, nothing is more important in establishing His identity than what evangelicals see as the most important event in all of human history: Jesus' death and resurrection.

The Death of Jesus

The consensus of our culture is that Jesus' death was an instance of an innocent person facing down injustice and dying for His commitment. Some see in Jesus' unjust death the revealing of the world for what it really is—in other words, they see that Jesus' death brings out the true colors of the worst of humankind. Some even see in His death an act of redemption—whereby the human race was enriched through the example of this man who was willing to pay the ultimate price for what He believed.

While all of those things may be true, they don't describe the essence of Jesus' death as evangelicals see it. The word that best describes the evangelical view of Jesus' death is the word *atonement.*

def•i•ni•tion _____

Atonement is the theological word used to describe the death of Christ as the payment for the penalty of human sin.

An easy way to understand the word is to see it in its parts: at-one-ment. For evangelicals, the death of Jesus was the act by which God made it possible for humans to be "at one" with Him. Humanity's sin separated us from a holy God. Harkening back to the Old Testament system of sacrifices for sin (where people would bring animals to the temple and then sacrifice them as examples of the fact that sin is so serious that only blood can atone—or bring forgiveness—for it), Jesus becomes the ultimate sacrifice.

This shows that for evangelicals, salvation is primarily focused on the forgiveness of individual moral guilt (although this idea is increasingly being challenged by evangelicals of a more postmodern bent—see Chapters 19 and 20). How the forgiveness of this guilt and the restoration of relationship with God takes place in the death of Jesus can be seen through several different metaphors.

Justification

The most prevalent metaphor evangelicals use to explain the significance of Jesus' death is the metaphor of a judge. Think of it this way: God, the perfectly righteous judge, must honestly evaluate the morality of humanity. To do less than this would be to abdicate His role as a truly righteous judge. However, being perfectly merciful as well as perfectly righteous, God declares the sentence ("the wages of sin is death"—Romans 6:23), and then takes off His judges' robes, steps down to the place of the defendant, and takes the punishment Himself.

Thus, justification takes place for sin. The proper punishment has been both levied and taken by God Himself. Jesus' death on the cross is the way this happened in real time and space. Jesus takes on the sin of all of mankind, and clears the way for a new relationship between God and humanity.

Ransom

However, evangelicals believe that there is more that takes place here than the simple payment of a debt. A second metaphor often used to describe Christ's death is the metaphor of ransom. In this line of thought, Jesus' death does more than clear the way for a new relationship, He actually exchanges His righteousness for the sin of human-kind. In other words, as Paul says in 2 Corinthians 5:21, "God made him who had no sin to be sin for us, so that in him we might become the righteousness of God."

Evangelicals believe that Jesus' death effected a transfer of His righteousness to their "account" with God. God sees them now the same way He sees Christ: perfectly "holy and blameless" (Ephesians 1:4). For people who are used to religion being about earning God's good favor through good works, this idea is very counterintuitive. But for evangelicals, it *is* the good news of the gospel. God offers all of this to us as a free gift through Jesus.

Reconciliation

One further metaphor completes the picture. Once sin has been justified and righteousness has been attributed to an individual, they can enjoy a reconciled relationship with God. Just as Adam and Eve "walked with God" in the Garden of Eden, evangelicals believe that people in today's world can experience an immediate and personal relationship with God. Thus, the death of Jesus not only effects a wiping away of sin, it is also the basis of a brand new opportunity to live out the destiny God had originally planned for us—a life in relationship with Him.

This new relationship with God enables us to live life to its fullest potential. Reconciled with our Creator, we are able to fulfill our created purpose—to be blessed by God and to be a blessing to others as we carry forward His kingdom (more on this in Chapter 9).

> ### In Their Own Words
>
> "The good news is that ... the kingdom of God ... is closer than you think. It is available to ordinary men and women. It is available to you. You can live in it—now."
>
> —John Ortberg in *The Life You've Always Wanted*

But Wasn't There a Better Way?

My friend whose story began this chapter asked me another important question not long ago. She said that she understood all of what I have just written about above, but she still had one question: why did Jesus have to *die* for all this to happen? God being God, didn't He have the power to do this any way He wanted? Wasn't there a less barbaric way?

This is a really important question (it probably deserves a whole chapter in and of itself, if not a whole book). In short, there is no easy answer. The best I've been able to come up with is that through suffering, Christ has taken on a radical identification with humanity. Jesus doesn't give pat answers because He Himself has lived with the questions. He Himself has gone the extra mile, turned the other cheek, taken up His cross, and become the light of the world. Jesus' death on the cross becomes both message and method—showing God's people how to redeem the world around them.

But of course, it doesn't end at the cross.

The Resurrection of Jesus

The resurrection of Jesus is either the greatest miracle of all time, or the greatest hoax in history.

Evangelicals believe that Jesus, after being laid in a tomb following His crucifixion on Friday, rose from the dead on Sunday. This is a belief based on faith, but on faith that rests on evidence, evangelicals would say. Indeed, many skeptics have investigated the resurrection, and come away convinced that the best explanation for the evidence we have is that Jesus did indeed rise, as the gospels record.

For instance, there are skeptics who say that the reason Jesus is seen alive after His crucifixion is because He didn't actually die before He was taken from the cross and placed in a tomb. This is not reasonable, counter evangelicals, according to the eye-witness evidence. Prior to His crucifixion, Jesus was beaten, which according to the savagery of the day, always resulted in massive blood loss. Having thus been greatly weakened, and already in critical shape, Jesus was *nailed* to a cross. Apart from the trauma and blood loss of having huge spikes driven through your wrists and ankles, crucifixion usually resulted in death by suffocation within hours, as victims struggled to pull their bodies up into a position to be able to take in air with each breath, and would finally run out of strength to be able to do so. Finally, after hanging on the cross for the better part of a day, and being judged dead by the guards, Jesus was stabbed in the side with a spear by the guards just to make sure He was dead. According to John (an eyewitness), the action brought forth "a sudden flow of blood and water" (John 19:34). What John did not know (he was not a physician) was that this constitutes clear medical evidence of the certainty of Jesus' death from the rupture of His heart.

Others have postulated that the disciples stole Jesus' body. This too is unreasonable, say evangelicals. In order to do so, the disciples (who had all scattered in fear at Jesus' arrest) would have had to overcome a Roman guard (consisting of anywhere from four to eight armed men) who had been posted at the site. It is highly unlikely that the guards would have been overcome, and beyond that it is even more unlikely that the Roman government would have made no effort to catch those who had done so (history records no such effort). As for theories that the guards may have fallen asleep, to have done so would have risked the death penalty, and anyway, who could sleep through the noise of a massive stone being rolled away from the mouth of the tomb?

The most important piece of physical evidence, however, is the missing body. Jesus' enemies, who had every resource available to them, and every reason to produce His body and put away all this nonsense once and for all, never did.

In Their Own Words

"Had the crucifixion of Jesus ended His disciples' experience of Him, it is hard to see how the Christian church could have come into existence."

—H. D. A. Major, quoted in *Evidence that Demands a Verdict*

Beyond the physical evidence, evangelicals point to the evidence of the disciples themselves. Perhaps we should believe in the resurrection, evangelicals assert, because those people who were closest to Jesus did. As a matter of fact, they believed it so much that most of them died martyrs' deaths for that belief.

Further, this small band of followers, based on the resurrection, birthed a planet-wide movement that has quite literally changed the world. One particularly strong piece of evidence: the fact that thousands of years later, billions of people come together each year at Easter to celebrate the resurrection.

"But maybe," you could say, "all of this was made up. Maybe the disciples got together and concocted this story."

Perhaps the experience of Chuck Colson, the convicted Watergate conspirator who later became a follower of Christ, is instructive here. Colson says that it was Watergate that proved the resurrection to him. Consider this: The Watergate conspiracy was perpetrated by some of the smartest and most powerful people in the world. But when the heat was on, this group, whose intense personal loyalty to the President had been strong enough for them to break laws for him, wilted in two weeks. That was how long it took one of them to turn state's evidence.

Compare that to the early disciples—eleven working-class men, facing every form of torture and abuse and death for their convictions, yet every single one of them, and many others besides, maintained to their deaths that they had seen Jesus alive.

Colson writes that as one who has lived through the conspiracy of Watergate, and as such, as an "expert in cover-ups" himself, that "nothing else but a resurrected Christ could have caused those men to maintain to their dying whispers that Jesus is alive and is Lord." He, like many before and many who will come after him, sincerely believes that the resurrection of Christ is a historic fact, convincingly established by the evidence, and "one you can bet your life upon."

For evangelicals, the evidence of the resurrection is compelling enough to do just that.

Lunatic, Liar, or Lord?

One final thought is helpful to summarize this chapter and put all of it into perspective.

C. S. Lewis, in his classic explanation of the faith, *Mere Christianity*, suggests that if we believe the primary historical documents of the gospels, logic dictates that there are only three possible responses to the person of Jesus. First of all, one may simply see Him as a lunatic. A person who sincerely believed He was God, but was wrong. Lewis asks, does the portrait of Jesus we get from history match this idea? Does Jesus belong in a mental institution along with others whose misguided God-complexes put them on the level of a person who thinks he is a poached egg?

Secondly, we can respond by believing that Jesus really did not believe He was God, but He lied about it. Again, this does not seem to match the character of the man we read about in scriptures.

So if Jesus was neither a lunatic or a liar, we are left with the option that "Jesus is Lord." In fact, this is an ancient liturgical affirmation, popular with the very first Christians, and used in church services around the world every week even to this day. It is the most basic theological affirmation that defines evangelicalism. Jesus' character, His works, His own claims, and ultimately His resurrection confirm for evangelicals His divine identity. (Not to mention His ongoing active presence in the lives of His followers today—see Chapter 9.)

And thus, to finally answer the question that titles this chapter, *that* is what all the fuss about Jesus is about for evangelicals.

The Least You Need to Know

- Evangelicals believe that Jesus was 100 percent God and 100 percent human. How? It's a mystery.

- Evangelicals believe in the divinity of Jesus because of His own claims, His works, and His character.

- Jesus' death, according to evangelicals, makes it possible for everyone to be reconciled to God.

- Jesus' resurrection was the ultimate proof of His divinity and His mission, according to evangelicals.

- According to evangelicals, Jesus as lunatic or liar doesn't square with the evidence. The solution for the question of His identity that most fits the evidence is to see Him as Lord.

Chapter 8

That "Born Again" Stuff

In This Chapter

- ◆ What evangelicals really mean when they say "born again"
- ◆ What evangelicals believe about "the image of God" in humanity vs. "original sin"
- ◆ Understanding what Jesus meant by "the kingdom of God"
- ◆ Is Jesus the only way?

Recently, I was watching a popular television comedy when an unusual moment in an otherwise normal scene caught my attention.

In the scene, a bunch of friends were standing around talking to one another, when one of them (not as well known to the others) declares something to the effect that she has been "born again." Suddenly, everyone becomes tense. The narrator of the show (who was also one of the people in the scene) says in a voice-over, "I'm not sure why it was suddenly so awkward, but I wish[ed] something would break the tension …"

The fact that writers see people expressing that they are "born again" as being socially uncomfortable enough to be a natural comedic moment is telling. Not to be too indelicate, but honestly, the reaction of the people in the scene (which is often mirrored in real life when someone expresses that they are "born again") reminds me of what I once heard someone else say: "It's sort of like what happens when someone farts in public."

How did it get this way?

In this chapter we'll take a look at exactly what evangelicals mean when they talk about being "born again." What exactly is conversion for an evangelical? And why does it make everyone else around them so nervous?

Bumper-Sticker Theology

The community I live in near San Francisco is very politically active. As a matter of fact, if you pull your car onto the 101 freeway (the sole main artery of the community), you will immediately become engaged in a political debate. How? Through the time-honored vehicle of bumper stickers. From "Practice Random Acts of Kindness" to "Visualize World Peace" to (my personal favorite) "What Would Scooby Do?" everyone has an opinion, and everyone wants to get his or her opinion out. As I drive around, every once in a while I see this one: "Christians Aren't Perfect, Just Forgiven." And every time I see it, it bothers me.

> **In Their Own Words**
>
> "Jesus is coming. Everybody look busy."
> —Bumper sticker

The bumper sticker represents a major, and unrecognized, problem between the vast majority of contemporary culture and Evangelicalism: reductionism. You see, bumper stickers are designed to communicate an important idea very fast. Recognizing the hurried nature of our culture, well-meaning Christians have tried to communicate the message of Jesus in a fashion that is consistent with that pace. The result is what I call "bumper-sticker theology." And the result of that has been threefold:

◆ The reduction of the actual gospel of Jesus into a prepackaged set of propositions that are intended to be easily understood in a sound-byte world

◆ An accompanying reduction in Christian practice that has left out important aspects of Jesus' teachings

◆ A resulting understandable reticence in contemporary culture as a whole to listen to the actual message of Christ communicated by people who are "born again" in the best sense of those words

However, this chapter presents us with a golden opportunity: to go back and look at what Jesus actually meant by being "born again" and to clarify what evangelicals mean when they use the terminology. Most of the time, evangelicals are using it as shorthand for some huge concepts that they have experienced, but that have gotten lost in the bumper-sticker translation.

The Human Paradox

The first of those concepts is the huge paradox of human nature.

When God created human beings, He called them "good" and "made in his image" (Genesis 1:27, 31). Based on Genesis and other scriptures, theologians have suggested that the image of God in humanity is reflected in our self-awareness, our capacity for moral understanding and choice, and our capacity to "rule." In a sense, God's "job description" commission to humanity (Genesis 2:28) was based on these things. God's intention is that humans would be, in effect, His junior partners in cocreating the ongoing story of our world. As God's representatives, working in partnership with Him, we would bring blessing to one another and to the creation around us.

However, that partnership was broken when Adam and Eve chose to go against God's will and do their own thing (Genesis 3). In this moment, evangelicals believe that the "disease" of sin was introduced into humanity and all of creation. Like a rock thrown into a pond (a very big rock), this choice by Adam and Eve had a ripple effect throughout all of creation, humanity, and history. Sin entered in and became an ongoing part of the story of each one of us, the creation around us, and the collective combinations of people, thought, and stuff that we call "culture."

Thus, all of us, while made in the image of God, are also affected by sin. This is the human paradox: our divinely given potential mixed with our propensity to sin. Contrary to what is often said about evangelicals, they don't believe that everyone is naturally "bad" (which is how the idea of "original sin" is often misunderstood). Instead, they believe that God's image resides in everyone. They also believe that the image of God in all of us needs to be cleansed from the negative impact of sin. Further (as we discussed in Chapter 7), they believe that Jesus' death is what makes that possible.

However, Jesus' gospel goes beyond the issue of the forgiveness of human sin. To move beyond the "bumper-sticker theology" that often substitutes in our culture for what evangelicals really believe, we must look a bit deeper into what Jesus himself taught and believed.

The Mosaic of the Gospel

At the very beginning of Jesus' public ministry, the Gospel of Mark summarizes His message (Mark 1:14-15, NASB):

> … Jesus came into Galilee, preaching the gospel of God, and saying, "The time is fulfilled, and the kingdom of God is at hand; repent and believe in the gospel."

In these verses, we see the primary content of Jesus' message, which we might say this way: "The kingdom of God is available to you." This somewhat dense concept (well coined and described by Dallas Willard in his seminal book, *The Divine Conspiracy*) basically means that through Christ, you can live in the way that you were originally created to live. You can once again live in partnership with God—in His "kingdom"—which is a metaphor that describes anytime or anywhere that what God wants done is being done. Jesus is saying that it really is possible to be blessed by God and to be consistently living in a way that is a blessing to others, as you cocreate the ongoing story of this world through practicing God's ways under the authority and protection of the benevolent king, God himself.

def•i•ni•tion

> The **Kingdom Of God** is a metaphor used by Jesus to describe the realm (anytime, anyplace) in which God's will is done. "Living in the kingdom" is a way of describing a lifestyle in which one practices God's principles consistently, and thus lives in an alternative way to the general surrounding culture.

The words "authority" and "kingdom" are loaded in today's culture. For many, they bring to mind past and current examples of totalitarianism and forced subjection. But the way Jesus used the concepts, and the culture within which He used them, created a meaning that was very different than what we might think of today. Throughout the scriptures, Jesus lays in the pieces of this meaning through His teachings and actions. He heals, forgives, challenges, confronts, judges, and brings comfort. As a matter of fact, I like to imagine Jesus as an artist, using each of His actions and teachings to contribute to a bigger overall picture that you could call "the mosaic of the gospel." And just like a mosaic, each piece is beautiful in and of itself. But when we see the whole—the nonreduced, total picture—we see an integrative beauty that describes in its totality the kingdom of God (and goes way beyond a bumper sticker).

For instance, in Matthew 12, Jesus heals a demon-possessed man who is both blind and mute. As He does so, He declares the presence of the kingdom. In Matthew 19, Jesus describes the single-minded commitment necessary for kingdom living after

He speaks about it to a rich young ruler. In Mark 10:14, Jesus declares that the kingdom of God belongs to those who are like children. As He sends out His disciples in Luke 9, Jesus instructs them to declare the nearness of the kingdom as they heal and preach. In John 3, He tells Nicodemus that the radical nature of the kingdom in a person's life is such that it is likened to a new birth (which we'll talk about later on in this chapter). What we see throughout Jesus' life is that He invites people into the kingdom in a myriad of different ways—and interestingly enough, He never once reduces His message to bumper-sticker theology. Instead, He creates an ongoing mosaic.

One way to understand all of this is to think of the kingdom using three metaphors:

- The *kingdom is a gift* to be received, often expressed in terms of forgiveness of sin.

- The kingdom is *a life to be inherited*, expressed through the alternative lifestyle that results from putting God first.

- The kingdom is *a mission to enter*, experienced as we engage with God in His mission of blessing the world around us.

Receiving, inheriting, and entering the kingdom are the biblical pathways to living it. Each of these words is used over and over in the New Testament to describe what it means to live as a Christ-follower. Each of them (as we will see in the next section) also matches up with a specific part of Jesus' statement in Mark 1:14-15. And the combination of these three things is ultimately what it means to be "born again."

"The time is fulfilled" = A Gift to Receive

First of all, in Mark 1:15 (NASB), Jesus says, "The time is fulfilled." What does that mean? It helps to think about it in the context of Jesus' world, where the Jewish people had been waiting for centuries to be free. For five centuries—twice as long as the entire history of the United States—they had been waiting for God to fulfill this promise. They had been in bondage to Egypt, to Babylon, and were currently in bondage to Rome. Every generation of Israelites wondered when they, as God's chosen people—the ones through whom God had promised to bless the world—would be freed to fulfill their mission. It was their belief that the Messiah would come as their deliverer to free them to accomplish this. He would be the powerful King who would come (some believed to overthrow the Romans) and set things right for their nation.

So along comes Jesus—no pedigree, no position of power—an unknown person from the wrong side of the tracks (Nazareth was not very well regarded in those days) who was the mostly pacifist illegitimate son of a carpenter. He shows up out of nowhere and declares, "The time is fulfilled—five hundred years of waiting are over—here I am." It must have been quite a shock, because He was nothing like what they expected.

The Gospel Truth

Most of Jesus' Jewish contemporaries were expecting the Messiah to be a political leader, not one whose "kingdom" would reside in the hearts and lives of people.

What they didn't understand, and what we need to understand, evangelicals say, is that Jesus was offering them (and us) a gift: the inbreaking of the kingdom of God not just in political terms, but in the context of our entire lives. As the climactic person of the history of the entire world, Jesus offers us the gift of access to a kingdom that is beyond political confines. So first of all, the kingdom is a gift to be received.

But what is received? According to evangelicals, it is the gift of authentic clarity and radical forgiveness, resulting in an opportunity to live the way we've been created to live. This is the gift of the King setting things right. But the offer of the gift is not the end of the process—as with all gifts, it needs to be received.

The language of receiving shows up throughout the New Testament. For instance, John says about Jesus (John 1:12, NLT), "But to all who believed him and accepted him, he gave the right to become children of God." In other words, the accepting of the gift is the gateway into the kingdom that Jesus has made available to us. We receive it aware of the undeserved nature of the offer—and thus our own sin. We recognize that this forgiveness is a gift that we need. Of course, we can also reject the offer, denying our need and choosing to continue to live the way we always have. Many of Jesus' contemporaries did just that. So do many people today. It is our choice. But Jesus says, the time is fulfilled—the *opportunity* is available.

"The kingdom of God is at hand" = A Life to Inherit

Secondly, in Mark 1:15 (NASB), Jesus says, "the kingdom of God is at hand." Those who understood His meaning were shocked by this, because they realized that He was saying, "I am the kingdom. It is at hand in my person." And Jesus spent His ministry demonstrating exactly that through His actions and words. Further, He taught His disciples that when He left them, they could carry on the inbreaking of the kingdom that He had made available. Evangelicals would say that the scriptures speak of this ongoing inbreaking possibility as a life to inherit.

We find references to this idea of inheriting the life of the kingdom throughout the New Testament. In one of them, (1 Peter 1:3-4), the apostle Peter says this, writing a letter to the early church:

> Praise be to the God and Father of our Lord Jesus Christ! In his great mercy he has given us new birth into a living hope through the resurrection of Jesus Christ from the dead, and into an inheritance that can never perish, spoil or fade …

Peter highlights here the eternal nature of this inherited life. Other places in the New Testament liken the inheritance to a new identity. For example, I Corinthians 5:17 says that in Christ, we become "new creations." Evangelicals point to this and other passages to show that the life we inherit is qualitatively different. So much so, in fact, that we can now live like different people.

Just after the Civil War, there are multiple recorded instances of slaves who had been freed, and yet who continued to serve their old masters. Although they had a new identity, they continued to live out of their old one. Evangelicals believe that the mosaic of the gospel calls people out of the slavery to self-centeredness that all of us, if we are honest, have experienced. Instead of living out of our old identity, we can live free—transformed from our naturally self-centered natures.

Thus, built into the concept of a life to inherit is the idea of transformation. We are now living in accordance with a new context. The gospel is not simply a new and better moral code that Jesus came to share, but an entirely new context of life—the kingdom is at hand—that enables real, authentic transformation to occur in our lives. Here is the good news: we *can* be changed! The kingdom can break in right now in our lives.

For evangelicals, this means that destructive habit patterns can be permanently broken. It means that relationships can be rebuilt. It means that people can actually live in unselfish love—that Jesus' command to "love your enemies" is not pie-in-the-sky wishful thinking, but a very possible reality. This is a qualitatively different life that we've inherited, evangelicals believe, not just a quantitatively longer life (i.e., a ticket into heaven). If we will enter the life we've inherited, evangelicals believe, we won't wind up at the end of our lives wishing we had really lived.

"Repent and believe" = A Mission to Enter

Finally in this passage, Jesus says, "repent and believe." Of all of the words that have gained unfortunate baggage in our day, these are some of the worst. Again, let's try to hear them in the context in which Jesus lived.

There is a Jewish historian who lived around the time of Jesus whose name was Josephus. As a young man, at one point Josephus was a commander in the Roman army, and in his autobiography he describes being sent out on a mission to sort out some rebel movements near Galilee. He describes his task as going to a bunch of hot-headed Galileans and trying to persuade them to stop their revolt and to trust him and a group of diplomats to work out a better solution. He says that he told them to give up their agendas and to trust him, Josephus, instead. And the words he used to do this are recorded by him as these: he said to the rebels, "Repent and believe in me."

Culture Clash! _____

Since "repent" literally means to turn around and walk in the opposite direction, try doing just that the next time you get into an overheated discussion with an evangelical friend. Coming back later to continue the discussion may prove to be more effective.

Josephus was not primarily calling the rebels to change their morality. "Repent" is actually a thinking word, not just a moral one. It comes from a word which means to exercise our mind. It also means to turn around. Essentially, Jesus is saying here that we need to change our minds. We need to look around us, and realize that a remarkable opportunity is in front of us. We then need to act on that opportunity, entering into the mission of God that we've been created to live out. In that context, then, we become not only the blessed, but those who do the blessing.

So the kingdom is a gift to receive, a life to inherit, and finally, a mission to enter.

Jesus defines that mission for His disciples in Matthew 28:19-20 (NASB). He says to them:

> Go therefore and make disciples of all the nations, baptizing them in the name of the Father and the Son and the Holy Spirit, teaching them to observe all that I have commanded you …

For evangelicals, making disciples of Jesus means introducing others to living in God's way through Christ. It means helping them to receive God's gift of blessing and to live out their inheritance as children of the King. It means encouraging them to join in the mission of the ongoing blessing of others and of all creation. And as true apprentices of Jesus, it means doing all of this in the way He did: through self-sacrifice.

The "Born Again" Connection

So what does all of this have to do with the "born again" stuff? Simply stated, evangelicals see being "born again" as a lifestyle that encompasses all three of the above ideas—receiving the gift of forgiveness and restoration, inheriting a life that is continually transformed through the presence of God, and as a result, entering into a life of mission with God. All of this is so radical that it is like being born all over again.

But also, within the metaphor of being reborn is the idea of a definitive personal moment of change. For some evangelicals, this does happen in an experience of "getting saved." Increasingly, however, for most people this is more of a process. Two words which I've found to help tremendously in describing this process are *recognition and reorientation*. Both of them together describe the response of a person to being called by God into this new lifestyle of following Christ. And each of them (again, to take us beyond the bumper-sticker mentality) deserves to be looked at in detail.

Recognizing the New Opportunity

Have you ever seen the famous picture that looks either like an old woman or a young woman, depending on how you look at it?

There are several popular versions of this same kind of optical illusion. In the particular one I'm thinking of, a person might see the crooked nose and wrinkled mouth of an old woman first. But if you look again, the nose turns into the smooth chin of a young woman, and the ungraceful mouth turns into a beautiful necklace on the young woman's neck. Pretty soon, you see the exact same picture in a completely different way.

Recognizing the opportunity of repentance is very similar. In biblical terms, it involves seeing the same picture (your life) in a completely different way than you have seen it in the past. Specifically, it involves recognizing that God is now and has always been at work all around you.

A Biblical Example of Recognition

There's an intriguing story in the book of Luke about John the Baptist (Luke 7:18-23). Jesus is starting to come into His own in His public ministry, and John's star is fading. As a matter of fact, John has been thrown in jail, and is perhaps quite depressed about his circumstances. In this context, he begins to wonder whether or not Jesus really is the Messiah (John had earlier publicly announced Him as such). So John sends his disciples to ask Jesus, "Are you the one who was to come, or should we expect someone else?"

The way Jesus answers them is fascinating. He has John's disciples hang around while He "cured many who had diseases, sicknesses and evil spirits, and gave sight to many who were blind." Most commentators believe that John's disciples watched Jesus in action for several hours. Finally, Jesus goes back to them and tells them to report to John what they have seen. And He tells them to tell John, "Blessed is he who keeps from stumbling over me" (Luke 17:23, NASB). Essentially, it's another way of saying to John, "Wake up and smell the coffee! Recognize what is happening right in front of you!"

Our Opportunities for Recognition

In our church, we have a little liturgical moment in almost every service where the worship leader says to the congregation "God is here," and the people respond, "He is among us." I've often thought that this should not just be something I do once a week, but that I should make it a practice several times a day. Because whether I recognize it or not, God is at work all around me all the time.

> **In Their Own Words**
>
> "God did not create the world and then leave it to function on its own."
>
> —Henry Blackaby, in *Experiencing God*

In the context of an experience of conversion for evangelicals, recognition means becoming aware of this fact. For many, it is quite a dramatic discovery, similar to what happens when you finally "see" the young woman in the young/old woman picture. She's been there all the time, but finally you have an "aha!" moment. You've just finally been able to recognize what's been there all along. In the same way, God has been there all the time in our lives, but for any number of reasons, we can become blinded (or closed-minded) to it.

For many, the difficulty in seeing it comes from very valid intellectual questions to which they have not been able to find satisfying answers. For others, it comes from skepticism based on bad examples of Christianity that they've experienced. For still others, it comes from moral habits that they don't want to change.

But I've personally seen what happens when someone seeks with great perseverance and finds an answer to the question that has stopped them for so long (often, quite to their own surprise). I've seen others change their minds based on recognizing that the bad examples in their past should not negate the possibility of good examples in their future (perhaps even their own). And I've been privileged to see people let go of moral failures that they did not even recognize up to that point had been damaging to them. In all of these cases, there is a recognition that God is indeed alive and at work all around them, and that their lives have to change—to turn around—in order to respond appropriately. And just like looking at the picture and seeing the two women instead of just the one, once you recognize God at work all around you, you can never see your world in the same way again.

I've also seen many people who never make that shift. The ones that sadden me the most are those who have closed their minds, and locked in on that position. In these cases, I often think of the words of C. S. Lewis in one of his *Chronicles of Narnia* books called *The Magician's Nephew*. In the books, a great lion, known as Aslan, represents God. And at a particular point in *The Magician's Nephew*, there is a character named Andrew who has closed his mind to the beckoning song of the Lion. Listen to how Lewis describes it:

> And the longer and more beautifully the Lion sang the harder Uncle Andrew tried to make himself believe that he could hear nothing but roaring. Now the trouble about trying to make yourself stupider than you really are is that you very often succeed. Uncle Andrew did. He soon did hear nothing but roaring in Aslan's song. Soon he couldn't have heard anything else even if he had wanted to.

I have all the respect in the world for those who diligently and sincerely seek out answers, and yet don't find them satisfying enough to believe. However, it must also be said that some of us don't recognize God at work—because we simply don't want to.

Either way, to understand the evangelical belief about being "born again," you must understand that it involves a *recognition* that God's kingdom—a gift to receive, a life to inherit, and a mission to enter—is indeed "at hand."

Reorientation

Recognition, however, is only part one of the conversion experience. Once we recognize that God is indeed alive and at work all around us (and in the process discover our own need for Him), we must respond. The best way to describe the response called for in order to be "born again" is to use the word "reorientation."

I read an article not long ago in my local newspaper about a man who engaged in a radical reorientation of his life. He decided to become a world-class backwards runner. As a matter of fact, backwards running become so important to him that he began to describe it as his new religion. In his mind, the opposite thinking required to run backwards, and even the physical differences involved in the act (using different muscle groups, a different sense of balance, etc.), enabled him to see life in a whole new way. As I read his story, I experienced an odd identification with him. According to evangelical beliefs, all followers of Christ are called to a similar kind of radical reorientation.

> **In Their Own Words**
>
> "I had too many questions without answers. Backward running let me attack my uncertainty and fear in a concrete way."
>
> —Joshua Davis, in *The Underdog: How I Survived the World's Most Outlandish Competitions*

Think about it: the truth is that all of us are pretty much oriented around one thing—us. As a matter of fact, psychologists tell us that we orient our lives around three basic things—our values, our priorities, and our ambitions. The common denominator? Us.

Once we recognize that God is at work around us—that He is indeed alive and real—that recognition calls us to change our orientation point. Jesus calls us to rearrange our lives around the new opportunity of living in the kingdom, or, to put it more bluntly, to arrange our lives around Him. Our values, our priorities, our ambitions begin to change. We place God in the driver's seat.

It's Hard to Be Humble

Of course, the difficulty of reorienting in this way cannot be overstated, as a story in the New Testament illustrates. In the story, a man who is described as young, wealthy, and powerful (a "ruler"), comes to Jesus. He is the type of person that we would say "has it all." Yet he comes to Jesus with a very important question: "Teacher," he says, "what good thing must I do to get eternal life?" (Matthew 19:16).

Even the phrasing of the question is fascinating. Apparently, the man is looking for one more thing to add to his list of accomplishments. He likely believes that there is some grand gesture by which he can assure his place with God. And Jesus' answer is equally fascinating, as it leads the man to come face to face with his need for reorientation.

First of all, Jesus answers him by saying, "Why do you ask me about what is good?" (Matthew 19:17) Here Jesus is challenging the man's definition of goodness. He wants him to see that it's not so much about what we do, but who we are—specifically, about our orientation point. So He tells the man to "Go, sell all your possessions …. Then come, follow me." (Matthew 19:21)

Jesus' challenge here is as appropriate for those of us in modern times as it was to the rich young ruler. Reorientation means that we don't need just a minor adjustment to our values, our priorities, and our ambitions. What we need is a full-on turn-around to the reality of living life in the kingdom that is available to us. Evangelicals would say that we need to center our lives, our relationships, our jobs, our finances, our recreation, our decisions—our everything—around Jesus. That is what reorientation is about.

> **The Gospel Truth**
>
> It's interesting to note that Jesus did not ask everyone who followed Him to sell everything they had. Thus, evangelicals are not of the opinion that wealth, in and of itself, is bad. For the rich young ruler, however, his possessions were the primary expression of his "lord"—what he had oriented himself around.

Jesus' suggestion to the man to sell everything is a challenge to him to do just that. Sort of like learning to run backwards, but with one big difference: for evangelicals, being "born again" means that we've finally begun to run in the right direction.

Tying It All Together

The five topics discussed above—the kingdom of God as a gift to receive, a life to inherit, a mission to enter, the idea of appropriating these through a recognition of our need for God and His work in our lives, and a reorientation of our lives around Jesus—are all brought together in a powerful narrative in John 3 from which we get the terminology "born again."

In the story, a religious leader named Nicodemus comes to Jesus to have a conversation. But rather than idle away their time in esoteric religious philosophizing, Jesus effectively ignores Nicodemus's polite conversation opener, and (seemingly out of nowhere if you read the passage) abruptly declares to Nicodemus: "I tell you the truth, no one can see the kingdom of God unless he is born again." (John 3:3). But Jesus' abruptness is calculated. What follows is a somewhat confused Nicodemus trying to figure out what Jesus means, and a very clear Jesus calling Nicodemus to a definitive decision regarding his acceptance of Jesus as the Messiah.

It is in the context of this conversation that we get perhaps the most famous words of scripture: "For God so loved the world that he gave his one and only Son, that whoever believes in him shall not perish but have eternal life." (John 3:16)

Being born again, then, is finally as simple as believing in Jesus. For evangelicals, this means trusting Him as the unique one who saves us from our sin and selfishness that has broken our relationship with God, practices that can be described as living in the kingdom of God.

According to the scriptures, the moment a person does this a new work happens in their souls. Theologians call it "regeneration"—a concept which is drawn from references throughout the New Testament to the idea that when a person believes (as described above), the Holy Spirit of God is literally "born" in the person's heart (see Ephesians 1:13-14 and 2 Corinthians 5:17 for examples). Thus, a work of God occurs in which the person is definitively brought from the "kingdom of darkness" (Colossians 1:13, NLT) into the kingdom of God. As a result, the Spirit of God begins a life-long process in cooperation with the person, making them progressively more and more like Christ (which we'll discuss further in Chapter 9).

This is a mysterious thing—which is why it took a whole chapter to finally get to this idea. Jesus describes it to Nicodemus by relating it to the wind (which in the original Greek of the book of John is the same word as "spirit"), saying (John 3:8):

> The wind blows wherever it pleases. You hear its sound, but you cannot tell where it comes from or where it is going. So it is with everyone born of the Spirit.

Just as you can't see the wind, but you can see its effects, so you can't "see" someone being born again. But you can definitely see the results in their lives.

This then, is what it means to an evangelical to be born again.

So Is Jesus the Only Way?

All of this brings us to a very important set of questions, perhaps the most prevalent ones in our culture with regards to Evangelicalism. Do evangelicals really believe that Jesus is the only way? Does reorienting around Jesus mean that you consider all other religions to be wrong? Does the idea of being born again mean that anyone who is not is going to hell?

Having set the foundation with our discussions of both Jesus himself (Chapter 7) and the idea of being born again (this chapter), let me now answer the above questions in order.

Evangelicals believe that Jesus, as He claimed, is "the way, the truth, and the life." (John 14:6, NLT). However, this has often been interpreted as being solely about His being "the way" to heaven and away from hell. A more accurate view of evangelical beliefs is that Jesus represents the way to the life we've been created to live—life in the kingdom. This life exists now, not just in the future. For evangelicals, Jesus is the teacher who shows that way.

This does not mean, however, that evangelicals believe that every other thing in every other religion is wrong. Indeed, they affirm the goodness of the teachings in other faiths. The point of departure for evangelicals with other faiths is primarily around the divinity of Jesus. They believe Him to be God, and thus to be worth following and worshiping as such, not just worthy of high admiration.

This then, helps us to understand better evangelical beliefs with regard to the question of heaven and hell. Evangelicals believe that Jesus' death is the only payment that can suffice for the sin of humankind. Therefore, they see Jesus' claims to be true with regards to the eternal destinies of those who do not follow Him. Although there is some debate about exactly what those claims are, as well as what is claimed in the rest of the New Testament (particularly among evangelicals of a more postmodern bent), in general, it is fair to say that most evangelicals believe that following Christ is the unique pathway to heaven. However, they also believe in the benevolence of God, and trust that God is both merciful and just. For many, this belief sustains them in their deep questions around this issue.

> **In Their Own Words**
>
> "Hell might have a place, but it can't get the last word … there's got to be a word after that ….Grace … the last word is always grace."
>
> —Casey, a character in Brian McLaren's "nonfiction novel" called *The Last Word and the Word After That*

Further, there is a surprising diversity among evangelical theologians with regards to what God's justice and benevolence means, especially for people in other cultures or other times who never had the opportunity to hear about Jesus. The common thread among all, however, is a belief in the lack of authority on the part of anyone but God to determine human destinies. Evangelicals (and again, sadly there are some) who judge individuals with regards to their eternal destinies do not fall within the teachings of Jesus in making those determinations.

A Final Word: From Morpheus to Jesus

In the final analysis, the idea of being born again carries with it an overriding question: is it worth it? Is following Jesus worth a radical reorientation? Is the gift received, the life inherited, and the mission to be entered worth arranging my life around?

Let me quote that great theologian, Morpheus, from the movie *The Matrix*. When Morpheus first meets Neo (the main character of the movie), Neo is still living in an artificial world, beginning to recognize that there is something more, and considering a radical reorientation of his life around it. Morpheus offers him a choice—a red pill, which will lead him to a reorientation, or a blue pill, which will make him forget all about it. As Morpheus offers the pills (and the choice) to Neo, he says this:

> Let me tell you why you're here. You're here because you know something. What you know you can't explain, but you feel it. You've felt it your entire life— that there's something wrong with the world. You don't know what it is, but it's there—like a splinter in your mind—driving you mad. It is this feeling that has brought you to me.

Evangelicals would suggest that one of the reasons that this movie had such resonance in our culture, is that what Morpheus says here is true of every one of us. We *know* there is something more—even if we can't explain it. And we seek after it—from backwards running to climbing the corporate ladder to trying to be the perfect parent. And yet the irony is, the more we try to find it in ourselves, the more elusive it becomes.

This is because, evangelicals would say, what we are searching for is not in ourselves. What we are searching for is the kingdom. The glimpses we've each had of that elusive something better—what our best poets and artists describe and paint and sing and make movies about—is the kingdom.

Here is what Jesus had to say about it (Matthew 13:44-46):

> The kingdom of heaven is like treasure hidden in a field. When a man found it, he hid it again, and then in his joy went and sold all he had and bought that field.

Again, the kingdom of heaven is like a merchant looking for fine pearls. When he found one of great value, he went away and sold everything he had and bought it.

In short—it's worth everything. What we're talking about here, evangelicals believe, is a new understanding of the possibilities of life. This is the life we've always yearned for in our deepest selves. Through Jesus, and uniquely through Jesus, the kingdom of God is available to you. If you recognize that, you have a choice. You can walk away—like the rich young ruler in our story ultimately did—or you can reorient around it. The choice, evangelicals (not to mention Jesus) would say, is up to you.

The Least You Need to Know

- ◆ "Born again" is shorthand for a personal conversion experience that evangelicals believe enables people to join in God's ultimate purpose for their lives.

- ◆ In order to be born again, individuals must recognize their need for Jesus, and reorient their lives around Jesus' teachings and practices.

- ◆ Evangelicals believe that the gospel is about more than just heaven and hell.

- ◆ Evangelicals believe that Jesus is the unique pathway to living in the "kingdom of God," which includes following the practices of Jesus in the here and now, and living in His presence after death.

Chapter **9**

But Does It Really Work?

In This Chapter

- ◆ Is "kingdom of God" living really possible?
- ◆ How do evangelicals define being "good"?
- ◆ What role do practices like prayer play in an evangelical's life?
- ◆ Why does God allow good people to suffer?

The last chapter ended with a very important question: is following Jesus to live out the ideals and practices of what He called "the kingdom of God" worth the commitment it takes to do so? This chapter explores an equally important, and perhaps even more foundational question: is it really even *possible* to live this way?

A friend of mine who goes to my church recently said to me, "All this 'kingdom of God' stuff sounds like utopia to me." Indeed, if all of this is simply pie-in-the-sky pipe dreams, then it is certainly not worth reorienting our lives around. In that case, the kingdom of God of Evangelicalism is more like the Magic Kingdom of Disneyland: an attractive illusion, even a short-term alternative reality—but ultimately not sustainable. Eventually, the ride ends and you have to go home.

In contrast, evangelicals would say that the realities of living life in the kingdom are not only consistently possible, but extremely practical.

Evangelical theology is not escapism; at its root, it is extremely realistic. Jesus Himself encountered the worst humanity had to offer, and yet His stubborn idealism ultimately triumphed. And therein lies the power of Evangelicalism, according to evangelicals. Indeed, they believe that following Jesus into a life of "kingdom" practices represents not just moral advancement, but the realization of the life that all of us have always wanted at our deepest levels. This truly is the "good" life, and it is sustainable. As one person put it, this life is not just morally good, but like "pizza and cold beer good." In this chapter, we'll explore more of what that life looks like and exactly how evangelicals believe that kind of life is attainable on a very practical, day-by-day basis.

The Good Life

Perhaps the best way to understand the evangelical point of view on "the good life" is to look at Jesus' definitive description of it, known popularly as the Sermon on the Mount. We've already listed a few excerpts from it in Chapter 7, but a global overview of it provides an orienting perspective with regards to the evangelical understanding of the possibilities and the resulting practicalities of their everyday faith.

The Greatest Sermon Ever Told

Jesus begins the sermon (Matthew 5:1-16) as any good preacher does, grabbing the attention of His audience. The beatitudes ("blessed are the ...") have come to be known as beautiful poetic statements of spirituality; however, to their original hearers they were likely quite offensive. In His introduction to the sermon, Jesus essentially turns the prevalent understanding of spirituality on its head. Being rich and successful are not definitive evidence of God's blessing, Jesus says—being poor in spirit is. Being strong and powerful (very important in the culture of the Roman empire) is not equal to success, Jesus says—instead, the meek will inherit the earth. He follows the beatitudes by telling those listening that they are to be the "salt of the earth" and "the light of the world"—preserving and displaying God's desires in the society around them.

Jesus goes on to further upset the apple cart (Matthew 5:17-48), taking six key religious principles of the day and reinterpreting them in ways that contrasted with the teachings of the prevalent leaders of Judaism. It's not enough to not murder, He says—you need to learn that anger itself is the spiritual equivalent of murder. Committing adultery is wrong, He says, but it is equally offensive to God to even look at someone else and want to commit adultery with them. This section comes to its climax with Jesus suggesting a near impossibility to His hearers: they are not only to love their neighbors, but also their enemies.

Following this (Matthew 6-7), Jesus goes on to teach about giving, prayer, fasting, priorities, money, worry, judging others, and the complete trustworthiness of God as a loving Father. Each of the teachings are brilliant in their clarity and their orientation toward the heart—and the practices—of the people.

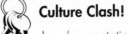

Culture Clash!

Jesus' expectations for His followers are high. For example, He says in Matthew 5:48, "Be perfect, therefore, as your heavenly Father is perfect." Although the statement refers more to a settled state of spiritual maturity than absolute moral perfection, verses like these are the reason evangelicals bristle when others say that "God is love" is all anyone really needs to follow.

Get Real!

But taken in their totality, they seem almost too good to be true. Indeed, many scholars have interpreted Jesus' Sermon on the Mount as being a description of an ideal that is beyond anyone's ability to actually live out. Thus, they say, the whole purpose of the sermon is to show that because we could never actually live this way, we need God to help us.

However, many evangelical theologians see it differently. Instead of seeing Jesus' message as a *pre*scription of a new set of (impossible) "laws" to live by, they see it as a general *de*scription of the kind of life that Jesus' followers are meant to live. Jesus is painting a picture here of the kind of life that is actually possible for His followers. He actually *expects* them to become the kind of people who consistently live as peacemakers, givers, faithful friends and lovers, merciful in conflict. He really wants them to become the light of the world.

According to these evangelicals, Jesus believes that it is possible for us to live in such a way that what God wants done gets done (or in other words, to live in God's "kingdom"). Not perfectly, but consistently. Evangelicals believe that Jesus' teachings here are a description of what is possible when one chooses to follow Christ. Living in the kingdom thus means living the kind of life that Jesus describes in the Sermon on the Mount. This should be the natural trajectory of the spiritual development of the followers of Christ. It is literally "happy" (the literal translation of the word "blessed" in the beatitudes) living.

But it still seems a tall order. Exactly how is it possible to live this way? Or to put it another way—how do evangelicals believe that such spiritual growth occurs?

A Model for Spiritual Growth

On my iPod, I have a playlist that I should probably keep a secret, but here goes: it's full of nothing but one-hit wonders. These are some of the best worst songs of all time. There's "Kung Fu Fighting" followed by "Ice, Ice Baby" and even (embarrassingly enough), "You Light Up My Life." (Just so you don't lose all respect for me, I always skip that last one.) Now since spiritualizing the playlist makes it seem more palatable, let me add this—I keep it because it reminds me of how *not* to grow spiritually.

One-hit wonders are a very popular means to spiritual growth in our culture, even in Evangelicalism. Many people believe that spiritual growth can be accomplished by finding *the* key—as evidenced by the plethora of best-selling publications that market themselves as such. But within the heritage of Evangelicalism are a variety of beliefs and practices that come together to create a sustainable whole. More than a one-hit wonder, they span the ages as proven methods of placing ourselves in a position for God to grow us. After studying evangelical theology for years, I believe that its primary principles for spiritual growth can be pictured in what I have come to call the *virtuous circle.*

With the concept of living out the practices of the kingdom of God as the center of the circle (which thus pictures the goal of spiritual growth), several key beliefs of evangelicals describe the process of growing toward the goal.

The center of the virtuous circle.

Kingdom
Living
Matthew 5 - 7

The Empowering Spirit

The first one has to do with the Holy Spirit. In the New Testament, a synonym for "life in the kingdom" is life "by the Spirit" (Galatians 5:16, 5:18, 5:25). Evangelicals believe that the Holy Spirit (the third person of the trinity, as we discussed in

Chapter 7), as He lives inside of believers, has the unique roles of initiating and empowering the spiritual growth process in their lives.

Throughout the Scriptures, the Holy Spirit is an initiator. In the Old Testament, the Spirit is seen coming upon individuals as a precursor for unique tasks to be accomplished (Judges 3:10, 6:34 11:29; 1 Samuel 11:6, 16:13; 2 Chronicles 20:14; Ezekiel 11:5). In the New Testament, the coming of the Spirit at Pentecost initiated the church (Acts 2). The Holy Spirit seals believers at the moment of salvation (Ephesians 1:13), initiating their entrance into the kingdom. In Paul's letters, the Spirit is the initiator of unique gifts for service (1 Corinthians 12:7) and growth.

Even more specifically, Jesus says in John 16:8 (NASB), "And [the Holy Spirit], when He comes, will convict the world concerning sin, and righteousness, and judgment." Conviction of sin is by definition an initiating act—the Spirit revealing a need to change and grow. Further, in John 16:13 Jesus states that the Spirit "will guide you into all truth." Evangelicals thus believe that it is the Spirit who not only authoritatively makes believers personally aware of their need to change, but shows them (through key steps that we'll discuss momentarily) the pathway to that change.

Beyond that, evangelicals believe that Spirit even empowers people to be able to make the change. This idea is evident throughout the New Testament, with perhaps the most dramatic teaching about it occurring in Paul's letter to the Ephesians, where He calls followers of Christ to "be filled with the Spirit." To be filled in this context means to be empowered by the Spirit, allowing Him to direct our thoughts and actions, opening up possibilities that go beyond our own natural character abilities.

> ### The Gospel Truth
>
> Evangelicals, often known as *charismatic*, believe that even the more dramatic gifts of the Holy Spirit (speaking in tongues, healing, etc.) should be practiced regularly in the modern world. For more information on these gifts (especially tongues), read 1 Corinthians 12-14.

Thus, for evangelicals, a conscious dependence on the Holy Spirit is foundational to true spiritual growth. Evangelicals would say that the process of growth is at its most basic level defined by placing ourselves in a position for the Holy Spirit to do His work in our lives. How a person places themselves in that position is described by the next piece of the virtuous circle.

The Holy Spirit in the virtuous circle.

Holy Spirit
Initializing, Empowering Role
Ephesians 5:15 - 6:9

Kingdom
Living
Matthew 5 - 7

The Practical Habits (Spiritual Disciplines)

Interaction with the Holy Spirit may seem mysterious, but the process through which it takes place is easily grasped. "… train yourself to be godly" says the New Testament (I Timothy 4:7). Just as athletes train their bodies for physical growth, people can engage in habits that train them spiritually. Evangelicals (as well as many other Christian traditions) often call these practices "spiritual disciplines." I like to call them spiritual habits.

Simply defined, these habits are activities that can be undertaken to lead to transformation. Whereas the Holy Spirit is the initiator and empowering force of growth, spiritual habits are the vehicles through which the growth takes place. Engagement in spiritual habits is a key part of the human responsibility in the divine/human partnership of spiritual formation.

def•i•ni•tion

Spiritual **habits of abstinence** are those activities (solitude, fasting, etc.) that enable one to disengage from the normal routine of life, providing space in which God can do His work in our lives. Spiritual **habits of engagement** are those activities that enable one to connect with God in an active way (prayer, Bible study, etc.), providing an intentional openness to hearing from God for the purpose of spiritual change.

Author Dallas Willard, in *The Spirit of The Disciplines*, makes a very helpful distinction between what he calls *habits of abstinence* and *habits of engagement*. Habits of abstinence would include practices such as fasting, solitude, or Sabbath rest. These are habits that make space in our lives, and that as a result enable us to respond to God. For instance, taking one day a week for rest readjusts our perspective a s we are refreshed, so that the pieces of our often hectic and certainly busy lives can be sorted through. Fasting causes us to recognize our need for God—

very tangibly represented by hunger. Solitude causes us to listen for God's voice in our lives as it removes us from the noise that consistently surrounds us otherwise. Other abstaining types of spiritual practices (e.g., silence, chastity, frugality, or sacrifice) enable similar connections with God. I often think of spiritual habits of abstinence as a way to avoid the scenario of having my hands so full that I am not able to receive a gift that God wants to offer me. As we make space for God, evangelicals would say, God meets us at the point of our most important (though often un-self-diagnosed) need.

Habits of engagement include activities like prayer, bible study, worship, service, and even celebration. These are practices that enable us to encounter God in an active way. For example, as we pray, we engage with God through seeking His wisdom or His favor. As we read or study the Bible, evangelicals believe that we engage with the very living word of God as He speaks to us. As we serve, we engage with God in His work of helping others, and as we celebrate we engage with God in His constant joy. Spiritual habits of engagement are like exercise for the soul—the more we do them, the stronger we get.

All of the habits, whether of abstinence or engagement, have one thing in common, according to evangelicals: they place us in a position to be changed. According to evangelical theology, much of our spiritual growth cannot be accomplished by direct effort or willpower. But through spiritual habits, God changes us. Thus, we find ourselves becoming more patient, not through focusing on patience, but through engaging in habits that enable God to train our souls. The ultimate outcome, then, is that we become the kinds of people who *naturally* live the kind of lives that Jesus describes in the Sermon on the Mount. I've often thought of engaging in spiritual habits like taking a ride on an elevator. I have the power to get on the elevator and press the button. But it is not my power that makes the elevator go up. Similarly, I can place myself in a position to be changed by engaging in spiritual habits, but it is God's power that actually makes the changes in my soul.

In Their Own Words

"Discipline: Any activity I can do by direct effort that will help me do what I cannot do now by direct effort.

"Spiritual discipline: Any activity that can help me gain power to live life as Jesus taught and modeled it."

—John Ortberg in *The Life You've Always Wanted*

The habits just listed are only a small sample of the kinds of exercises that can be utilized. They are only limited by our own imagination and initiative, according to evangelicals. I've known people who practice a daily prayer-hike; others who practice artistic creation (painting, songwriting, etc.); and others who simply sleep for a full eight hours a night or a specified period of time in order to place themselves in a position to experience spiritual growth from God. Perhaps the most prevalent exercise that evangelicals engage in is popularly known as the "quiet time"—a daily devotional time (usually anywhere from 15 minutes to an hour) set aside for prayer, Bible reading, and often journaling.

Overall, a spiritual "training" program should be a balanced and consistent exploration of and engagement in a variety of spiritual habits suited to the personality, season of life, and individual circumstances of each believer. This kind of an effort offers the opportunity to train our souls so that we can become the people that we do not have the ability to become by direct effort or willpower. Rather, evangelicals believe, the habits enable us to train in such a way so that our souls are formed, and we thus become naturally able to live a kingdom lifestyle.

Spiritual habits in the virtuous circle.

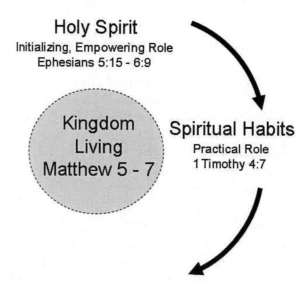

Holy Spirit
Initializing, Empowering Role
Ephesians 5:15 - 6:9

Kingdom Living Matthew 5 - 7

Spiritual Habits
Practical Role
1 Timothy 4:7

The Sustaining Community

We live in a very individualistic culture. Study after study shows that the average American is becoming less and less connected to the people around them. Part of this is the result of our ever-increasing busyness, and part of it is our ingrained western worldview of individualism. All of it can very easily send our process of spiritual formation down an unintended, yet harmful pathway.

One of the clearest expressions I've ever read of this danger came in a book called *Habits of the Heart* by sociologist Robert Bellah, in which he interviewed people from lots of different backgrounds about their faith journeys. One woman, whose name was Sheila, explained her experience this way:

> I believe in God. I'm not a religious fanatic. I can't remember the last time I went to church. My faith has carried me a long way. It's Sheilaism. Just my own little voice.

The problem with "Sheilaism" or (place your own name inside of those quotation marks) any other personal "ism," according to evangelicals, is that it doesn't square up with the overwhelmingly communal orientation of spiritual growth described in the scriptures. The modern world's focus on individualism has nearly snuffed out the intended communal emphasis in spiritual formation, even for evangelicals. The growth of an individual's soul is typically seen as one more step on the individual self-actualization ladder. Spiritual formation becomes a matter of pursuing the betterment of "my" soul. Even being a part of a church community is primarily a connection that is made out of self-interest. Worship gatherings can often be described as individuals "consuming" their weekly spiritual recharge diet—a collection of people having individual experiences with God.

> **In Their Own Words**
>
> "A society of many virtuous but isolated individuals is not necessarily rich in social capital."
>
> —Robert D. Putnam, Professor of Public Policy at Harvard, in *Bowling Alone: The Collapse and Revival of American Community*

To counter this, evangelicals believe that community provides the sustaining role of spiritual formation. As the Holy Spirit initiates and empowers, and spiritual habits provide the practical vehicles for growth, involvement in the community of faith sustains the growth process. This happens both through the encouragement of others walking the same road and through the challenging and balancing of our individual perspectives that occurs in the context of community. Another way to say this is that the sustaining community is the context of spiritual growth.

Acts 2:42-47 gives a snapshot of the early church's growth. Note the use of plural pronouns (I've italicized them) in the passage:

> *They* devoted themselves to the apostles' teaching and to the fellowship, to the breaking of bread and to prayer. Everyone was filled with awe, and many wonders and miraculous signs were done by the apostles. All the believers were

together and had everything in common. Selling *their* possessions and goods, *they* gave to anyone as he had need. Every day *they* continued to meet together in the temple courts. *They* broke bread in their homes and ate together with glad and sincere hearts, praising God and enjoying the favor of all the people. And the Lord added to *their* number daily those who were being saved.

Spiritual growth is intended to happen in the context of community, according to evangelicals. Christians are designed to grow as a group at least as much as they are designed to grow as individuals. As the above passage shows, a symbiotic experience develops as a group of individuals form a new identity as a community, following the biblical mandate to "teach and admonish one another" (Colossians 3:16). Indeed, one could even make the case, based on the above passage, that growth happens through the group first, resulting in individual growth, instead of through individuals first, resulting in group growth.

> ### In Their Own Words
>
> "Authentic redemption moves from personal salvation to inclusive fullness in community and in corporate ministry."
>
> —Gilbert Bilezikian, in *Community 101*

Community in the virtuous circle.

Of course, individual identity does not disappear in this context. People are still responsible to pursue growth on their own. However, in contrast to the overwhelmingly individualistic mindset of our culture, in community our individual identities are enhanced by a sense of a larger group identity. Thus, the third step in the virtuous circle, past the initiating and empowering work of the Holy Spirit and the practical role of spiritual habits, is the sustaining role of "the body of Christ" (see I Corinthians 12), or the community.

Actualizing Obedience

The final step in the virtuous circle is the actualizing step of obedience. For evangelicals, obedience means an ongoing commitment to follow the principles of Christianity, evidenced in moment-by-moment decisions to do what is right. Empowered by the Holy Spirit, strengthened through spiritual habits, and sustained by the ongoing connection in community, obedience becomes a very natural outflow of a life focused on Christ.

A clear expression of this concept for evangelicals comes in John 15:5, where Jesus says, "I am the vine, you are the branches. If a man remains in me and I in him, he will bear much fruit ..." Later in the New Testament, Paul identifies the "fruit of the Spirit" as character qualities such as love, joy, peace, patience, kindness, goodness, gentleness, and self-control (Ephesians 5:22-23). These are very practical character qualities that create the ability to make the right choices at the right time and in the right way in the everyday experiences of life. Thus, obedience—the actualization of faith—really does come as naturally as a vine bears fruit. The vine does not have to strain—the fruit comes naturally from the DNA of the vine.

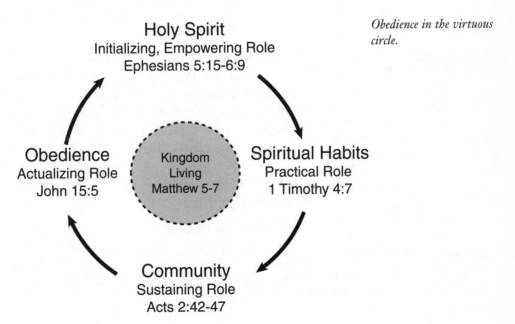

Obedience in the virtuous circle.

Perhaps most interestingly, the fruit is also naturally self-replicating. In other words, as a person obeys God, they find out that the experience really is very good—which opens them up further to the work of the Spirit, which leads to further engagement in spiritual habits and community, which leads to further obedience. Thus, the virtuous circle feeds on itself, and the cycle of growth continues—centered around the new reality of living in the kingdom of God.

Living It Out: Work and Wealth

Let's take a look at how this evangelical paradigm of spiritual growth might work itself out in the very specific and practical scenario of vocation, and the even more practical issue of personal finances.

Evangelicals believe that there is intrinsic spiritual value in work, and thus in every vocation. Many see their jobs as a "calling" from God—the specific coming together of the unique gifts and talents they've been given by their Creator with the specific mission they've been given to be a blessing to the world around them. Thus, as the Holy Spirit (at the top of the virtuous circle) leads them to a new job opportunity, a typical evangelical would pray over the decision (exercising a spiritual habit), seek counsel about it from trusted Christian friends (engaging in community), and then make a decision based on all of the above, intended to be in obedience to God's desires for them. Having chosen, to the best of their ability, according to God's will, the evangelical would thus experience the blessing of God, and be motivated to continue to follow Him—starting the circle all over again.

The Gospel Truth

Over the past few years, about ⅔ of Americans have given some money away to a nonprofit or religious organization; generally less than 5 percent of them gave away 10 percent or more of their income (a practice often called "tithing"). Evangelicals were the most likely of all groups surveyed to have tithed.

—Source: *The State of the Church: 2006* by The Barna Research Group

---

But what about in a more difficult scenario? Let's take it a step further. Work creates wealth. And although evangelicals do not believe that being wealthy is wrong in and of itself, they do believe that the Bible teaches that few things have the potential to trip us up more than a focus on gaining wealth. So let's say our evangelical friend above does really well in their job, and starts to make a very good living. What do they do with that money?

Most likely, according to evangelical theology, they would begin to experience a conviction from the Holy Spirit to practice the spiritual habit of giving. However, they may not be ready to part with their money quite so easily. Thus, through spiritual habits such as prayer, or exposure to the word of God (which has much to say about money as an alternate God), and perhaps even through a discipline of abstinence such as fasting, they would begin to see the importance of the needs of others. As they observed their peers in the community of faith in the practice of giving, they would be sustained in this conviction. Finally, out of a genuine desire to follow Christ, they would decide to give. The blessing that resulted (and many evangelicals would affirm the counterintuitive sense of freedom that giving brings) would motivate them to listen to the Spirit even further about giving, starting the cycle all over again.

Reality Checks

This all sounds great, but what happens when things don't turn out quite so well? What happens to their faith, for instance, when an evangelical decides to follow what they see as God's pathway into a new job, and it turns out to be a fiasco? Or what happens when something even more dramatic takes place? A crippling accident or disease? The death of a loved one? The victimization of a child?

If evangelical theology really "works"—if it is not just pie-in-the-sky utopianism— then it must provide satisfying answers for these kinds of questions. This is an age-old topic ("Why do bad things happen to good people?") that deserves its own book (at least). A short answer to how these kinds of experiences are dealt with in evangelical theology would be to say that the question is usually answered in one of three ways:

- **Suffering is corrective.** Sometimes, evangelicals would say, we bring suffering on ourselves through our own choices. God, as a faithful Father, allows a measure of suffering to cause us to turn back toward Him.

> **In Their Own Words**
>
> "Suffering is God's megaphone to rouse a deaf world."
> —C. S. Lewis in *The Problem of Pain*

- **Suffering is growth.** At other times, evangelicals believe that suffering, though undeserved, can be used by God to grow us in our spiritual lives. "The testing of your faith produces endurance" says James 1:3 (NASB). Sometimes we experience suffering because of the sin that surrounds us in the world—the natural consequences of the acts of others, or the spoiling of creation. At these times, evangelicals believe that God will take the bad and transform it into the goodness of an opportunity to grow closer to Him.

♦ **Suffering is an opportunity to trust**. At times, even the above two answers do not satisfy. Honest evangelicals will often admit that they do not know why certain kinds of suffering occur. However, they will often affirm, even in their doubts, a trust in the sovereignty and wisdom of God. Ultimately, they hold on to their faith by saying with Job (Job 1:21, NASB), "The Lord has given, and the Lord has taken away; blessed be the name of the Lord."

Obviously, this last kind of faith is not easy to come by. In my own experience, evangelicals who are the strongest in their faith tend to be the ones who have put in the most time and effort into listening and responding to the Spirit in their everyday lives, "training" through the spiritual habits, connecting into community, and expressing their beliefs through obedience and service. Just like athletes, those who train the hardest experience the greatest results.

Pigpen Theology

Maybe you remember Pigpen, from the old *Peanuts* cartoons by Charles Schultz. Pigpen's defining characteristic was that everywhere he went, a little cloud of dust surrounded him, or more accurately, emanated from him. It was the result of his lifestyle—the fruit of his habits—and it affected everyone who got close to him.

I see Pigpen as a great picture of the calling of evangelicals. Jesus said that we are to be a "light of the world." Instead of dust, I believe Jesus' intent was that we are to be little emanations of light wherever we go. The light should surround us like Pigpen's cloud, and it should affect everyone who gets close to us. This "light"—from the simple kindness of common courtesy, to a willingness to give our very lives for the sake of others—should be the natural fruit of our habits. And the combination of all of our lights, according to evangelicals, should be bright enough to change the world.

But that's what the next chapter is about.

The Least You Need to Know

♦ Evangelicals believe that it is possible to live consistently, although not perfectly, the kind of lifestyle described by Jesus in the Sermon on the Mount.

♦ The virtuous circle is a way of describing the evangelical viewpoint of the process of spiritual growth and transformation.

◆ Evangelicals believe that spiritual habits place a person in a position to be spiritually transformed by God.

◆ Suffering does not necessarily negate the faith of evangelicals; at their best, evangelicals see it as an opportunity to increase their faith.

Chapter 10

Who Needs the Church?

In This Chapter

- What makes a church a church?

- How are evangelical churches organized and governed?

- Why do evangelical churches put so much emphasis on sharing their faith with others?

- What do evangelical churches believe about the end of time?

You can find some great stuff on the Internet.

Not long ago, I decided to do a search to find the oddest, weirdest church I could find. I found more of them than I could count.

For instance (and I'm *not* making this up), I found the Church of the Charismatic Pineapple, the Chapel of the Snoring Possum, and the E-Commercial Church, whose motto is disarmingly honest: "Believe and get rich." I also found the Church of the SubGenius, which makes the list because the goal of the church is not the attainment of spiritual maturity, or of nirvana, or of being one with the cosmos—the goal is the attainment of "slack."

There was also the Church of the King, which doesn't sound so weird until you realize that the King—is Elvis. When I logged on, I saw a picture of a bunch of guys standing around an altar taking communion—all dressed like Elvis (complete with matching sequined white jumpsuits, long sideburns, and Elvis sunglasses). Perhaps somewhat related to this church I also found Beer Church, whose 100,000 worldwide members from 26 countries have given away over $40,000 in the last few years to charities, through beer-themed activities.

One might be tempted at first to laugh the previous examples off. But if you think about it, why shouldn't they call themselves churches? They express a common loyalty to something they see as highly esteemed (which could be called worship), they engage in rituals together (the Elvises at communion), and they even give money away, evidencing a sense of mission. As humorous as they might sound, they raise an important question: what is a church?

What Is a Church?

Many in today's culture see the church as a quaint idea, but not really necessary for spiritual growth. Our highly individualized western world mindset has convinced us that spiritual growth is really a personal thing. Thus, the church might be a nice add-on, but is not vital to our spiritual growth. Some even go beyond this, believing that the church—as evidenced by its history—is actually quite dangerous. Thus, they see parodies of the church such as some of the ones mentioned above as healthy correctives that serve to challenge the status quo.

When it comes to church, evangelicals have historically been in the forefront of challenging the prevailing norms. Theirs is an innovative tradition. However, it is held in place by a bedrock set of beliefs about the definition and purpose of the church. For them, the church is not an organization, it is more aptly described as an organism. It is the living, breathing, growing, changing, literal "body of Christ" (1 Corinthians 12:27). It encompasses both the totality of the worldwide movement of Christians, and is also represented in each individual local expression of that movement (local congregations).

> **The Gospel Truth**
>
> In addition to "the body of Christ," other metaphors for the church in the New Testament include the bride of Christ, a flock (with Jesus as the shepherd), a family, and an army.

The Greek word for church (ekklesia) used in the New Testament comes from the Greek verb *kaleo* (to call) and the preposition *ek* (meaning "out of"). Literally then, *church* means "the called out ones." Although in popular vernacular the word *church* usually refers to a building, evangelicals (and most other Christian traditions) recognize that the building is simply the place the church meets. The "church" is properly defined as God's people. Evangelicals believe that these people are called out on a mission—extending the kingdom of God.

The Purposes of a Church

Acts 2:42-47 is a good look at what evangelicals see as a picture of a healthy church. Although we referenced this passage in Chapter 9, it bears looking at again in more detail here. It is a six-verse snapshot of the first century church, as believers in Jesus began to spontaneously band together:

> They devoted themselves to the apostles' teaching and to the fellowship, to the breaking of bread and to prayer. Everyone was filled with awe, and many wonders and miraculous signs were done by the apostles. All the believers were together and had everything in common. Selling their possessions and goods, they gave to anyone as he had need. Every day they continued to meet together in the temple courts. They broke bread in their homes and ate together with glad and sincere hearts, praising God and enjoying the favor of all the people. And the Lord added to their number daily those who were being saved.

In this passage, we see five purposes of the church that define it for evangelicals:

- ◆ The purpose of corporate worship (what they did as they met together in the temple courts)

- ◆ The purpose of spiritual growth (devoting themselves to the apostles' teaching)

- ◆ The purpose of community (signified by their unusual commitment to "having everything in common")

- ◆ The purpose of service (" … they gave to anyone as he had need")

- ◆ The purpose of extending the faith (as evidenced by the new people who were "being saved" on a daily basis), often called evangelism or mission

These five purposes are the basic building blocks of the church for evangelicals. Let's look at each of them in more detail.

Worship

"To worship God is to ascribe to him the worth of which he is worthy" according to the *Evangelical Dictionary of Theology.* It is helpful in considering what the concept of worship means to a modern evangelical to break the concept up into a more specific and a more generalized meaning.

In general, to worship means to live a life that is oriented around God. When we orient ourselves in this way, it gives God the worth He deserves in our lives—or, as in our definition above, it ascribes to God "the worth of which he is worthy." Thus, one can say that virtually every activity of the evangelical church has the goal of worship in mind.

A more specific application of worship comes in the church's purpose to provide corporate opportunities for people to express together the worthiness of God. This is typically known as a worship service. A defining characteristic of evangelicals has been their high level of creativity in seeking out modes of worship most appropriate to each generation. Jesus told His followers to worship Him "in spirit and in truth," and evangelicals have been remarkably innovative in this. Connecting with the "spirit" of each arriving generation, they have upheld the truths of scripture in an amazing variety of ways. From the revivals of Finney's day to barefooted Jesus-people-acoustic guitar worship services, all the way to today's emergent churches that often feature an artist painting a huge canvas as the congregation sings, evangelicals put great effort into their worship experiences.

All of this is in the service of the church's fulfillment of what Jesus said (Matthew 4:10), quoting the Old Testament scriptures: "Worship the Lord your God, and serve him only."

Spiritual Growth

A second key purpose of the church is the spiritual growth of its participants. In Colossians 1:28, the apostle Paul articulates this purpose well, saying, "We proclaim [Jesus], admonishing and teaching everyone with all wisdom, so that we may present everyone perfect in Christ."

The word *perfect* here can also be translated as "mature." The idea behind it is not absolute flawlessness, but consistent kingdom living. Evangelicals believe that the church is tasked by God as the entity which teaches and encourages (another word for "admonish" used in the verse above) people to live in this way. Often, evangelical churches call this process "discipleship" or even "apprenticeship to Jesus."

The apprenticeship model is intriguing as a way of understanding this purpose of the church. Apprentices learn not just by gaining information, but by *doing*. First, the master shows them what to do. Then the master helps them as they try it. Soon, the student is accomplished at the task, and over time is even able to take on an apprentice of their own. Thus, apprenticeship involves both understanding a foundational corpus of knowledge about something, and then learning to live it out. Apprenticeship also happens in community; by definition it cannot happen with only one person.

The church, then, helps to make apprentices to Jesus by helping people to gain an ever-growing knowledge about kingdom living, and helping them to live it out. The ultimate master is Jesus, but within the church, individuals help one another along as they apprentice to their common Lord. This communal effort of growth is what evangelicals see as a key function of the body of Christ.

In Their Own Words

"[O]rdinary people who are [Jesus'] apprentices, gathered in the name of Jesus and immersed in his presence, and taking steps of inward transformation as they put on the character of Christ: that is all that is required."

—Dallas Willard, describing the purpose of the church as spiritual growth in *Renovation of the Heart*

Community

This brings us to a third purpose that evangelicals see as key to the church: community.

Within the church, community works itself out on several levels. First of all, there is the social level—providing the venue for people to connect with one another and simply enjoy being together. It also works on a functional level—a group of individuals working together to carry out the commission of Christ to extend the kingdom to others. It works even further on an intimate level—providing the kind of close and deep interaction that is necessary for real life change to occur.

At their best, evangelical churches are unique in their ability to provide a safe place for the development of the level of relationship it takes for deep life change to occur. As the people of the church evidence deep commitment to one another, they begin to open up about their struggles as well as their joys. In that context, encouragement and accountability and healing can take place. Experiencing the Spirit of God working through His people to help each other through difficult times is one of the most rewarding parts of being involved in an evangelical church.

Contrary to the overwhelmingly individualistic ethos of our culture, evangelicals believe that the church is a place of belonging. As the Living Bible translation of I Corinthians 12:27 puts it, "All of you together are the one body of Christ, and each one of you is a separate and necessary part of it."

Service

A fourth purpose that evangelical churches claim as their own can be summarized under the heading of service.

Following the teachings of Jesus about the practical outworking of their faith, most evangelical churches see part of their role as bringing good news to the community and the world around them. Speaking of Himself in Mark 10:45, Jesus said that, "[T]he Son of Man did not come to be served, but to serve ..." Evangelical churches see this and other similar biblical teachings as a clear mandate to find ways to help others.

One unique aspect of this in most evangelical churches is the concept of spiritual gifts. In several places (Romans 12, I Corinthians 12, Ephesians 4, and I Peter 4 among others), the New Testament mentions (and sometimes lists) special abilities that are given to believers in Christ for the purpose of service. Beyond natural abilities or talents, these gifts include prophecy (i.e., seeing the truth of a situation and proclaiming it), mercy (the unique ability to empathize with others and thus reach out to them in extraordinarily helpful ways), and even healing (usually given more prominence in more "charismatic" evangelical churches). Leadership, service, and faith are examples of other spiritual gifts mentioned. Although beliefs about these gifts and their operation in the church vary in evangelical churches, there is a general consensus that God does indeed enable His people in unique ways to do His work.

> **In Their Own Words**
>
> "You are a minister; therefore, you have a ministry."
>
> —Bruce Bugbee, writing to lay people in his book on spiritual gifts titled *What You Do Best in the Body of Christ*

As each member of the body of Christ discovers and implements their giftedness, the church serves with a supernatural power that is well beyond the natural abilities of its participants. As a result, the church's purpose of serving is carried out in ways that go well beyond the sum of its individual parts.

Evangelism/Mission

The word *evangelism* carries with it a terrible stigma in our culture today. From big-haired women and big-headed men staring at you through a television camera, to goofy people who hold up signs at football games, to your friend who inappropriately tried to "convert" you at a party, the idea of sharing the message of Christ with others has been tarnished almost beyond repair. That's why I prefer to use the word *mission* here.

There is no doubt that Jesus called His followers into a mission to extend His kingdom. In what is known as the Great Commission, the book of Matthew closes with Jesus saying to His disciples:

> All authority in heaven and on earth has been given to me. Therefore go and make disciples of all nations, baptizing them in the name of the Father and of the Son and of the Holy Spirit, and teaching them to obey everything I have commanded you. And surely I am with you always, to the very end of the age.

This call to "make disciples" is the impetus for evangelicals' dedication to sharing their faith with others. From individuals sharing their faith with their friends, to churches organizing city-wide campaigns, to international missionary efforts, evangelicals have earned their name through their effort in this regard.

Admittedly, this effort has gone awry at times. (I have a gift for understatement.) However, to be fair one must also consider the large numbers of evangelicals who are *not* big-haired or big-headed, and who have a genuine concern to help others in this regard. These folks see the extending of Jesus' invitation to life in the kingdom to others as analogous to the biblical value of offering hospitality.

Throughout the scriptures, hospitality is an important vehicle for service to others. It goes well beyond our modern conception of the idea; the story of the Good Samaritan (Luke 10:27-37) in the New Testament helps us to understand the lengths to which Jesus calls His followers to go to help others. For evangelicals, evangelism thus means saying and *showing* that the kingdom of God is at hand. Believing that one should not be done without the other, many evangelical churches find ways to help with the practical needs of their communities as a part of their mission. Food pantries, divorce recovery workshops, job training—these kinds of activities are much more prevalent in evangelical churches than most people realize.

In addition, most evangelical churches work hard to equip their people to be able to clearly explain Christianity to others who are interested in developing a relationship with God. Often this includes a thoughtful telling of their own spiritual story, connected with an explanation of the basic tenets of the Christian understanding of how Jesus offers personal forgiveness and new life. Often this kind of teaching is put together into "evangelism training" seminars offered by churches. The downside of these seminars has been their huge contribution to the reductionism of the gospel we discussed in Chapter 8.

In Their Own Words

"Preach the gospel—if necessary use words."
—Francis of Assisi

Having been through many of these, my experience is that they feel very much like a sales seminar—complete with defined message points, canned answers to common objections, and even "closing" techniques. However, the upside to these has been their enormous influence in mobilizing evangelicals to share their faith. This mobilization is one of the keys to the overall strength of the movement. Further, it is important to remember that the basic impetus for this type of training for evangelicals has been to share a life-changing message in the most effective manner possible.

Through both practical service and verbal witness, evangelicals have moved far beyond local church efforts at evangelism. Huge world-wide efforts to spread Christianity (usually known within Evangelicalism as "mission work") are evident literally all over the planet. Through denominations, parachurch organizations, and individual local church mission activities, evangelicals give millions of dollars a year and enormous amounts of personal time to reach out. They spearhead international relief efforts, build homes and hospitals, create schools, and connect with people one-on-one in enormously creative efforts to fulfill their calling.

However it is done, evangelicals see sharing their faith as an imperative that comes directly from God. They see it as a key part of the mission of the church. And they see it as a genuine opportunity to help others. Further, as we'll see in Chapters 19 and 20, evangelicals of a more postmodern bent are expanding the traditional definition of evangelism into a much wider-ranging implementation of mission.

The Practices of the Church

In one of the first churches I served in, I got into big trouble.

I moved a picture.

Not just any picture, mind you, but the picture of Miss Mable. Miss Mable—who had started the Sunday School class that had met in the same room for more years than I had probably been alive. Miss Mabel—whose picture was on the wall of that room. People threatened to leave the church over it. I was flabbergasted.

That was my introduction to a lesson that proved to be one of my most important: it's usually not the theology of an evangelical church that causes people to wonder about it—it's the practices of the church. In my experience, most people understand and even respect the need for a church to have and hold to a set of core beliefs. But when those beliefs get turned into action—when you start moving Miss Mabel's picture around—then you're in for some adventure. (For the record, I stand by my decision. I'm not bitter or anything.)

Evangelicals are curiously bipolar when it comes to the practices of the church. On the one hand, they work hard to make sure the church is as relevant as possible to the world at large. On the other hand, they are just as likely as any other kind of church to have their own ways of doing things, and just as likely to resist change. Let's take a look at a few practices that define the evangelical church.

Worship Styles

We begin with the one that has both created the most growth and caused the most internal disagreement in evangelical churches: worship styles.

The explosion of growth in evangelical churches in the late '60s stemmed in large part from the cultural relevance of churches being birthed out of the Jesus Movement. One of the defining characteristics of these churches was the use of rock music in worship services. This was controversial at the time, and over the years lots of evangelical churches struggled and even split over the issue, as the music of the baby boomer generation made its way into churches throughout the land.

Today, the typical evangelical church does make use of soft-rock music in its services, replacing or sometimes mixing traditional hymns with *praise choruses*. This practice is far from universal, however, as many mainline, and even "high" church denominations, hold to evangelical beliefs, yet follow a more traditional format. Some churches even create separate services on Sundays featuring different styles of music, usually called a traditional service and a contemporary service.

def•i•ni•tion

A **praise chorus** is a song (not a hymn) sung by evangelicals in a church service. Another (painfully accurate) definition: "Three chords, four verses, twenty minutes."

In addition to adopting modern musical styles, many evangelical churches have become quite adept at other communication vehicles. Drama, multimedia presentations, live painting, dance—all of them and more are practiced with regularity and often (especially in the megachurches) with great skill by evangelical churches.

Often the churches that tend to be the most prolific in their use of these forms are also the least liturgical in their approach; eschewing the following of an annual liturgical calendar and instead opting to design their services around the particular "felt needs" of the people of their community. For example, in my current church we often do a summer series based on blockbuster movies and other current media—exploring their spiritual themes and using them as jumping-off points to engage people with the principles of scripture.

Similarly, many evangelical churches are thematic in their services. The music, drama, and/or the multimedia of the day often reinforce a specific theme that the pastor will expound on in his or her message. Additionally, most evangelical church pastors tend toward a conversational tone as they preach, forgoing both the formal lecture approach of more traditional mainline churches and the yelling and sweating approach most often associated with fundamentalist churches.

Overall, the worship styles of most evangelical churches are intentionally designed to be culturally relevant. Evangelicals are passionate about making sure in this way that everyone feels welcome in their midst, and that the message of Christ is not discarded simply because its vehicle of delivery is out of date.

Rites of Passage and Sacramental Observances

Evangelical churches also tend to be less liturgical regarding rites of passage and sacramental activities (often called *ordinances*). Spread as they are among so many denominations (along with many nondenominational churches), they engage in a variety of practices, such as:

- Baby dedications
- Infant baptisms
- Adult or teen baptisms
- Communion
- Confirmation
- Joining the church

The specific ordinances observed and their manner of observation varies from church to church.

Ordinances such as the above are often observed informally. For example, I've been involved with countless baptisms conducted at local lakes, rivers, or even backyard pools (including my own) that were connected with a relaxed family picnic for those involved, their friends, and anyone else who wanted to come. The actual ritual of baptism is no less solemn in these cases; on the contrary the meaningfulness of the observance is often enhanced by its lack of pretension. The authenticity of hearing people tell their stories as they are baptized, surrounded by their community in such a normal, family-like atmosphere, is quite fresh and moving.

As we've seen is often the case with evangelicals, in their liturgical observances, they innovate. From special coming-of-age ceremonies, to creative wedding rituals, to family "quiet times," the scope and variety of evangelical liturgies are quite vast. Again, this is a reflection of the entrepreneurial spirit that is historically characteristic of Evangelicalism.

Community Life

The community life of the church is very important to evangelicals. Helping people to connect in more intimate venues than a public worship service has been a key to the growth of evangelical churches. As a matter of fact, in most of them, the primary organizational "infrastructure" of the church is built around the development of community life, typically organized into various types of smaller group gatherings.

In more traditional evangelical churches this often takes place in a Sunday School class, where adults gather in small groups to study the Bible and get to know one another better. Baby boomers seem to prefer what are often called "small groups"— usually meeting in the homes of participants during the week, where a less formal atmosphere fosters even more personal relationship building.

> **In Their Own Words**
>
> "Disciples are made in relationship."
>
> —Jeffrey Arnold in *The Big Book on Small Groups*

Some evangelicals have taken this a step further, forming "house churches." These are seen by many as the wave of the near future for Evangelicalism. A house church is just what it sounds like—a church that meets in a home. Although the concept has been around for quite a while, it seems to be more and more attractive to younger evangelicals, who are searching for more organic and less institutional church forms. The most dynamic of these small churches are often connected through a network in a particular area, which allows them to share resources, encourage one another, do local mission work together, and multiply more quickly. Historically, house churches have been enormously successful in worldwide Evangelicalism, particularly in countries where persecution prevents the organization of larger church bodies.

It is widely recognized by evangelical church leaders that the community life of the church is not an add-on. One of the most prevalent distinctives of evangelical churches is the attention they pay to the development of smaller communities inside of the church. Studies have proven over and over that these communities, more than any other single factor, create and sustain the growth of evangelical churches.

Giving

Obviously, another key factor in the growth of a church is its ability to remain financially healthy. Nearly all evangelical churches are funded solely by the gifts of the participants in the church. Very few receive any help from a larger denominational body. As a matter of fact, evangelical churches that are part of a denomination typically give part of their revenue to the denomination to help sustain it.

def•i•ni•tion

Tithing is the practice of giving away 10 percent of your earnings.

The practice of *tithing*, or giving 10 percent of one's income, is an important part of how evangelical churches raise their resources. Many evangelical churches teach that tithing is a biblical commandment, just as important to a life of obedience as not murdering or not committing adultery. Some even teach that God calls individuals to tithe first to the church, only giving to other organizations afterward. Other churches are less stringent in their beliefs, seeing the New Testament scriptures as teaching what is known as "grace giving"—releasing Christians from the obligation of the tithe, but calling them instead to a standard of "giving as they've been given to" by God. Even in this case, however, most evangelicals would say that the tithe is the minimum benchmark for grace giving.

According to pollster George Barna, in practice less than 10 percent of evangelicals actually tithe, even though the teachings of the majority of churches that they attend espouse the practice. However, evangelicals are much more likely to both tithe and/ or give to their church than nearly any other segment of the American population. Many give much more than a tithe. Overall, this is because evangelical churches are very good at teaching people that giving habits are a clear reflection of a person's heart. Evangelicals believe that giving is a spiritual habit, designed to help people remember that God is the owner of everything, and humans are simply the managers of what God has given them. This concept is often called "stewardship" in evangelical churches. Further, evangelicals believe that giving demonstrates trust in God, and encourages an overall approach to life that counters the materialistic worldview of today's culture. Overall, they believe that giving demonstrates a wise, contented, and ultimately missional lifestyle.

Church Leadership

One of the most intriguing practices of evangelical churches is how they govern themselves. People often think of the pastor as the head of the church (in human terms), but that approach is actually uncommon. Typically, there is a plurality of leadership, usually called an Elder or Deacon board, that holds the final leadership reigns in a church. These boards are made up of the members of the church; usually the Pastor (the Senior Pastor, in a multi-staff environment) sits on the board as both a member and as one who is ultimately accountable to the board.

Typically, a church board will delegate authority for the day-to-day operations to the Pastor, often including responsibility for the hiring and firing of the other staff. Further, the board (similar to any nonprofit) helps make directional decisions for the church, and carries the legal and fiduciary responsibility for the church's operations.

The intriguing part of all of this is that many evangelical boards operate on a consensus model of decision making. In other words, they often don't vote on matters before them. Instead, following what they believe to be the pattern of the early church reflected in the New Testament book of Acts, they will continue to talk and pray over situations until they come to a consensus. This is often a much slower way of "doing business," but it's been fascinating to me to see how this process often results in people's minds changing through prayer and interaction with one another. In these cases, consensus does not always mean unanimity, but will often be a beautiful demonstration of true Christian humility—one person giving up their ideas in deference to what they believe God is saying to the rest of the group. (Of course, it doesn't always work that way, but in my experience it happens much more often than people realize.)

Some evangelicals believe that church boards and Senior Pastor roles should only be filled with men, reflecting a further expansion of the views of authority that we'll talk about in Chapter 12. Others, reflecting a different point of view on the same scriptures, believe that women and men are to serve equally in leadership in the church. Indeed, the number of women serving as Pastors in evangelical churches continues to rise.

The Future of the Church (and the World)

I have a friend who told me recently that he didn't go to college because he was convinced that Jesus was coming back so soon, it wouldn't matter.

That was over 20 years ago.

Today, he still believes in the second coming, but he has completed his degree. As his faith matured, his understanding of what the Bible actually means in all of its pronouncements regarding the future has become more nuanced. In both his more literalistic stage, and his current, more mellow stage, he is a picture of the spectrum of evangelical beliefs with regard to the future.

Taking the Bible as seriously as they do, evangelicals have always been very serious about the future of the church (i.e., the worldwide body of Christians, not just the individual local bodies). They believe that the prophecies about the end of time are to be listened to, although exactly what these prophecies mean is the subject of vast disagreement. In this last section about the church, we'll sketch out a few of the major areas of importance in this regard within Evangelicalism.

The End of the World as We Know It

The theological word for the study of "last things" is eschatology. For evangelicals, the word has both a doctrinal and a practical meaning. Doctrinally, it means digging into the scriptures to try to understand what God has said about the consummation of the age of humanity.

While there are lots of careful and reputable theologians who have written in this realm, there are lots of others who are not so careful. Unfortunately for Evangelicalism, the not-so-careful ones often have the loudest voices, and the novelty and shrillness with which they speak is what often gets the most attention from the media. Further, the sensationalism of fictionalized accounts of the end of the world (often written by evangelicals) have made it even tougher to have an intelligent conversation around these issues. But let's try anyway.

The basic elements of evangelical eschatological theology (say that three times fast) include …

- **The second coming of Christ.** This belief is based on the New Testament accounts of what Jesus Himself said, and on what the apostles later wrote about (especially in the book of Revelation). Evangelicals believe that Jesus will return to Earth to consummate the kingdom He began, and inaugurate a new age.

- ◆ **The "rapture."** This is the belief of some evangelicals that when Jesus comes again, those who believe in him will be suddenly snatched away to meet him in the air.

- ◆ **The tribulation.** This is the belief of some evangelicals that prior to the end of the world, believers in Jesus will go through terrible persecution.

- ◆ **The millennial rule of Christ.** This is the belief of some evangelicals that when Jesus returns, He will set up a thousand-year reign on earth, prior to the beginning of a new age.

- ◆ **Final judgment.** This phrase summarizes many beliefs of evangelicals about God's final act of setting things right with both humanity and creation.

- ◆ **Heaven.** This is the belief of evangelicals in a conscious, eternal afterlife with God.

- ◆ **Hell.** This is the belief of most evangelicals in a conscious, eternal afterlife without God.

You'll notice in the above list that I qualified quite a bit (i.e., the belief of "some" or "most" evangelicals). This is because there is quite a bit of disagreement about exactly what is predicted, and particularly about the order in which what is predicted will take place. All of this gets extremely complicated, and is very subjective, based, as much of it is, on the interpretations of symbolic literature in the Old and New Testaments. It is also way beyond the scope of this book. (I would recommend *The Complete Idiot's Guide to the Bible*, especially the chapter on Revelation, if you want to dig into this some more.)

The Sweet Here and Now

This brings us to the more practical definition of eschatology. In addition to it being the study of "last things," many theologians also define it as being a practical living out of the hope of the consummation of God's purposes. This is where most evangelicals (crazy fiction books and goofy movies aside) actually live.

Most of them are functional agnostics about the order of events predicted in the Bible. Quite frankly, they really don't care. What they do care about is the hope that is represented in an eschatological viewpoint of life. They care about the hope of Christ returning to consummate His kingdom, the hope of God setting things right for all humanity and creation (a clearer way of understanding the idea of judgment), the hope of resurrection, and the hope of a new, better, and ongoing relationship with God after death. At its best, then, eschatology encourages evangelicals to live with a forward-looking mentality, and to engage in God's mission in the here and now in anticipation of God's completion of His work.

The Dream Come True

The book of Revelation gives an incredible picture of the future of the church (7:9-10). Here is what the apostle John writes, as part of His vision of the future:

> … I looked and there before me was a great multitude that no one could count, from every nation, tribe, people and language, standing before the throne and in front of the Lamb. They were wearing white robes and were holding palm branches in their hands. And they cried out in a loud voice:

> "Salvation belongs to our God,
> who sits on the throne,
> and to the Lamb."

This picture of a church that encompasses the entire planet, that is pure (symbolized by white robes), that is prevailing (symbolized by the palm branches), and that is worshipping, is quite literally the dream come true—both for the church, and for God Himself.

For evangelicals, the church of here and now is the dream *coming* true. More than a group of people who join together to celebrate Elvis, or beer, or even to do good works, the church for evangelicals is *super*natural in nature. It is God's people on a mission to do God's work.

And, evangelicals believe, it will prevail.

The Least You Need to Know

- ◆ Most evangelicals see the church as defined by five purposes: worship, spiritual growth, community, service, and evangelism/mission.

- ◆ The practices of evangelical churches are as varied as the movement itself.

- ◆ Evangelical churches believe in a second coming of Jesus.

- ◆ Most evangelicals don't have a definitive belief about the sequence of events at the end of the world.

Part 3

What Would Jesus Do? Evangelical Hot Buttons

Evangelicals are a counter-cultural bunch—sort of. While on the one hand, their devotion to their theological beliefs as presented in Part II of this book lead them to lifestyles that are often out of sync with contemporary culture, their beliefs also have led to the creation of an alternate culture— a sub-culture that seems to have its own rules of conformity. And whether or not this sub-culture actually reflects the core of their faith, it often defines evangelicals in the public mind.

This section focuses on several of the issues that define the personal morals of evangelicals. Why are sex, "family values," abortion, and creationism (among other issues) so important to evangelicals? Is this where the focus should be? Or, in the now famous words of bumper-stickers everywhere: What Would Jesus Do?

Chapter 11

Sex, Drugs, and Rock 'n' Roll: Evangelicals and Personal Morality

In This Chapter

- ◆ Why do evangelicals seem so hung up about sex?
- ◆ Do evangelicals hate gays?
- ◆ Are all evangelicals tee-totalers?
- ◆ Do evangelicals advocate censorship of the media?

In a widely read book that is an evangelical classic called *The Pursuit of Holiness* (1978), author Jerry Bridges wrote:

> God has called every Christian to a holy life. There are no exceptions to this call. It is not a call only to pastors, missionaries, and a few dedicated Sunday School teachers. Every Christian of every nation, whether rich or poor, learned or unlearned, influential or totally unknown, is called to be holy. The Christian plumber and the Christian banker, the unsung housewife and the powerful head of state are all alike called to be holy.

For those outside of the evangelical lifestyle, this kind of a statement is quite intimidating. The thought of being "holy" conjures up ideas of a stiff and prim person who, as Mark Twain once put it, is a "good man in the worst sense of the word." Why would anyone aspire to that?

Indeed, many who claim to be good are simply self-righteous. This is because their habits of obedience to certain standards place the standards in first position, instead of the heart. In other words, they expect rules to form their heart, instead of the other way around.

For evangelicals, living a "holy" (literally "set apart") lifestyle grows *out* of being "spiritually formed" in the way that we discussed in Chapter 9. As God aligns their hearts with His good desires, God's people begin to align their behavior accordingly. In this chapter, we'll explore some of the more obvious ways that evangelical lifestyles thus differ from the prevalent culture around them.

Let's Talk About Sex

For a guy who was single and celibate, Jesus left behind a group of followers who have a lot to say about sex.

Indeed, one of the places where evangelicals seem most out of sync with the rest of society is in their beliefs about personal sexual morality. While roughly half of Americans approve of sex outside of marriage, for example, only a scant 7 percent of evangelicals do, according to a 2003 survey by pollster George Barna. And where at least 30 percent of Americans approve of same-sex sexuality, only 5 percent approve who are evangelicals. Why is it that evangelicals have such strong feelings toward these issues, and why is it that they feel everyone else has to believe what they do? Can't they just "live and let live"? Are they just prudes?

God Loves Sex

It is a surprising thought for many people that God is not a prude. Not only did He invent sex, according to the Bible, He gave it as a gift to human beings. The evangelical point of view is that God's good gift is to be cherished and used wisely—and not just for procreation.

From the beginning of humanity, the Bible sees sex in a positive light. The second chapter of Genesis, which records the beginning of the human race, shows this point of view in a passage that describes Adam and Eve seeing each other for the first time (Genesis 2:23-24):

The man said, "This is now bone of my bones and flesh of my flesh, she shall be called 'woman,' for she was taken out of man."

For this reason a man will leave his father and mother and be united to his wife, and they will become one flesh.

"One flesh" here literally means the sexual act. Adam's obvious excitement about Eve (the original Hebrew text above is more like poetic verses—much more animated than English translations convey), displays an attraction that is much more than platonic. In a sophisticated and discreet—yet unmistakable—way, the author affirms the goodness of sexual attraction. This is echoed throughout the Old and New Testaments, far from the stereotype of a prudish religious point of view.

> **In Their Own Words**
>
> When it comes to sex, married evangelicals mix it up with the best of them. Some chapter titles from a widely popular evangelical book on sexuality in marriage called *Intended for Pleasure* include: "One Flesh: The Techniques of Lovemaking," "For the Pre-orgasmic Wife: Fulfillment Ahead," and "All Love, All Liking, All Delight."

The Old Testament book Song of Solomon, for example, is an extended love poem essentially about a man and a woman responding to one another physically. Through poetic metaphors and some surprisingly graphic word pictures, the book very obviously shows the biblical intention for sexual pleasure. For instance, in Song of Solomon 7:6-9, the man speaks to his beloved, who will become his bride:

> How beautiful you are and how pleasing,
> O love, with your delights!
> Your stature is like that of the palm,
> and your breasts like clusters of fruit.
> I said, "I will climb the palm tree;
> I will take hold of its fruit."
> May your breasts be like the clusters of the vine,
> the fragrance of your breath like apples,
> and your mouth like the best wine.

Not only does this passage show a delight in sexuality, it shows that its purpose is not solely procreation. Indeed, within the context of marriage, evangelical teaching encourages sexual freedom and exploration, based on the desires of both partners.

In the New Testament, the apostle Paul, writing to the first century church in Corinth (I Corinthians 7:3-5), confirms this:

> The husband should fulfill his marital duty to his wife, and likewise the wife to her husband. The wife's body does not belong to her alone but also to her husband. In the same way, the husband's body does not belong to him alone but also to his wife. *Do not deprive each other* except by mutual consent and for a time, so that you may devote yourselves to prayer. *Then come together again* … (Emphasis mine.)

In this case, not only does Paul affirm sexual expression, he actually recommends it!

The Context for Great Sex

This recommendation, however, comes in a specific context. Because evangelicals believe that sex constitutes a sacred bond, they also believe that it should take place within the boundaries of a sacred covenant. This is the promise represented by marriage.

Look again at Genesis 2:23-24. In saying that the man is to leave his parents and cling to the woman as they become "one flesh," the passage shows that sexuality is intended as the beginning point for a new primary relationship—a new family. Again, the apostle Paul, in I Corinthians 7:2, says:

> But since there is so much *immorality* [a word which, by the way, has a root meaning of "idolatry," which will become important in the discussion of homosexuality later in this chapter], each man should have his own wife, and each woman her own husband.

Evangelicals believe that marriage is more than an agreement to live together. The level of mutual commitment involved literally means that lives are at stake—it is like a blood oath. This is why the gift of sex is seen as the consummation of that oath—two people giving themselves to one another, completely and without limits. In this view, sex is intended by God to be a unique intimate fulfillment of a promise. And the bonds of that promise create a healthy context not only for this intense level of intimacy, but also for the creation of new life.

True Love Waits—For What?

Thus, as the popular evangelical teen slogan "true love waits" shows, personal sexual morality for evangelicals is based on a commitment to abstention outside of marriage. But abstention from exactly what?

Certainly intercourse—but beyond that, it depends on who you ask. Generally, evangelicals agree that because ultimate sexual union is reserved for marriage, other forms of sexual expression outside of that are to line up with that ethic. One way to accomplish this is for unmarried couples to refrain from sexually oriented activity that results in desires that cannot be consummated. Another way is to make sure that the level of physicality in an unmarried relationship is equivalent to the level of emotional commitment. Another general principle is for couples to keep in mind their own emotional and spiritual maturity when setting boundaries for themselves.

> **The Gospel Truth**
>
> An estimated 2.5–3 million teenagers have signed pledges to remain sexually abstinent before marriage through the Southern Baptist Convention's True Love Waits campaign.

Overall, there are no set rules. Evangelicals span the spectrum from those who eschew any kind of sexual context in their relationship (i.e., some will not even kiss until they are engaged) to those who see almost anything outside of intercourse as fair play (although the extremes of this attitude would be unusual for a truly faithful evangelical). In general, committed evangelicals tend to be very careful about the level of sexuality involved in their relationships, believing that the good gift that God has given is worth preserving for the context in which one can experience its most ultimate enjoyment and fulfillment.

Evangelicals and Alternative Sexuality

The evangelical perspective that sex is a gift to be enjoyed within the marriage covenant also informs their beliefs with regards to alternative sexuality. For evangelicals, gay, lesbian, bisexual, and transgender sexuality are all things that fall outside of the biblical covenant of marriage. Further, (and perhaps more importantly), they see sexuality as intimately related to personhood, which encompasses not just the physical, but also the spiritual identity of humans as male and female.

Back to the Beginning ... Again

Once again, the Bible is normative for evangelicals on this issue, not the norms of contemporary culture. And once again, the biblical basis for how evangelicals understand this issue goes back to Genesis. For evangelicals, the creation account provides the foundational understanding of human sexuality. Basically, they believe that the first book of the Bible teaches heterosexuality as God's design.

> **In Their Own Words**
>
> "Sexuality and spirituality are intricately connected."
>
> —From *Authentic Human Sexuality: An Integrated Christian Approach* by Judith and Jack Balswick

Further, within the Old and New Testaments, there are at least nine instances where homosexual activity is specifically and clearly condemned. The most comprehensive teaching in this regard comes in the first chapter of the book of Romans in the New Testament. A walk through Romans 1:19-27 (in the updated language of a modern Bible translation known as *The Message*) is helpful in gaining a clear understanding of the evangelical point of view, and avoiding the stereotypes that often go with it.

In the passage, the apostle Paul is speaking to the fledgling first century church in Rome. A cosmopolitan center, the city was no stranger to many of the experiences of modern cities, and was thus quite familiar with (if not a center of) alternative sexual expressions. As Paul begins to lay out a comprehensive argument for the credibility of Christianity for the young believers in Rome (the book of Romans is perhaps the most systematic theological argument in the entire New Testament), he starts by pointing out the obvious (Romans 1:19-20):

> But the basic reality of God is plain enough. Open your eyes and there it is! By taking a long and thoughtful look at what God has created, people have always been able to see what their eyes as such can't see: eternal power, for instance, and the mystery of his divine being. So nobody has a good excuse.

Basically, Paul's point here is that in the created order, God has clearly revealed Himself to everyone. There is no excuse not to respond. However, Paul points out next that not everyone does respond (Romans 1:21-23):

> What happened was this: People knew God perfectly well, but when they didn't treat him like God, refusing to worship him, they trivialized themselves into silliness and confusion so that there was neither sense nor direction left in their lives.

They pretended to know it all, but were illiterate regarding life. They traded the glory of God who holds the whole world in his hands for cheap figurines you can buy at any roadside stand.

Paul's argument here is that humans, because of their self-centeredness, refused to acknowledge God, and instead created gods (idols) for themselves—the "cheap figurines" mentioned in the passage. Made to conform to human desires, these gods were much easier to live with. They did not challenge human behavior in the way that the authentic God's "glory" did. This carried with it consequences, some of which Paul enumerates further (Romans 1:24-27):

> So God said, in effect, "If that's what you want, that's what you get." It wasn't long before they were living in a pigpen, smeared with filth, filthy inside and out. And all this because they traded the true God for a fake god, and worshiped the god they made instead of the God who made them—the God we bless, the God who blesses us. Oh, yes!

> Worse followed. Refusing to know God, they soon didn't know how to be human either—women didn't know how to be women, men didn't know how to be men. Sexually confused, they abused and defiled one another, women with women, men with men …

According to Paul, the progression of this idolatrous mindset led to confusion about the identity of both God and humans. Eventually, this developed into outright rebellion against God, including sexual deviations from the created order. It is important to trace Paul's line of thought here:

- ◆ Humans refused to acknowledge God as God.

- ◆ In God's place, they created "gods" of their own.

- ◆ This led to genuine confusion about the identity of God, which led to …

- ◆ Genuine confusion about the identity of humans.

Herein lies the basic evangelical argument against alternative sexual expressions. The bottom-line evangelical belief about sexuality outside of a heterosexual context is that *it falsifies the human identity as sexual beings, just as idolatry falsifies the human identity as created/spiritual beings.* Again, the key issue here is personhood—and a belief that there is purpose, dignity, and meaning in our creation by God as male and female.

Nature or Nurture?

Thus, it is obvious that evangelicals generally fall on the "nurture" side of the "nature or nurture" debate with regard to the origins of alternative sexual expressions. Thoughtful evangelicals point out that there is no scholarly consensus anywhere in contemporary culture with regard to biology as the cause of homosexuality. Regardless of an overwhelming (and uninformed, evangelicals would say) cultural acceptance of that idea, in actuality no definitive evidence has come to light to prove that homosexuals are born without a choice.

The Needed Mea Culpa

However, thoughtful evangelicals will also admit that the evangelical community has in general taken a simplistic, even demonizing approach to this issue. The best evangelical scholars point to alternative sexuality as a complex psycho-social issue involving biology, culture, environment, morality, behavior, and volitional choice. And the best evangelical leaders readily confess that many Christians have turned homosexuality into some sort of special class of sin, somehow worse than others. This kind of thinking is decidedly unchristian, and blatantly hypocritical. (Statistics show that straight evangelicals are just as "fallen" in the arena of sexual sin as are their gay and lesbian counterparts—just with different issues.)

> **Culture Clash!**
>
> To help an evangelical have a substantive discussion about gay and lesbian issues, remind them that (1) Jesus was a friend of the outcast, and that (2) he commanded that his followers look at their own sin before looking to the problems of others (Matthew 7:3).

Thus, those in the evangelical community (and sadly, there are some, though most are technically fundamentalists, not evangelicals) who march with "God hates fags" signs and spew hateful slogans are in fact not representative of true biblical Christianity. Evangelicals who take the commands of Christ seriously condemn these sorts of extremist and mean-spirited points of view, and are embarrassed by the actions that flow from them.

Actions Speak Louder Than Words

Regardless of their point of view with regard to the causes of homosexuality, evangelicals are in clear agreement about this concept: At the level of action, everyone is responsible for his or her own choices.

Thus, regardless of any sort of genetic disposition or nurtured tendency, people are responsible for choosing how they live out their sexuality. In view of the clear record of scripture, evangelicals believe that the only God-honoring (and thus ultimately fulfilling) sexual union is to take place between a man and a woman within the bonds of marriage. Clearly then, engaging in homosexual activity is prohibited, as are many of the other sexual practices that have become the norm in a culture that erroneously equates sexual *gratification* with essential personhood.

For evangelicals, healthy sexual behavior is a choice, just as is healthy behavior toward food or exercise, or even the development of healthy attitudes and behavior toward other potentially addictive substances such as alcohol. Each of us have predispositions toward certain kinds of sin, and each of us are responsible for our actions in regards to them. Certainly human sexuality is complex and multifaceted, and thus a simplistic approach is naïve. However, at the bottom line, evangelicals believe that regardless of our sexual tendencies, we are all responsible for how we act on them.

> **In Their Own Words**
>
> "Exodus affirms reorientation of same sex attraction is possible. This is a process, which begins with motivation to, and self-determination to change based upon a personal relationship with Jesus Christ."
>
> —"Healing Statement" from Exodus International, a controversial evangelical ministry to homosexuals

Although they may differ on the level of change that is possible in the life of a gay or lesbian person's sexuality, evangelicals are—quite literally—eternal optimists when it comes to the ability to live a "good" life. They believe that with God's help, everyone has the power to change. This includes change in issues as complex as human sexual behavior. Believing that God wants only the best for His children, and that the Bible is a guidebook for finding that "best," the faithful truly expect to be able to choose to live in accordance with the biblical principles that represent the pathway to authentic sexual freedom.

Smoking, Drinking, and Better Living Through Chemistry

Beyond sexuality, the second thing most people think of when considering the differences in evangelical morality and public morality at large is the attitude of evangelicals toward smoking, drinking, and drugs. Although not as strict as some religious groups (faithful Mormons, for example, will ingest nothing that contains caffeine), evangelicals tend to be more conservative than the rest of society.

Believing that the body is "the temple of the Holy Spirit" (I Corinthians 6:19), evangelicals believe they have a God-given responsibility to care for their health. This is the primary reason that most evangelicals disparage smoking. Add to that a commitment to "be in subjection to the governing authorities" (Romans 13:1; NASB), and you have two of the most important evangelical reasonings against illegal drug use. In addition, both smoking and drug use (particularly in teens) are widely assumed by evangelicals (and others) to be gateways to potentially more destructive behavior.

The issue of drinking, however, has a much less clear-cut evangelical consensus. A look at the theology and history behind various evangelical attitudes toward alcohol provides an interesting glimpse into the evolving evangelical mindset.

What Would Jesus Drink?

The Bible is clearly against drunkenness. Ephesians 5:18, for instance, clearly states: "Do not get drunk on wine …." There are several biblical narratives where drunkenness leads to awful consequences—for example, Lot committing incest with his daughters in Genesis 19:31-36. Further, passages such as Proverbs 23:29-35 show the potential problems of abuse, reminding the reader, "Who has woe? Who has sorrow? Who has strife? Who has complaints? Who has needless bruises? Who has bloodshot eyes? Those who linger over wine, who go to sample bowls of mixed wine." Overall, evangelicals are in agreement that drunkenness is bad, and that alcoholism is a serious problem.

However, the lines are less clear with regard to drinking in moderation. Those who imbibe on occasion point to Jesus' miracle of turning water into wine at a wedding and the apostle Paul's advice to his protégé Timothy to "use a little wine because of your stomach and your frequent illnesses." (I Timothy 5:23) Further, the Christian ordinance of communion—a key part of weekly worship for many—is a reenactment of Jesus' last supper with His disciples that *features* wine.

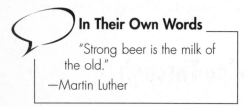

In Their Own Words

"Strong beer is the milk of the old."

—Martin Luther

However, tee-totaling evangelicals point out that Jesus' culture was different. They contend that water in those days was often less sanitary than wine, and thus it was more necessary to drink wine in Jesus' day. They also point to the enormous modern difficulties associated with alcoholism. In an effort to both be careful with their own lives, and to uphold the biblical principle of "not causing your brother to stumble," many evangelicals abstain completely.

In general, the average modern evangelical takes a nonjudgmental stand with regard to alcohol use, recognizing that use or abstention is a personal choice that is not bound by scripture (with the exception of abuse). This is a fairly recent consensus in Evangelicalism, however. From the prohibition movement in the 1920s (led by religious conservatives) to evangelical flagship Wheaton College's 2003 revamp of its "Community Covenant" allowing for "Christians to exercise their freedom responsibly, carefully, and in Christ-like love," with regards to drinking, evangelicals have come quite a long way.

> **In Their Own Words**
>
> "The slums will soon only be a memory. We will turn our prisons into factories and our jails into storehouses and corn-cribs. Men will walk upright now, women will smile, and children will laugh. Hell will be forever rent."
>
> —Evangelist Billy Sunday, in a sermon celebrating the passage of Prohibition in 1920

See No Evil, Hear No Evil

Wheaton's "Community Covenant" is also instructive with regards to modern Evangelicalism's attitudes toward the consumption of media. It reads:

> The Wheaton College community also encourages responsible freedom in matters of entertainment, including the places where members of the College community may seek it, such as television, movies, video, theater, concerts, dances and the Internet. The College assumes its members will be guided in their entertainment choices by the godly wisdom of Philippians 4:8: "Whatever is true, whatever is noble, whatever is right, whatever is pure, whatever is lovely, whatever is admirable, if anything is excellent or praiseworthy, think about such things."

Again, this is a long way from times past, when some of the boundary markers for Evangelicalism included never going to movies and never dancing. As quaint as these attitudes seem today, evangelicals of times past were biblically grounded in their attitudes. And although the general consensus has loosened up quite a bit, evangelicals are generally still quite a bit more conservative than the culture at large with regard to what kind of media they will expose themselves to.

A key scripture passage that defines and explains evangelical attitudes in this regard is Romans 12:1-2. It states,

> Therefore, I urge you, brothers, in view of God's mercy, to offer your bodies as living sacrifices, holy and pleasing to God—this is your spiritual act of worship. Do not conform any longer to the pattern of this world, but be transformed by the renewing of your mind. Then you will be able to test and approve what God's will is—his good, pleasing and perfect will.

The idea of "renewing the mind" in this passage is crucial. Recognizing that our thoughts precede and determine our actions, evangelicals want to make sure both to fill their minds with good things, and avoid filling their minds with things that are harmful. As the old computer programming adage goes, "garbage in, garbage out."

This desire to live with a different mindset than the world around them leads evangelicals to take very seriously media which does not fall within what they see to be a biblical worldview. Thus, staying away from media that glorifies unbiblical attitudes is very important to them. At times this has caused them to be accused of censorship (and at times that accusation has been correct), as they have tried to influence the values of the culture around them. But to be fair, society at large must be willing to honor the desires of people who, for example, want to protect their children from influences they see to be harmful. Thoughtful evangelicals certainly do not condone censorship; but many will fight to try to impact the prevailing culture toward wholesomeness in the media.

This desire to "hear no evil, see no evil" is one of the primary reasons for the meteoric popularity of media produced by evangelicals for evangelicals. From Christian rock music to Veggie Tales videos (cartoon Bible story allegories featuring animated vegetable characters), Christian media is a multi-million dollar industry. (For more detail on Christian media, see Chapter 16.)

Culture Clash!

The metal band Judas Priest, when accused of putting Satanic messages on their songs that could be heard if played backwards, responded by commenting that if they really had "backmasked," they would have said something more productive, like, "Buy more of our records."

Keeping It All in Perspective

To the outsider, Evangelicalism seems to be defined by the kinds of behavioral characteristics described in this chapter. Sex, drugs, and rock and roll seem to be the antithesis of Evangelicalism, and for most people, the evangelical attitude likely seems a bit extreme.

But it is important to remember that evangelical attitudes toward personal morality are, at their best, outgrowths of an inner personal spirituality (see Chapter 9). It's easy to see how evangelicals act differently, and even easier at times to laugh it off as vestiges of a bygone era. In a culture of sound-bites, it is much harder to recognize the deep personal values that drive evangelicals to dance to a different beat (sometimes quite literally!). Perhaps the way forward in an increasingly polarized culture is a commitment on the part of evangelicals and nonevangelicals alike to listen to each other more, and talk at each other less.

The Least You Need to Know

- Evangelicals believe that intercourse is to take place only within the bonds of heterosexual marriage.

- Evangelicals believe that alternative sexual expressions (gay, lesbian, bisexual, transgender) are outside of God's best for human spiritual and physical identity as male and female.

- Evangelicals believe that they have a God-given responsibility to care for their body, and are thus typically against smoking and illegal drug use.

- Evangelical attitudes about drinking are less clear; some drink, some don't— although all would agree about the harmfulness of drunkenness or alcohol abuse.

- In an effort to keep themselves free from harmful influences, faithful evangelicals tend to be careful about their media consumption.

Chapter 12

Family Matters

In This Chapter

- What is a family?
- Do evangelicals think husbands are superior to their wives?
- Do evangelicals spank their children?
- What do evangelicals believe about divorce and remarriage?

A few years ago, the We Are Family Foundation created a video to be distributed to 61,000 schools in the United States. Intended by its creators to promote tolerance and diversity following the September 11 attacks, its content created a media frenzy when Dr. James Dobson, head of the evangelical Focus on the Family organization, took a swing at it in a speech at a black-tie event in Washington D.C., which included members of Congress. Calling it a "pro-homosexual video" because of We Are Family's stand on tolerance toward alternative sexuality, Dobson's criticism stemmed from his belief that this was another part of an ongoing attempt to "re-define the family" by liberals. The media frenzy resulted from the fact that at the center of the firestorm was none other than that well-known political operative—SpongeBob Squarepants.

The story that got out (although incorrect) was that Dobson had called down wrath upon SpongeBob because the cartoon character was gay.

def•i•ni•tion

Family values describes a combination of loosely connected evangelical and conservative beliefs regarding the nuclear family and its operation in society; it connotes support for "traditional" morality in general. The term has been a widely used political buzzword since the early 1980s.

This is the kind of stuff that late-night comedians' dreams are made of. And this is also the kind of stuff—both Dobson's concerns, and the media's misportrayal of them—that describes the highly charged atmosphere surrounding evangelicals' *family values.*

Although younger evangelicals (particularly "emerging church" types—see Chapters 19–20) are increasingly questioning the biblical basis of the traditional family model historically upheld by Evangelicalism, the model is in fact well ensconced in the minds of most in the movement. Evangelicals believe that the family unit is ordained by God, and a foundation of both spiritual growth and cultural stability. And yet, even as the definition of family remains relatively secure within Evangelicalism, the ways in which it gets lived out are much more diverse than most recognize. As a matter of fact, two of the most internally controversial topics within Evangelicalism are covered in this chapter: the roles of men and women in the family, and divorce.

What Is a Family?

Dobson's own words (found on his website—www.family.org) are instructive for understanding the basic evangelical definition of family:

> [W]hat is the traditional definition of the family? It is a group of individuals who are related to one another by marriage, birth, or adoption—nothing more, nothing else. The family was divinely instituted and sanctioned in the beginning, when God created one man and one woman, brought them together, and commanded them to "be fruitful and multiply." This is where we begin, and this is where we must stand.

Going back to Genesis 2:24 in the creation narrative once again, many evangelical theologians see at least three biblical purposes for marriage and family, all based on an exclusively heterosexual model that they believe the Bible teaches:

- The creation of new, independent lives and households: "For this reason a man shall leave his mother and father ..."

- In that context, the creation of new primary relationships: "... and be united to his wife ..."

◆ In that context, the development of mutually completing relationships: "… and the two shall become one flesh."

Popular evangelical shorthand that is sometimes used for this is that the purpose of marriage and family is to "leave, cleave, and weave."

Living It Out

Implicit in the three purposes are some other things. Evangelicals believe that part of their responsibility in starting and caring for a family is creating a sense of mission within the family. The commands to "Be fruitful and multiply," and to "fill the earth and subdue it" (Genesis 1:28, NASB), are seen by evangelicals as a calling to "steward" (or manage) God's good gifts to them. Many see nurturing a household in which Godly character can be developed as key to this mission. As husbands, wives, and children learn from their primary environment the basic character lessons of life, these growth experiences enable them to take God's character into the world around them. Indeed, many evangelicals would look at their lives in concentric relational circles—first their relationship with God; second, their relationships within the family; and third, their resulting relationships with the rest of the world.

This God-ordained order of relationships is a spiritual lynch-pin for many evangelicals, carrying with it innumerable practical consequences. The deep, intensely intimate connection that it ties between an individual, God, and family is the reason for the incredible intensity evangelicals bring to their public debates about family issues. In short, they see these issues as core to their spiritual identity.

Most also believe that God uses even the tough parts of their marriage and family life to develop this identity. Evangelicals believe that marriage is not a 50/50 commitment arrangement between two people, but that both partners must enter into it with a willingness to give 100 percent, even if one partner does not reciprocate at times. They take Jesus as their model in this, "Who, being in very nature God, did not consider equality with God something to

In Their Own Words

"When we establish Divine Order in our home, it creates an atmosphere in which Jesus feels at home: the Holy Spirit is then able to do His work of teaching and leading us into the kind of family life for which God created us."

—Larry Christenson in *The Christian Family*

be grasped, but made himself nothing, taking the very nature of a servant …" (Philippians 2:6-7). Though both evangelical partners typically strive to enter into a marriage with this commitment, how that servanthood should play itself out is the cause of one of the most intense internal controversies currently afoot within the movement. Because it is so important in contemporary Evangelicalism, we will look at evangelical attitudes toward the roles of husbands and wives in depth.

Marriage: Rocking the Roles

Within the marriage bond, typical evangelicals have historically advocated a "man-is-the-head-of-the-household" approach. In the past few decades, however, this interpretation of the biblical record has been increasingly called into question within evangelicalism. Currently, there are somewhere between four and six (depending on who you ask) definable theological viewpoints within the faith community that define men's and women's roles in marriage, in the church, and (to some degree) in society as a whole. The two ends of the spectrum are generally called the *complementarian* point of view, and the *egalitarian* point of view.

"I Got Gaps": The Complementarian Perspective

When Rocky Balboa made his famous on-screen profession of love for Adrian in the movie *Rocky*, he explained his feelings by saying "I got gaps, she's got gaps … we fill each other's gaps." This would be an essential (though certainly less than theologically nuanced) explanation of the complementarian point of view.

def•i•ni•tion

Complementarian describes the belief of some evangelicals that men and women are created to have different, complimentary roles in the family, the church, and (to some degree) in society. In this view, men have a core role of leadership, and women of support and nurture.

Evangelicals who hold this more traditional point of view believe that men and women are created by God with different roles that are complementary to one another. Simply put, men are designed to be the leaders, and women are to function in a subordinate, supportive role in the family, in the church, and to some degree even in society at large.

These perspectives are based on what complementarians see as a theme clearly woven throughout the Bible. For instance, in Genesis, Eve was created as a "helper" for Adam; and in several New Testament passages, women are instructed to "submit" to their husbands. Perhaps the most oft-quoted such passage is Ephesians 5:22–24:

> Wives, submit to your husbands as to the Lord. For the husband is the head of the wife as Christ is the head of the church, his body, of which he is the Savior. Now as the church submits to Christ, so also wives should submit to their husbands in everything.

Complementarians take the above passage as a universal command for the order of all families. In addition, they generally advocate that a married woman's primary focus is to be on the nurture of her home and children. This is based on Bible passages such as Titus 2:5, where younger women are instructed "to be self-controlled and pure, to be busy at home, to be kind, and to be subject to their husbands, so that no one will malign the word of God." A married man's core role is consequently to provide loving leadership for his family, being a benevolent patriarch who engenders family participation in decisions, but retains the final word.

Why Would Anyone Do That?

Although all of this sounds extremely counter-cultural in the twenty-first century, those who follow this pattern believe that it is not only biblical, but deeply practical.

They point out that one of the primary causes of divorce and family upheaval in contemporary society is the confusion and the resulting self-protecting (or simply selfish) behavior that is often brought into marriage relationships. Scriptural clarity in family roles gives partners the structures they need to flourish, and thus the freedom to drop their guards.

When everyone lives in the way they were actually created and gifted to live, according to complementarians, true fulfillment and harmony are the result.

> **In Their Own Words**
>
> "I have no problem accepting within my womanhood the equality of creation and personhood, while recognizing that my divinely bestowed womanhood is uniquely suited to the divinely assigned task."
>
> —Dorothy Patterson in *Recovering Biblical Manhood and Womanhood*

But Is This Fair?

To those who raise the issue of fairness, complementarians point out that there is an important distinction between *personal role* and *personal worth*. In contrast to a culture that values people based on their position in life, Christianity focuses on the inherent value in every person.

Submission, then, is the privilege of following the example of Christ, who although He is equal to God the Father in the Godhead, chose to submit Himself in His role as God the Son. Wives (and children) thus have the spiritually privileged position of service—a key, counter-cultural quality of Christ-followers.

The Promise Keepers

The strength of the complementarian point of view in Evangelicalism in the past few years can be seen in the phenomenal popularity of the Promise Keepers movement. Started in 1990 by former University of Colorado head football coach Bill McCartney, Promise Keeper gatherings have drawn over five million men to huge stadium and arena rallies across the country, in addition to other smaller events. The gatherings feature contemporary singing, praying, and men bear-hugging one another and chanting "J-E-S-U-S" like they're cheering for their favorite football team.

Touting the "Seven Promises of a Promise Keeper," the organization seeks to help men live lives of integrity in their relationships to God, their families, and the world around them. A key component of the Promise Keeper credo encourages men to develop close and accountable relationships with a small group of other men, to help one another fulfill their promises. These promises include commitments to "moral, ethical, and sexual purity," and a strong commitment to a local church. All of the promises are founded upon the conviction that God has uniquely called men into leadership roles—in the home and the church in particular.

At the organization's peak, it drew hundreds of thousands of men (organizers say close to a million) to Washington D.C. for its "sacred assembly of men" (1997), and over one million men to various regional rallies across the United States. (1996). In addition, tens of thousands of Promise Keeper "small groups" have arisen in local churches, providing ongoing connections between men and the group. Between its rallies, sales of Promise Keeper Bible study materials, partnerships with denominations, and other ancillary spin-off groups, the Promise Keeper organization at one time had an annual budget as high as $76 million. In recent years, the organization has intentionally scaled back and focused more attention on racial reconciliation and social service in addition to family issues.

Separate and Equal: The Egalitarian Perspective

In contrast to the male-dominated family and church model, a growing number of evangelicals interpret the *same* Bible passages quite differently. Led by groups such as Christians for Biblical Equality and with the support of such influential mega-churches as Willow Creek Community Church in suburban Chicago (see Chapter 18) and the newer "emergent" evangelical churches (see Chapters 19 through 20), this group can be identified theologically by the term *egalitarian*.

Egalitarian evangelical Christians (how's that for theological hair-splitting?) also point to Genesis as the foundation point for their perspective. But contrary to complementarians, they believe that male hierarchy is nowhere recommended in scripture for contemporary Christians.

Their perspective can be generally summarized this way:

def•i•ni•tion

Egalitarian describes the perspective of some evangelicals that men and women, while distinct in their sexuality, are to share equally the authoritative roles in the family, in the church, and in society at large.

- The subordination of woman to man in Genesis 3 came as a direct result of the fall of humanity (when Adam and Eve chose to disobey God for the first time in Genesis 3, thus introducing sin into the world).

- Therefore, the battle of the sexes for domination is indeed real, but it is part of the "curse" of the fall.

- When Christ redeemed humankind from the consequences of sin, the historic consequence of the domination of one sex over the other was broken.

In Christ, therefore, the curse of the fall is redeemed, and men and women can again live in equality (i.e., mutual submission) and true harmony as they pursue God's mission of being a blessing to His creation. This "creation/fall/redemption" pattern is consistent with what evangelical theologians on both sides of the issue would agree is an overall pattern and theme throughout the Bible.

Egalitarians also point out that …

- The word "helper" used of Eve in Genesis 2 is the same Hebrew word that is often used in the Old Testament for God Himself (as in Psalm 33:20, where the writer says "We wait in hope for the Lord; he is our *help* and our shield.")

♦ There are actually four Hebrew words used for "helper" in the Old Testament that connote subordination, none of which are used in the Genesis account.

♦ With regard to the order of creation argument (i.e., that Adam was created first, and therefore is meant to be dominant), egalitarians point out that the animals were created before Adam. Does that mean humans are to be in subjection to them?

A New Norm: All Are One in Christ

With regard to New Testament teachings about the family and male/female relationships, egalitarians point to Galatians 3:28 as the "normative" passage for all Christians as they live in new, redeemed community with one another. The verse reads, "There is neither Jew nor Greek, slave nor free, male nor female, for you are all one in Christ Jesus."

Egalitarians believe that this verse is the baseline for interpreting other New Testament passages that seem to imply female subordination in the home or in the church. They point out that complementarians tend to treat other verses as "normative," whereas this verse, which deals with the foundational identity of Christians, should be the norm.

But What About All Those Passages About Submission?

Pointing to examples of women leading in authoritative roles in both the Old and New Testaments, egalitarians see the female-restricting passages as exceptions that are culturally based. They see them in the same category as scriptures which, for example, forbid women from braiding their hair (I Timothy 2:9-10):

> I also want women to dress modestly, with decency and propriety, not with braided hair or gold or pearls or expensive clothes, but with good deeds, appropriate for women who profess to worship God."

Passages like this have universal truth in them (i.e., women are to be humble and lead simple lives, just as men are), but are also connected to specific cultural practices of biblical times. Braided hair, for example, was sometimes associated with specific cultic worship or even with prostitution in the first century. Thus, passages that seem to imply female subordination are to be interpreted with careful attention to context, and with the norm of Galatians 3:28 in mind, according to egalitarians. They point out that interpreting more confusing scripture passages by applying clearer scriptural "norms" is one of the most important principles of evangelical scriptural interpretation.

> **Quote Head**
>
> "As a wife and mother, I have little use for the traditional roles the pro-family movement thinks are so crucial to the health of family life. Neither does my husband … We make decisions together, we are both equally responsible for our children's well being, and we both find we need work that gives us a sense of satisfaction and purpose."
>
> —Lynn Marcotte in "E-Quality Journal," Fall, 2005 (a publication of "Christians for Biblical Equality")

Slavery and Equality: An Interpretive Method

Egalitarians point to the issue of slavery as an example of how to properly interpret biblical texts that seem to imply female subordination. The apostle Paul seems to advocate slavery in some of his letters (Ephesian 5:5, for example, says, "Slaves, obey your earthly masters …")—and yet no responsible evangelical scholar would agree that this is binding today.

Instead, they would say that Paul actually advocated the freeing of slaves (the entire New Testament book of Philemon was written in defense of a runaway slave), and was making an exception due to the specific local circumstances in Ephesians 5:5. Similarly, Paul's instructions for women that advocate a subordinate role are to be interpreted as specific to their particular local context.

The Ultimate Example

Finally, egalitarians point to the example of Jesus Himself. Jesus was quite a radical in His day, running with a band of followers that included both women and men—pretty much unheard of for a first century rabbi. Further, He broke many of the conventional rules for rabbis of the time—speaking to women (even women of "known reputations") freely in public, and even including them in His band of disciples. And it was those women, egalitarians remind us, to whom Jesus gave pride of place by revealing Himself first to them following His greatest and most important miracle—His resurrection.

Come Together

Confused yet?

All of the theological hair-splitting may seem excessive, but it is actually a testimony to the high view of scripture that is characteristically evangelical. No committed evangelical family that I know of would simply say, "Who cares what the Bible says about this? Let's just do what we want!"

Where all evangelicals come together on these issues is around a shared desire to live out healthy male/female relationships in a sexually confused culture. What may seem like an overemphasis on these male/female issues in Evangelicalism is partially fueled by a shared conviction that sexually, contemporary culture is in free-fall.

As previously mentioned, evangelicals believe that in our sexual identities, our very personhood is at stake. The relationship of men and women in their most foundational human context (the family) is thus primary to our spiritual identities. Further, these relationships also inform and shape the environment in which the next generation develops.

Raising Kids

Whether or not they're watching SpongeBob, the kids of evangelicals are blessed (or burdened, depending on your point of view) with a plethora of resources that surround their parents regarding child-rearing. Indeed, books, CDs, and videos on Christian parenting make up a large segment of the huge Christian retailing industry.

Perhaps the single most influential resource over the years has been Dr. Dobson's *Dare to Discipline*, which has sold millions of copies since its first publication in 1970. An antidote to the more permissive style of parenting that was burgeoning as baby boomers began to have children, the book's no-nonsense appeal made it a standard for parents looking for a biblical guide to setting boundaries for their children. Indeed, Dobson notes in the introduction to the book that:

> In a day of widespread drug usage, immorality, civil disobedience, vandalism, and violence, we must not depend on hope and luck to fashion the critical attitudes we value in children. That unstructured technique was applied during the generation which is now in college, and the outcome has been quite discouraging. Permissiveness has not just been a failure, it's been a disaster!

The Importance of Authority

Dobson's focus on discipline (which he defines more as setting boundaries than as punishment), points out a key characteristic of the evangelical approach to child-rearing: a focus on helping children learn to relate properly to authority.

This is a huge focus for evangelicals because of their belief in a God who is in authority over them. For evangelicals, a key part of character development is learning how to place oneself in a proper role of submission to authority. Just as adults must learn how to recognize the goodness of God's authority as protection over them, so children must learn the goodness of boundaries that exist for their own healthy development. And the place where that happens first and foremost is in the home.

Culture Clash!

To spark an interesting discussion with an evangelical friend who is a fellow parent, invite them over to watch an episode of *The Osbournes*. (I'm serious—read on.) After the show, talk about the incidents of both expressed authority and unconditional love by Ozzy and Sharon that you both saw.

A good way to understand this is to think about the Ten Commandments. The commandments to stay away from murdering, stealing, and adultery, for instance, are all about submission to a higher authority than our individual desires or emotions. Ultimately, these boundaries protect us and form the basis for a healthy culture. Evangelicals believe that a child first learns this type of obedience in relationship to his or her parents, and that these lessons form the basis for their understanding of the protective authority of God over them as adults.

Thus, raising a child with healthy boundaries is even more than an expression of parental love—it is seen by evangelicals as a part of their God-given overall mission to the world. They believe that as a child develops his or her character in the home, they will take that character out to the world around them—becoming a blessing to the world and a part of God's mission for all human beings.

Sparing the Rod—or Not

Evangelicals accomplish this mission in as many different ways as there are parents. In that context, many believe in administering corporal punishment to children, and many do not believe in it. For those who do, spanking is usually seen as a last resort, and is advocated as being undertaken only for the purpose of discipline, not out of anger, and surrounded with both explanation to the child and (once the episode is over and the child has become repentant) expressions of love.

Indeed the expression of unconditional love for children is actually *the* central guiding principle behind evangelical parenting philosophies. Recognizing that they have been unconditionally loved and accepted by God, evangelicals strive to offer that same kind of love to their children, empowered by the reality that (in the words of Paul from Romans 5:5) "God has poured out his love into our hearts by the Holy Spirit, whom he has given us."

Divorce

Because of the strong spiritual connection of marriage and family, divorce is taken very seriously by evangelicals. How can that which God has made "one flesh" become two? Thus, typically evangelicals will work very hard to hang on to their marriage, even it if it is troubled. Even so, many evangelical marriages end in a split. There is a fair amount of controversy over how divorce should be treated in Evangelicalism, and this controversy has been the source of much sadness for those caught in it as divorcees. In short, most evangelicals believe that divorce is biblically permissible under certain circumstances, only a few believe that it is absolutely prohibited. The real question is under what circumstances divorce is sanctioned by scripture.

The Gospel Truth
The rate of divorce for those who claim to be "born again" (often a larger group than those who are defined as "evangelicals" by pollsters) is virtually the same in the United States. as the rate of divorce among those who claim no "born again" experience.

There are nine passages in the Old and New Testaments that most scholars point to with regard to the divorce question. The four most important are:

- ◆ Adam and Eve (Genesis 2)

- ◆ Mosaic Law regarding divorce (Deuteronomy 24:1-4)

- ◆ Jesus' teaching on divorce (Mark 10:11-12; Matthew 19:9)

- ◆ Paul's teaching on divorce (I Corinthians 7:10-16)

The cultural and contextual surroundings of the teachings make it impossible to pronounce a clearly definitive position. Although there is a spectrum of beliefs, most evangelicals (based on the passages cited above) believe that divorce is permissible in instances of sexual infidelity. Some, however extend that further, believing that both the spirit of the teachings and the proper application of cultural analysis of the passages extend the "divorce clause" for sexual infidelity into emotional infidelity, or even emotional abandonment.

The Bible and Remarriage

From the standpoint of biblical interpretation, the bigger and even more controversial question is around the issue of remarriage after a divorce.

Again, there are several primary texts used, mainly from Jesus' teachings and the teachings of Paul. Evangelicals are even more divided on their interpretations here than they are on their interpretations around the divorce question (as discussed above).

Essentially, one perspective is that remarriage is not an option, because regardless of the physical status of the couple (together or separated) the spiritual status remains the same—one flesh. Thus, remarriage (and the accompanying sexual union) actually represents adultery, since the kinship status in God's eyes between the original couple has never been broken. In this view, remarriage is only permissible in a situation where one of the spouses is no longer alive.

On the other hand, those who advocate remarriage believe that the biblical teachings are not as strict. They point to both the qualification of the absolute standards in the texts themselves (Paul, for instance, advocates the remarriage of an abandoned spouse under specific circumstances), and the practical complexities of navigating new relationships (i.e., couples who have remarried and subsequently become converts, for instance) under such absolute standards. Generally, these scholars believe that remarriage is consistent with scriptural teachings if the people involved have done their best to reconcile with former spouses, but have been unable to do so.

For the most part, those evangelicals who are more lenient on divorce tend to have the same type of approach to remarriage following a divorce. Those who are more strict on divorce are also more strict on the issue of remarriage.

Another Mea Culpa

For all the theological wrangling over divorce and remarriage, the reality is that both happen all the time in Evangelicalism. Unfortunately, there is still a stigma attached in some evangelical circles, even though such treatment is decidedly unbiblical. This is one of those places where the love of Christ and the grace of God should be overwhelmingly clear to those who have had to walk through the difficulties. So, taking on authority that is certainly not mine to take (but I'll do it anyway): on behalf of evangelicals everywhere, I offer an apology to those who have been treated badly by the church because of these issues. The thoughtlessness with which you have been treated is inexcusable—so I pray that you will find the big love of God's big family in a faithful family of believers who will support and encourage you.

After all, family matters.

The Least You Need to Know

- Evangelicals believe that a family is made up of individuals who are related to one another by heterosexual marriage, birth, or adoption.

- Some evangelicals believe that the Bible teaches that men have a core role of leadership and women of nurture in the family, the church, and to some degree in society at large.

- Others interpret the same biblical passages differently, believing that women and men are to share equally all roles and responsibilities.

- Key issues for evangelicals with regard to child-rearing include unconditional love and respect for authority.

- Evangelicals have differing views on divorce and remarriage, depending on their interpretation of various scripture passages related to these issues.

13

A Matter of Life and Death

In This Chapter

- ◆ The biblical foundations for Evangelicalism's pro-life stance
- ◆ Evangelical answers to pro-choice arguments supporting abortion
- ◆ Controversial tactics that have been employed by evangelicals in the abortion debate
- ◆ Enterprising evangelical responses to the practical needs of unplanned pregnancies

In 1999, veteran photojournalist Michael Clancy was hired by *USA Today* to photograph what was at the time a breakthrough surgical procedure at Vanderbilt University Medical Center. A twenty-one-week-old fetus was to be operated on in-utero for spina bifida.

According to Clancy, during the procedure there was an amazing surprise moment: a tiny hand reached out of the surgical incision in the mother's uterus. Dr. Joseph Bruner, the surgeon, put his finger under the hand, and according to Clancy, Samuel Armas (the child who was born later and to whom the hand belonged) closed a grasp around the surgeon's finger. Clancy snapped several close-up pictures, catching on film the astounding moment. In that moment, Clancy switched from being pro-choice to pro-life.

The pictures created quite a controversy upon their publication. While Clancy maintains that indeed, the child reached out and then grasped the surgeon's finger, Dr. Bruner later claimed that he pulled the child's hand out to pose for the picture. What difference does it make? All the difference in the world if you're involved in the highly politicized debate surrounding abortion. Pro-lifers know that the picture could give great credibility to their cause. Pro-choicers recognize the potential damage to their efforts to sway opinions if Clancy's side of the story is true. Both sides continue to stand by their version of the story behind the photograph. And the photographs themselves (which eventually ended up in *USA Today*, *Newsweek*, and across the globe in other publications) stand as a symbol of the incredibly strong emotions on both sides of the abortion debate.

Choosing Life: Evangelicals and Abortion

Evangelicals line up solidly and passionately on the pro-life side of the debate. Even before the 1973 *Roe vs. Wade* Supreme Court decision, evangelicals were in the fore-front of fighting abortion. The reason? Simply put, evangelicals believe that abortion involves killing. As the popular bumper sticker says, "It's a child, not a choice."

Culture Clash!

Evangelicals prefer the term "pro-life" as opposed to "anti-abortion" to define their position, just as those on the other side of the abortion debate prefer "pro-choice" as opposed to "pro-abortion." However, politics being what they are, each side routinely disregards the other's preference …

With an estimated 1.3 million abortions happening each year in the United States, evangelicals have galvanized perhaps their most potent political power behind this issue. And they seem to have made a difference. According to experts, since 1990 the number of abortions performed in America has been steadily declining, in part due to the aggressive efforts of pro-lifers in legislation, education, and other pro-life programs. And much of that effort has come from evangelicals. Although they may have somewhat different opinions on exactly what legislation should be enacted regarding abortion, they are very consistent in their belief that abortion, as it is practiced today, is a national tragedy.

The Biblical View of Abortion

How can evangelicals be so sure about what others see as a moral quandary filled with shades of grey? Once again, the evangelical's reliance on the Bible as their guide is the key reason for their passionate surety. Evangelicals point to at least six clear ethical themes in the Bible that inform their view of abortion.

The Sanctity of Human Life

Evangelicals believe that all human life is sacred. This is seen in the Genesis creation account, where humanity is uniquely delineated as made "in the image of God." It is also seen in the prohibition against murder in the Ten Commandments in the Old Testament (Exodus 20:13), as well as in multiple similar Old Testament regulations given to protect life. (See Exodus 21:22-25 for an instance in which an unborn child is treated the same as an adult for purposes of levying justice toward an assaulter.) In the New Testament, Jesus' consistency in His treatment of all people, regardless of their social status or physical capabilities, showed His belief that all human beings matter to God.

Speaking to the Corinthians (1 Corinthians 6:19-20), Paul takes it a step further, proclaiming, "Do you not know that your body is a temple of the Holy Spirit, who is in you, whom you have received from God? You are not your own; you were bought at a price. Therefore honor God with your body." Paul shows here that human life is sacred not just because it is human, but because it is also uniquely connected to the divine. Thus, Paul's statements are an echo of the sanctity of life perspective seen all the way back to Genesis.

In the strongest possible terms, the Bible both declares and implies that human life is sacred, and that God's desire is that it be protected.

The Personhood of the Fetus

In Jeremiah, God says to the namesake of the book, "Before I formed you in the womb I knew you, before you were born I set you apart; I appointed you as a prophet to the nations." (Jeremiah 1:5) Evangelicals point to this verse as just one of multiple places in both the Old and New Testaments where there is a clear and consistent biblical ethic that life begins at conception. For example:

- In Job 31:15 (NKJV) the writer, speaking of God, says, "[D]id not the same One fashion us in the womb?"

- In Psalm 51:5, David relates a sense of personhood from conception when he says, "Surely I was sinful at birth, sinful from the time my mother conceived me."

◆ In the New Testament's stories of the birth of Jesus, the same Greek word (brephos) is used for both a baby in the womb and a baby outside of it. In Luke 1:44, Elizabeth says to her cousin Mary, upon Mary's visit while they were both pregnant, "As soon as the sound of your greeting reached my ears, the [brephos] in my womb leaped for joy." And in Luke 2:12, the angels speaking about the newly born Jesus say to the shepherds, "This will be a sign to you: You will find a [brephos] wrapped in cloths and lying in a manger."

But perhaps the strongest of all passages showing that the Bible teaches that life begins at conception is seen in the poetry of Psalm 139:13-16, where David writes of God:

> For you created my inmost being;
> You knit me together in my mother's womb.
> I praise you because I am fearfully and wonderfully made;
> Your works are wonderful,
> I know that full well.
> My frame was not hidden from you
> when I was made in the secret place.
> When I was woven together in the depths of the earth,
> your eyes saw my unformed body.
> All the days ordained for me
> were written in your book
> Before one of them came to be.

Here we see a very clear picture of personhood in the womb. David even goes so far as to say that God had a master plan for his life that was fully developed even before David was born. To evangelicals the evidence is clear: from the perspective of the Bible, life begins at conception. Abortion happens to a live person in the womb, not a blob of tissue.

The Sovereignty of God in Matters of Life and Death

Because of His rulership of all of creation, and because of the unique status of humankind, evangelicals believe that God alone has prerogatives over human life and death. "See now that I myself am He!" says God in Deuteronomy 32:39, continuing, "I put to death and bring life ..."

God, as creator, has exclusive rights to decide death and life. Because evangelicals see a fetus as a life, they see it as a usurpation of God's role for an individual person to decide the fate of that life. Indeed, abortion to evangelicals is tantamount to "playing God."

The Gospel Truth

The "pro-life" stance of many evangelicals does not always include support for the abolition of capital punishment. Although an anti-abortion stance is pretty much a consensus issue in evangelicalism, there are a variety of views on capital punishment (see Chapter 15 for more information).

The Biblical Ethic of Love and Nonviolence

Jesus' message of nonviolence is clear. He encouraged His followers to "turn the other cheek" (Luke 6:29) and to "do to others what you would have them do to you" (Matthew 7:12). With the recognition of the fetus as a person, this teaching becomes applicable to abortion.

Evangelicals believe that abortion is violent. They cite study after study showing that babies in the womb can feel pain, especially in the case of late-term abortions. They also point out that a baby in a womb is to be loved with the same level of respect given to a person no longer in the womb.

The Biblical Value of Helping the Helpless

Multiple teachings in both the Old and New Testaments encourage those who are strong to watch out for those who are weak. Evangelicals argue that no one is weaker than a defenseless child in the womb.

The Biblical Value of Self-sacrifice for the Good of Others

In Philippians 2:3-4, Paul says, "… in humility value others above yourselves, not looking to your own interests, but each of you to the interests of others." Evangelicals believe that parents should be willing to make sacrifices in their own lives in order to preserve the innocent life of an unborn child.

The Biblical Reality of the Special Love of God for Children

Throughout the Old and New Testaments, the Bible displays a special affection of God toward children. For example, in Psalm 127:4, children are called a "heritage" and even a "reward" from God to their parents. Jesus said that we all must receive the kingdom of heaven "like a child" (Mark 10:15), and famously told His disciples to "Let the little children come to me, and do not hinder them, for the kingdom of God belongs to such as these." (Luke 18:16)

Practical Answers to Common Issues

Beyond the biblical basis for a pro-life stance, evangelicals advocate a host of practical arguments against a point of view that advocates abortion. Most evangelicals feel that the prevalent culture (in particular the media and the education establishment) has presented a distorted view of abortion that is overwhelmingly biased. Evangelical answers to some of the common arguments in favor of abortion are listed below.

"Abortion is about freedom of choice."

This would be true, evangelicals argue, if abortion was simply the removal of a woman's own tissue from her body. But once another life is involved, everyone's freedom of choice must be considered. In an abortion, the unborn child has no choice.

Many evangelicals see the choice issue as an example of moral relativism. Thus, even the idea of being "personally against abortion, but for freedom of choice" (as is often politically popular) strikes the evangelical mind as a lack of moral clarity (and perhaps even a lack of moral courage). In freedom of choice versus freedom to live, life should always win.

> **Quote Head** _____
>
> "The comparison between a baby's rights and a mother's rights is unequal ....
> [O]ne person's right to a preferred lifestyle is not greater than another person's right to a life."
> —Randy Alcorn, in *Pro-Life Answers to Pro-Choice*

"No one knows when life really begins—that is a religious question, not a scientific one."

Although questions about the human soul are certainly religious in nature, the biological definition of life is clear, according to evangelicals. They point out that the entire genetic code of a child is present at the time of conception—a different genetic code than that of its mother or father. Further, they note that as pregnancies progress, human life becomes more and more viable outside of the womb; and with today's scientific and medical advances, the age of viability is younger and younger. Indeed, among scientists there may be disagreement as to exactly when human life begins, but there is a large body of scientists who believe—on a scientific basis—that it begins at conception.

"Abortion prevents unwanted children from being born into bad situations."

Certainly, no one wants to see a child suffer. For evangelicals, abortion is the ultimate expression of suffering for a child—unwanted death. Further, evangelicals would say that the "quality of life" argument has far-reaching social implications with regard to the protection of the handicapped, the elderly, and the infirmed. They insist that the sanctity of life must be society's benchmark, not the quality of life. Otherwise, who makes the decisions as to whose life is qualitatively fit?

"Legalizing abortion provides safety for women. Illegal abortions would be very unsafe."

While it is true that legalizing abortion has lowered the risk to the mother, many evangelicals would argue that it has resulted in less safety for untold numbers of children who would be alive today if abortion were not legal. Evangelical ethicists argue that it is wrong to try to stop one evil by legalizing another (even greater) one.

Culture Clash!

For evangelicals, abortion is about the taking of a life. For them, the issue of choice pales in comparison. To get to a substantive discussion with an evangelical regarding abortion, be prepared to answer the question, "If what is in the womb is not a child, then what is it?"

"What about the hard cases—like rape or incest or where the mother's life is at risk?"

This is where many evangelicals part ways. Some are in favor of a consistent ethic of protecting unborn life. Others (probably the majority) recognize that certain situations present untenable choices no matter which path is chosen, and thus believe that Christians who truly seek God's will may come to different conclusions.

Responding to the Crisis

Particularly in the years since *Roe vs. Wade*, evangelicals have taken an active stance toward what they believe to be a moral crisis in America. The response of the evangelical community can be described in several ways.

First of all, evangelicals have sought to bring their views into the public eye. Through their involvement with sophisticated media and political organizations (see Chapter 15), they have mobilized thousands, and at their best, have tried to provide for substantive debate on the issues at hand.

Networking through groups like the National Right To Life Committee, founded in 1973, evangelicals have been a powerful voice in the pro-life movement. Although not specifically evangelical in its mission, the NRL is a good study in the prowess of the evangelical political agenda. Since its modest beginning, the organization has grown into the nation's largest and most effective pro-life lobby, with over 3,000 local chapters, 50 state affiliates, and millions of supporters. They provide education, lobbying and media communications through the NRL Political Action Committee, federal and state legislative offices, a medical ethics department, and a legal department. They seek to identify and support pro-life political candidates, and reach out through programs to churches, colleges, and minority groups. Overall, they may be the largest single organization focused on the pro-life agenda. Their growth and prowess speaks to the strong support they have built in audiences that include evangelicals, but go well beyond the movement as well.

Secondly, in more controversial responses, evangelicals have taken a page from the playbook of the civil rights movement and engaged in civil disobedience. This has included everything from picketing abortion clinics to staging sit-ins at medical facilities, blocking the entrances for patients and medical workers. Although controversial, this type of response can be seen at one level as logical if evangelicals indeed believe that lives are at stake.

Undoubtedly, the most controversial organization connected to these kinds of activities is Operation Rescue/Operation Save America. Founded in 1986 by Randall Terry, the organization is specifically Christian, and more accurately described as fundamentalist than evangelical. Through the 1980s and 1990s Operation Rescue (as it was called then) organized mass demonstrations at abortion facilities throughout the country, resulting in tens of thousands of Operation Rescue volunteers being arrested. Although it mimicked the tactics of civil disobedience groups, Operation Rescue's demonstrations were known to be quite acrimonious. Indeed, Randall Terry has been denounced by most evangelical leaders, and is no longer the leader of the organization he founded. The organization currently sports a picture of its present director, Rev. Philip Benham, baptizing Norma McCovey (Jane Roe in *Roe vs. Wade*) on its website—McCovey has now become an evangelical herself.

Yet Another Mea Culpa

Although some of the demonstrations of Operation Rescue and groups like it have been true to the spirit of civil, non-violent disobedience, others have not. Tactics such as "sidewalk counseling"—where pro-lifers passionately try to convince those going into abortion clinics not to go through with the abortion—can often turn into yelling matches and can traumatize the women who are targeted. Further, some pro-lifers who started out with a peaceful civil disobedience strategy have become more uncivil in their rhetoric and actions as time has passed.

In addition, there have even been cases of violence in the pro-life movement. Such violence is abhorrent to those who truly seek to follow the example of Jesus, and certainly not embraced by the evangelical community.

The best, most compassionate, and most Christ-like responses from evangelicals have come in the form of social service agencies geared to provide practical help to women (and men) who are faced with unwanted pregnancies. "Crisis pregnancy centers" are at work in nearly every major

> ## In Their Own Words
>
> "The violence perpetrated by James Kopp and others represents a rejection of the prolife movement. In my judgment, violence only begets more violence. Such actions work a profound disservice to the prolife community. These people may be antiabortion, but they're not prolife."
>
> —Ken Connor, President of the evangelical Family Research Council, responding to the conviction of extremist James Kopp, who killed abortion provider Dr. Barnett Slepian

U.S. city, mostly run by evangelicals. These agencies work to help women have their babies by providing counseling to the mothers and fathers, prenatal and postpartum care, shelters or half-way homes for abused and unwed mothers, parenting education, financial assistance, job training, and even compassionate and effective adoption assistance. For many, these centers are a picture of Evangelicalism at its best.

The Debate Goes On

Nearly four years after the picture of Samuel Armas's hand appeared across the globe, Samuel himself appeared before a U.S. Senate subcommittee at a hearing about pioneering medical procedures. As living proof of life before birth, the smiling toddler stood as a strong reminder of the pro-life position. As Senator Sam Brownback (R-Kansas), Committee Chair, noted after questioning Samuel and his parents, "There is little debate about whether the child in-utero is alive; the debate is over whether or not the child is a life worthy of protection."

For evangelicals, that protection is both a biblical imperative and a societal norm worth fighting for.

The Least You Need to Know

- ◆ Evangelicals believe that abortion is the taking of a human life.

- ◆ Evangelicals believe that the Bible clearly teaches that life begins at conception.

- ◆ Evangelicals believe that the value of freedom of choice involved in abortion pales in comparison to the value of the protection of the life of the unborn child.

- ◆ Evangelicals are abhorred by and reject the violence of some in the pro-life movement.

- ◆ Evangelicals have been in the forefront of caring for the practical needs of unplanned pregnancies through agencies and programs that provide help.

Chapter 14

School Daze

In This Chapter

- ◆ The spectrum of evangelical beliefs about creation and evolution
- ◆ Are evangelicals against sex education?
- ◆ What's all the fuss about prayer in schools?
- ◆ Evangelical homeschoolers

They call it "teaching the controversy."

In dueling op-ed pieces in the *San Francisco Chronicle* recently, Stanford neurology professor Robert M. Sapolsky squared off against Stephen C. Meyer and John Angus Campbell, senior fellows at The Discovery Institute, a conservative public policy think tank. Sapolsky, calling those who support teaching alternative scientific hypotheses to evolution people with "Jed Clampett" profiles, said, "[T]he rank and file of intelligent design supporters is most likely to come from the parts of the country with the lowest literacy rates, the lowest percentages of high-school graduates and the lowest rates of government investments in education." Meyer and Campbell shot back in their piece that, "A good education presents students with competing perspectives held by credible experts, and offers them the skills to judge these views themselves."

It certainly is controversial. But what is popularly known as the *intelligent design* debate is only one of many battlegrounds where evangelicals fight for what they perceive to be their right to free expression in the schools. School prayer, school choice, sex education, and higher education are some of the primary venues. These are emotional issues that are correctly perceived by all sides as being about much more than education. They are about the character of our culture.

In this chapter we'll look at some of the hot-button issues in education for evangelicals that span both the personal and the cultural. Hopefully, in the process we'll break through some stereotypes and enable conversation that goes beyond controversy to understanding.

The Beginning of the World as We Know It

A 2006 Gallup poll showed that eight out of ten Americans believe that God guided creation in some capacity. A few years earlier, a group of one hundred scientists with doctorates from Yale, Princeton, Stanford, and Cal-Berkeley (among others) published a full-page magazine advertisement in *The Weekly Standard* (October 1, 2001) that was headlined, "A Scientific Dissent from Darwinism." They stated: "We are skeptical of claims for the ability of random mutation and natural selection to account for the complexity of life." This kind of support from both the public at large and the scientific community, evangelicals say, is not reflected in the curriculum of public schools today.

The issue, according to evangelicals, is scientific integrity. Over the past several decades, much evidence has come out regarding holes in evolutionary theory, yet almost none of it has made its way into what is taught by the average biology or physics teacher. To be clear, most evangelicals are not in opposition to the idea that living things evolve. The issue that raises its head from school boards to academic journals has more to do with the fact that the evidence for the hypothesis of a directed process of the development of life (i.e., intelligent design) is routinely skipped over. Evangelicals would say that the scientific evidence for intelligent design and against random mutation is very strong, yet mostly ignored by an academic community that is biased against something that so threatens its status quo.

> **The Gospel Truth**
>
> Most evangelicals are not opposed to evolution. They are opposed to the idea of a random, *undirected* process of creation. They believe that God is behind all of creation, regardless of the processes he chose to make it happen.

Evangelicals face an uphill battle, however, in part due to their own history. In 1909, the popular Scofield Reference Bible included in its notes a timeline created by Bishop James Ussher (in 1650) tracing the genealogies of the Bible back and thus setting a definitive date of October 23, 4004 B.C., as the date of creation. For some reason, this date got imbedded into the minds of many fundamentalists and even some evangelicals. This kind of goofiness has created a reputation that evangelicals really *are* about as smart as Jethro and Ellie Mae. Yet over the years, the level of sophistication within their ranks has steadily grown.

Creation Science

For instance, in 1963, Dr. Henry Morris founded the Creation Research Society (now called the Institute for Creation Research), in conjunction with writing several books that brought forward geological evidence of a great flood (i.e., Noah and the ark), and perhaps more importantly, questioned the philosophical basis of prevailing scientific approaches to the origins of the earth and mankind. Although much of his work was not accepted by the scientific community at large (including many evangelical scientists today), his assertion that all scientists studying the origins of the earth work from a specific interpretive framework (admitted or not) was an important step. In popularizing the reality of the existence of philosophies of science, he helped evangelicals integrate faith with the modern scientific method that has as its touchstone the observation of repeatable phenomena. According to Morris, since origins by definition are not repeatable or observable, all scientists work from a bias of some kind of "faith."

Morris thus popularized "Creation Science," which although much less sophisticated (and often criticized for being scientifically inaccurate), was a forerunner of the modern intelligent design movement.

> ### In Their Own Words
>
> "There is no longer any justification for doubting or scoffing. God has given men overwhelming evidence, both in Scripture and in science, that he created all things and that he controls all things."
>
> —Henry Morris, in *The Beginning of the World*

The Modern Intelligent Design Movement

Today's intelligent design movement is made up of a wide range of evangelicals. Some believe in the Genesis story as literal fact (including the six 24-hour days of creation);

most do not. Led by people like former UC Berkeley Law Professor Phillip E. Johnson (author of numerous books, including *Darwin on Trial*), and biochemist Michael Behe of Lehigh University, intelligent design proponents put forward arguments such as the following in contention to the universal acceptance of neo-Darwinism:

◆ They do not believe that the fossil record supports macro evolution (mutations that create whole new species).

◆ They are skeptical that random mutation could have produced the incredibly delicate balance that enables human life.

◆ They believe that the "irreducible complexity" of certain organisms (meaning that without even one single part the organism would cease to function) creates questions around the idea of evolution due to natural selection.

◆ They believe that the incredible complexity and fine-tuning of our planet's place in the universe, and the similar complexity and fine tuning of living things—all of which together enable life—more logically leads to a hypothesis of intelligent design.

Basically, intelligent design proponents believe that because there is a design, there must be a designer. They believe it is scientifically impossible to prove that nonlife has produced life.

There is much, much more to this debate. As a decidedly right-brainer, I would suggest that if you are interested in pursuing this area further, you pick up a copy of *The Case for a Creator* by evangelical author Lee Strobel. It is a good overview of the arguments in this arena for the nonscientist. If you want to go a bit deeper, Phillip Johnson's *Darwin on Trial* and Michael Behe's *Darwin's Black Box* are standards in the field.

Beyond creation science proponents and intelligent design advocates, many evangelicals would fall into what I would call the "shrugged shoulders theistic evolution" box. They are content to believe that God uses the process of evolution to do his work. However, they are saddened by the anti-God bias they see in science in the public schools, and would like to see more openness toward and less ridicule of students of faith.

School Prayer

Ridicule can also go in the opposite direction. Just ask Dr. Patricia Kilzer, of Munford High School, just outside of Memphis, Tennessee. As the faculty advisor for the school's student chapter of the ACLU, Kilzer recently experienced a bit of ostracism from other teachers when the ACLU demanded that the traditional prayers before and after the Munford High graduation ceremony be cancelled.

"People say I am a God-hater. I simply believe in the Constitution and equality. I am very tolerant of other religions and that to me is what we're supposed to be," she said in an interview with the local newspaper. She also said that as a result of the incident, other teachers in the school seem reluctant to make eye contact with her in the halls, and even turn their heads to look the other way when she passes.

The students at Munford High, however, did not take such a laissez-faire approach to the whole situation. When the traditional time came for the prayer at the graduation ceremony, principal Darry Marshall instead asked for a moment of silence. As the crowd stood with bowed heads, most of the 286 seniors pulled out their own copies of the Lord's Prayer and began reciting it out loud. When the crowd of about 1,500 people in the football stadium saw what was happening, spontaneous cheers erupted from the stands.

Based as it is on a much less technical set of arguments than evolution vs. intelligent design, the controversy around school prayer generally carries more developed opinions from rank-and-file evangelicals. In order to understand those opinions, it is helpful to take a look at an overview of the issue from a historical perspective.

> **Culture Clash!**
>
> To understand an evangelical's feelings about public prayer, it's helpful to realize that most see it as an issue of being restricted from the free expression of their religion.

The Supreme Court on Prayer

"Congress shall make no law respecting an establishment of religion …" says the first amendment to the constitution.

Twentieth century courts have tended to interpret this to essentially mean that the framers intended separation of all religious expression from public life. Not so, claim evangelicals, who point out that the Constitution itself was hammered out in the context of meetings that often began with daily prayer. Evangelicals further explain that the first amendment concerns "an establishment of religion," not "*the* establishment" of religion. In other words, the amendment was intended as a safeguard regarding the establishment of a single religion by the government. This is quite a ways from a religious cleansing of culture that amounts to a religion in and of itself, according to evangelicals—the "religion" of secular humanism.

Indeed, secular humanism has become the de facto religion of America, say many evangelicals. As regards the issue of prayer in public schools, they say that a summary of influential court cases in the twentieth century shows a clear trend in this direction:

♦ *McCollum v. Board of Education* **(1948).** This ruling established that it is a violation of the first amendment for religious leaders to lead optional or voluntary religious instruction in public school buildings.

♦ *Engel v. Vitale* **(1962).** This is perhaps the most important of the modern cases, determining that any daily recitation of prayers in public schools is unconstitutional.

♦ *Abington School District v. Schempp* **(1963).** In this case, the court struck down any daily school-directed reading of the Bible, or recitation of the Lord's prayer.

♦ *Lemon v. Kurtzman* **(1971).** This ruling established what has come to be known as the three part "Lemon test" regarding violations of the First Amendment. To avoid violation, any school activity must first of all have a secular purpose, secondly not advance or prohibit religion, and third not foster excessive entanglement between the government and religion.

♦ *Stone v. Graham* **(1980).** In this case, the Court struck down a state law that required schools to post the Ten Commandments.

♦ *Wallace v. Jaffree* **(1985).** Deeming the purpose of the practice to be religious rather than secular in its intent, the court struck down a state law requiring a moment of silence ("meditation or voluntary prayer") in schools.

♦ *Lee v. Weisman* **(1992).** This case disallowed a private individual from offering prayer at a public school graduation. The importance of graduation, according to the court, compelled the students to be there (even though attendance was voluntary). Thus, students who were subjected to the suggestion of bowing their heads were having their Constitutional rights violated.

♦ *Santa Fe Independent School District v. Jane Doe* **(2000).** Here the Court struck down the opportunity for a student to open football games with a prayer, citing that the practice "unquestionably has the purpose and creates the perception of encouraging the delivery of prayer at a series of important school events."

While many evangelicals see these cases as proper boundaries for a pluralistic society, many others do not see it that way. They note that in each of these cases the focus was on the establishment clause of the first amendment. However, they point out that we must remember the more complete context of the amendment:

"Congress shall make no law respecting an establishment of religion, or *prohibiting the free exercise thereof* …" (Italics mine.)

Many evangelicals suggest that the virtual court doctrine in the twentieth century has been a downgrading of the free expression of religion. It is important to note here that evangelicals are not the only ones seeing this trend; they are often joined in their efforts to extend religious expression in schools by other Protestants as well as Catholic and Jewish believers.

> **The Gospel Truth**
>
> One example of the fact that the issue of school prayer is not just an evangelical issue: *Lee v. Weisman* involved a Jewish rabbi offering a prayer at a public graduation ceremony.

The Basic Arguments

The result of all of this from many evangelicals has been a cry for more freedom to pray in the public school systems. We can summarize some of the most oft-used arguments this way …

♦ **Banning school prayer represents a restriction of religious freedom.** Especially in the way the courts have ruled over the past decades, many feel that the protection afforded by the free exercise clause is being demeaned. They view some of the restrictions being placed on them as violations of their freedom to exercise their religion without government interference.

♦ **The Court's decisions are essentially establishing a national secular religion.** Some go a little far with conspiracy theories here, but many evangelicals believe there is validity to the idea that secular humanism has become the real (yet unrecognized) religion of public America.

♦ **The majority of Americans are in favor of voluntary prayer in public schools.** Many believe that the Supreme Court judges have taken a role on themselves which unfairly skews the balance of power in our government. They are legislating from the bench. If a vote were taken on this issue today, polls show that prayer in school would be allowed.

◆ **Banning school prayer leads to a decline in morality.** It's a bit of a red herring, but some point to the rise in everything from murder rates to teen pregnancy since 1962 (the *Vitale* case) and declare a direct connection to "taking God out of the schools."

◆ **The religious connection is seen in other government institutions.** Congress opens each session with prayer; "In God We Trust" is displayed on our currency; the President takes the oath of office on the Bible; the Ten Commandments are displayed in the Supreme Court building. If religious expression is accepted in these institutions, many evangelicals ask why it should have to stop at the schoolhouse door.

Evangelicals Against School Prayer

Evangelicals who advocate for prayer in public schools, however, are not the only evangelicals out there. A growing and significant number have a very different opinion. They point out that Christianity demands love of neighbor, which includes sensitivity to those of other religions. They also point out that the pluralism of our culture would require either equal time for prayers of other religions, or very tepid nonsectarian praying that would encourage the vapid spirituality of an already vastly uncommitted culture. Finally, they say that the enormous energy going toward this issue is taking the focus off of really important issues such as the plight of the poor in our culture.

As always, however, the most shrill voices are the ones that make the best media stories. Speaking of which …

Sex Education

"Screw Abstinence" declared the headline of the official NARAL Pro-choice America's website not long ago, advertising a "Screw Abstinence Party" sponsored by the organization. According to the accompanying press release, attendees were invited to "Throw up your hands and say it out loud: Screw Abstinence!" The party featured guests such as a group called Toys in Babeland featuring tips on sex toys, as well as a comedy group performing a sex ed class (which could likely include a parody, one could assume from tone of the website information, of what the ad called the "dangerous" abstinence-only-until-marriage point of view).

The vitriolic nature of the ad and the event itself are evidence of a huge divide between those who are more liberal in their sexual ethics and those who are more conservative. Evangelicals see these kinds of initiatives as further proof of the fact that the goal of those who seek to liberalize sex education is more than just the dissemination of information: it is the reversal of the personal values that evangelical parents work very hard to instill into their kids. Calling the abstinence-only-until-marriage point of view "dangerous" is quite offensive to those who believe it to be the best way. Additionally, evangelicals would see such a statement as clear evidence that those who claim to be neutral and open-minded in their sex education viewpoint certainly are not.

In Their Own Words

"One has to ask: What do sex toys have to do with our children?"

—From a Focus on the Family response to the "Screw Abstinence" Party invitation

According to recent polls, the overwhelming majority of Americans believe that sex education should be taught in schools. Surprisingly, this includes evangelicals. However, the content of the desired curriculum is quite different for evangelicals. Most would prefer that sex education be taught through a program that is at least neutral on such issues as premarital sex and alternative sexualities.

Why do evangelicals feel this way? The reasons go beyond their commitment to biblical sexual ethics (see Chapter 11). Some of the more common reasons for their concern include …

- **Sex education is not values-free.** There is no such thing as values-free sex education, say evangelicals. The debate in this arena, although often unspoken, has always been about what values will be taught.

- **Focusing on contraceptive methods encourages kids to experiment.** An article on the Concerned Women for America website cites the example of a group of male students who got into a contest to see who could get the most sex. "They teach us condoms this and condoms that, but they don't teach us any rules," one young man in the group was quoted as saying.

- **Safe sex is not so safe.** Some sex ed curriculum, according to evangelicals, can lull kids into a false sense of security about sex. In addition to the risk of STDs, evangelicals are concerned that the emotional health of kids who engage in early sex is at risk.

◆ **Overall, the government should not be overruling the values *that parents are teaching their kids*.** Many evangelicals see that the more comprehensive sex education curricula that is taught in schools very often diametrically opposes their own point of view.

◆ **Citizens should not be forced to pay for something that violates their religious conscience.** Evangelicals see it as a violation of their religious freedom to have to pay (with their tax dollars) for something they so completely disagree with from both a religious (and practical) point of view.

On the other hand, evangelicals see abstinence-focused sex education as helpful. General reasons for this include:

◆ **Abstinence-based curricula represents the highest health standard.** If the goal of sex education is the promotion of good health, teen abstinence is the best way to go, say evangelicals. The benefits of teen abstinence are well-established, including reduced physical and mental health risks.

◆ **Abstinence-based models are comprehensive.** Curriculum includes material on STDs, condoms, teen pregnancy, HIV, relationship skills, and the benefits of marriage. According to a 2004 Heritage Foundation study, nonabstinence programs devoted a total 5 percent of the page content to abstinence as a choice, and 0 percent to healthy relationships and the benefits of marriage.

◆ **Abstinence-based instruction is more realistic about the downside of early sexual activity.** The realities of the high risks associated with teen sexuality are well established. Advocates of abstinence-based models believe that the clearer goals and values of the model enable teachers to be more honest with students about the dangers of high-risk behavior.

Obviously, this is not a topic that is going away anytime soon. Hopefully, as the debate continues, all sides will learn to listen more, and spout slogans ("Screw Promiscuity"?) less.

Public, Private, and Homeschools

"Some would say that Sally should be in preschool," begins the 30-second TV spot, complete with strains of "for unto us a child is born" from Handel's *Messiah* played in the background. "But Mom knows that institutional preschool damages children."

The shot across the bow is unmistakable, aimed at the overwhelming majority of professional educators who advocate school at an earlier and earlier age in our culture. The ad continues, as the camera features close ups of a young mom and a little baby with blonde curls and dimples, playing with flowers in a field: "And Mom knows that the best place for Sally to thrive, learn, and grow, is right in her loving arms. That's why Sally's Mom is considering homeschooling." As the organization's website address appears at the bottom of the screen, the baby's smiling face fills the screen, and the final pitch is given. "Come join the millions of Christian families that have discovered the blessings of private Christian homeschooling," the announcer says, with the voice of a young child finishing the ad (and adding a very obvious emotional pull) by announcing the website address.

> ### In Their Own Words
>
> "I like homeschooling because it's more fun and I can watch TV over lunch ... If I need help with a subject, I can get it. If I understand a subject, I can move on."
>
> —Danny, age 11, quoted in *School Choices* by Jan Sheble

The ad (part of a national campaign, which has been titled "Preschool Damages Children" by its creators) is actually quite a soft sell for an organization that also features videos of Tim LaHaye (author of the *Left Behind* series) telling parents that public schools "brainwash" children with secular humanism. "It's time to get our kids out of public schools!" he declares.

The passion and emotion behind this issue finds its way into public communication that—yet again—as we've seen several times in this chapter, lacks nuance. Indeed, there are those among fundamentalists and evangelicals who believe public or even private schools are damaging to the healthy development of children. However, within Evangelicalism, there are those with quite opposite points of view. Indeed, my experience as a pastor has been that there are few issues that cause more internal strife, both in churches and within Evangelicalism as a whole, than strong opinions regarding the education of children. Perhaps because everyone recognizes how much is at stake.

Following, we discuss three options for school choice, and the general attitudes of evangelicals toward each one.

Homeschooling 101

Christians are not the only ones homeschooling their children. The trend is on the upswing throughout the United States. However, for most evangelicals, the impetus to homeschool comes from a sense of their biblical calling as parents. This includes the calling to protect their children's spiritual lives from negative outside influences, as well as the calling to give them the very best education possible. For many, homeschooling is the obvious choice. The general reasons for that choice include …

- **The advantages of completely individualized curriculum.** Every person learns differently. The one-on-one nature of homeschooling provides the opportunity for the student to have the curriculum arranged solely around them. Further, as most homeschool teachers are the parents of the students, there is the advantage of the intimate knowledge that the parent has of what the child actually needs. Because of this, homeschoolers claim that studies show that the average homeschool student outscores the average public school student by 15 to 30 percentile points on standardized tests.

- **The assurance of shared values.** By teaching their kids at home, parents can be assured that the values they want their kids to learn are being reinforced at all times.

- **The convenience of homeschooling.** This includes the fact that homeschoolers can have a much more flexible schedule than their peers; especially considering the fact that the one-on-one academic experience takes much less time than a classroom experience. Most homeschoolers complete their work in only a few hours each day. For many homeschool families who nurture their total family experience very carefully, the extra flexibility in their schedule is a bonus, enabling more quality family time together.

Often, homeschoolers will band together for extra-curricular activities, outings, or specialized instruction. Many parents find their primary social relationships in local homeschooling support groups, connecting with other parents of similar values and lifestyles.

Private Schooling

Homeschooling is not for everyone, however. Quite a few evangelical parents who are not interested in public schooling or homeschooling choose private Christian schools for their children. Typically, these schools are populated by children whose parents are looking for a combination of the advantages of a smaller school combined with a desire to see their kids receive specific spiritual growth opportunities. Overall, the reasons many evangelicals choose this option include ...

◆ **The specific religious worldview of the school.** Parents concerned about the values espoused by teachers and students in public schools often choose a Christian school for their child to insure that what their child is being taught is consistent with biblical principles. Many believe that Christian schools are indispensable in helping their child to develop a Christian worldview.

◆ **Smaller class sizes.** Though not as highly individualized as homeschooling, the smaller classes of Christian schools provide for more interaction between student and teacher, and teacher and parent.

◆ **The positive peer influence of other students in a Christian environment.** Although not all kids in a Christian school are personally Christian, the environment of the school encourages students to develop in their faith together. This often results in positive reinforcement of Christian values as students grow up together in their faith.

> **Culture Clash!** _____
>
> For a great (and satirical) look into issues of conformity in Christian schools, check out the 2004 movie *Saved!* starring Mandy Moore and directed by Brian Dannelly. Watch it with a friend whose point of view is different from yours—it's an absolutely great discussion starter.

Although the conformity (and at times the financial cost) of Christian schools can be stifling to some, many evangelicals see them as an excellent alternative for their children's education. Further, many parents and students choose an evangelical college experience. Again, the similar worldview and the academic environment of these schools (many have very high academic standards) are keys to such choices. In addition, many Christian colleges and universities provide expanded ministry opportunities (i.e., domestic and overseas mission trips, student fellowship groups, etc.) for students that are very attractive to evangelicals.

Public Schooling

In the face of all of this, the vast majority of evangelicals (up to 90 percent, according to recent research) still choose public schools for their kids. Some evangelicals would say (and here we hit a bit of the internal strife of these issues) that these parents simply are not being thoughtful enough about what they're doing. However, others claim that the public school experience is not only a better choice for their child's education, it's also a better choice for their child in enabling them to "salt and light" to the world around them.

In general, the reasons evangelicals choose public schools include …

- **The opportunity for both students and parents to be significantly connected to their communities in a redeeming way.** In other words, the relationships built through what is our culture's primary social network for kids enable Christian families to engage with and be "good news" to people in a very natural environment.

- **The extracurricular opportunities.** Many public schools offer athletic or arts programs that simply are not available elsewhere. Evangelical parents whose children are oriented in those kinds of ways often choose the public school to enhance their children's opportunities.

- **The diversity factor.** Many evangelicals want to expose their children to diverse worldviews and lifestyles as a way of preparing them for the real world. These parents feel that they can best prepare their children for the tough choices ahead by mentoring them through those kinds of choices while in school.

Regardless of the reasons, most evangelicals choose public schooling for their kids, and many involve themselves in everything from volunteering in the classroom to running for the school board. As a matter of fact, it is those evangelicals who are most active at the public school level who often create the kinds of controversies much of this chapter is about.

And this same impetus in evangelicals to be involved in and influence their public setting brings us to the focus of our next chapter.

The Least You Need to Know

- Evangelical beliefs about creation run the gamut from literal six-day creationists to theistic evolutionists.

- Although not against teaching kids about sex, most evangelicals are skeptical of the values behind public school sex education.

- Some evangelicals see the lack of opportunity for prayer in public schools as a restriction of their religious freedom. Others do not.

- Some evangelicals believe homeschooling to be the right choice for their children, some believe private Christian schooling to be best, but the majority have their kids in public schools.

Part 4

Mission Possible: The Cultural Impact of Evangelicalism

The evangelical impact on contemporary culture is undeniable. From politics to rock and roll, and from megachurches to Habitat for Humanity, it is obvious that evangelicals are on a mission.

In this section, we'll explore that mission. We'll find out, for example, that while "evangelical" and "conservative" seem to be the norm politically, there is a growing number of evangelicals who are more interested in poverty than gay marriage. Along the way, we'll also look at the pervasiveness of evangelical media, the amazing influence of several contemporary megachurches, and the equally amazing work being done world-wide by evangelical parachurch and relief agencies.

Through all of this we'll see that evangelicals do believe that they are a people sent on a mission—and they do believe that it is possible to change the world.

Chapter 15

The Fight for the Right: Evangelicals and Politics

In This Chapter

- ◆ Are all evangelicals Republicans?
- ◆ Do theology and politics actually mix?
- ◆ Are evangelicals environmentalists?
- ◆ Is the Christian Right getting left behind?

He was the golden boy with the golden touch. Head of a major and highly successful national political lobbying group at the young age of 29, on the cover of *Time* magazine at age 33, and a close advisor to the President of the United States by age 39. But at age 45, Ralph Reed, the former head of the Christian Coalition, and the one that *Time* had once christened "The Right Hand Of God," suffered a humbling political defeat due to the issue he had used so successfully against others in the past: his personal moral values.

In his first ever run for political office in 2006, Reed lost as a candidate for Lieutenant Governor in his home state of Georgia. The primary reason? An ethics scandal that tied him to another lobbyist (Jack Abramoff) who had recently been convicted of tax fraud, tax evasion, and bribery. But this was not just guilt by association. Reed, whose choir-boy image was built in part on his moral opposition to gambling, had taken money for his political consulting firm (through Abramoff) from Native American casinos. Reed, who had been claiming to work hard to stop gambling, was simply working for casinos who were trying to stop their competition (other Native American casinos) from opening.

For Reed, it was a case of "the Lord giveth, and the Lord taketh away." For the Christian right, it was a wake-up call. For seasoned and cynical observers, it was simply another day in politics. However you look at it, Ralph Reed's story provides an excellent picture of the possibilities and the perils of Christian politics. In this chapter, we'll take a look at both.

Christian Politics: An Oxymoron?

Jesus said, "[R]ender to Caesar the things that are Caesar's and to God the things that are God's" (Luke 20:25, NASB). For some Christians this has meant staying out of politics. But for others, particularly as the "born again" idea became popular and even hip in the late 1970s, Caesar's things and God's things began to converge. As the stock of Evangelicalism rose culturally, many began to see its potent political potential.

Further, they saw that the connection of Christianity and politics has lots of historical and theological precedent. Historically, some examples include:

♦ The "covenant communities" of Puritans, which were formed around mutual commitment to one another under God, and which influenced the political philosophies of those who created the American system of government.

♦ The social action movements that arose out of the Second Great Awakening, particularly under Charles Finney (see Chapter 2).

♦ Historical movements such as abolitionism and temperance in the United States.

♦ The biblical referents often used by Martin Luther King, Jr. in the civil rights movement.

All of these and more were part of the consciousness of evangelicals that played into the rise of the modern Christian right in the late 1970s and early 1980s.

Evangelicals were further encouraged down this pathway by influential evangelical theologians such as Francis Schaeffer, who advocated that all the world is God's, and that the dividing line between the "secular" and the "spiritual" that had arisen in the ethos of our culture was actually a theo-logical inaccuracy. In more recent years, people like Jim Wallis of the Sojourners (an evangelical, but not part of the Chris-tian Right) have been calling on everyone to realize that Christianity is always per-sonal, but never private. Indeed, according to Wallis, national budgets are "moral documents" that reveal the priorities of the nation. Remembering Jesus' call to care for "the least of these" in every culture, many evangelicals believe that they are called by God to influence society for the good of all.

> ## In Their Own Words
>
> "Caesar is not to be put in the place of God, and we as Christians, in the name of the Lordship of Christ, and all of life, must so think and act on the appropriate level."
>
> —Francis Schaeffer in an address titled *A Christian Manifesto*, delivered to Coral Ridge Presbyterian Church in Fort Lauderdale, Florida in 1982

There is a spectrum here that may be surprising. Some evangelicals, for example, border on what is often called "dominionist" thinking—the idea that the United States has a manifest destiny to be a "Christian nation." This is often coupled with the notion that America needs to be "taken back" for God. The extremes of these positions look to create what is almost a theocracy, although these extreme points of view are not very influential in Evangelicalism at large. More typical are those whose theology leads them to the idea that Christians should strive for political power in order to create laws and a culture that reflect the goodness depicted in the scriptures. There is no desire here to force everyone to live in a specifically Christian nation; it is more a conviction that the nation should reflect Christian values that are universal in application (i.e., respect for life). The rub, of course, comes when one begins to ask *which* values are universal (e.g., traditional marriage verses homosexual marriage).

On the left side of the spectrum are Christians who believe that the poor, the environment, and a consistent respect for life (e.g., no capital punishment) are the values that Christians should spend their energy and resources on promoting. The spectrum here is also wide. There are Christian Democrats, Christian pacifists, Christians who oppose a capitalistic agenda in government, Christian environmentalists, and even Christian gay rights supporters (Jimmy Carter, for example, supports legal domestic partnership status for homosexual couples). This is the growing edge of evangelical political involvement, as we will see later on in this chapter.

The Theology of Politics

Both the left and the right side of the spectrum are in fairly consistent agreement on several theological principles that underlie their activities.

First of all, there is what is known in evangelical circles as *"stewardship."* The word comes from a Greek word that basically translates into modern parlance as "management." Throughout the Bible, God's call to humanity to be careful managers of his gifts is unmistakable. For evangelicals, this means the management of their individual gifts and callings, the management of their time, the management of their possessions, and in a broader sense, the management of God's creation in a just and proper way.

The Genesis account records God's calling to mankind to "fill the earth and subdue it" (Genesis 2:28). In its context, this is a broad directive from God to his creatures to care for all that he has given them. The human structures of government are certainly a part of that calling, and are especially important since they affect so many areas of life. In order to be good stewards, many evangelicals believe that God calls them to participate in the political arena.

Closely related to this idea, yet distinct from it, is an idea that is best expressed in the New Testament book of Colossians. Speaking of Jesus, it says (Colossians 1:15-16):

> He is the image of the invisible God, the firstborn over all creation. For by him all things were created: things in heaven and on earth, visible and invisible, whether thrones or powers or rulers or authorities; all things were created by him and for him.

This passage proclaims that Christ is Lord over every aspect of human existence. This includes the social systems and structures that make up the political world. Thus, many evangelicals feel that it is inaccurate to say that religion and politics don't mix.

A third theological principle common to evangelicals, both left and right, is the New Testament calling to responsible citizenship. In I Timothy 2:1-2, Paul says:

> I urge, then, first of all, that requests, prayers, intercession and thanksgiving be made for everyone—for kings and all those in authority, that we may live peaceful and quiet lives in all godliness and holiness.

Praying for our leaders is an intimate form of involvement. It shows an underlying principle of being caring participants in our social environment. As good stewards, many evangelicals believe that they are called to not only pray for their government, but also to participate in it to bring to pass the kinds of actions on the part of the government that will enable the culture to live "peaceful and quiet lives in all godliness and holiness."

This then leads to a fourth common theological conviction, perhaps the most important one, that encompasses a wide range of political philosophies and activities: the calling of the kingdom.

We've already discussed how the kingdom of God for Jesus was a huge concept that was a way of describing what is happening when God's will is being done (Chapter 8). In the context of politics, the implications of this are that the policies and activities of the government would enhance that process, and not be a hindrance to it in any way. Of course, exactly *what* God's will would be is often up for debate (even between evangelicals). But the over-arching call of Jesus to love one's neighbor—and even one's enemy—translates into a powerful motivation for evangelicals who want to see our society reflect that ideal as much as is humanly possible. And the fact that this calling of the kingdom is so central to the core of the faith and lives of evangelicals explains why politics often becomes so passionate for them.

> **The Gospel Truth**
>
> For evangelicals, the kingdom of God does not just reside in the hearts of people. Its availability extends outward into all realms, including the political and social.

So, how does all of this play out in the real world? To understand all of this, we will begin by digging a bit deeper into evangelical history and profiling some of the key leaders and organizations that have made up the Christian right.

The Moral Majority

Although predated by an organization called The Christian Voice (established in 1978), which pioneered some of the grassroots activism that defines much of the Christian right, the Moral Majority soon became the most well-known modern Christian right organization after its founding in 1979.

It was founded by the Reverend Jerry Falwell, who had gained a following through his *Old Time Gospel Hour* television broadcast, and who had been urged to get into politics by many as the tide of evangelicals in power was rising around the time of Jimmy Carter's election (1976). Evangelicals were being given a place at the political table for the first time in the century, and Falwell, with his very public persona, was naturally a part of it.

According to organization insiders, the movement was begun in a sort of "ready, fire, aim" approach. After becoming dissatisfied with Jimmy Carter's values as President, a group of influential evangelicals (mainly megachurch/media pastors) including Falwell began to see the need for an alternative political group that would more consistently address their issues. Originally, the intent of the group was to influence the 1980 Republican Party platform, and to do it by coalescing grassroots support around issues based on the Ten Commandments. The revolutionary idea to fundamentalists (who routinely broke ranks over almost anything) was to gather a group together around bigger issues, who might not agree on *all* issues. The "discovery" of this very normal political approach combined with the rising tide of evangelical power in the culture at large quickly created an organization that was very strong.

Its early platform, was "pro-life, pro-family, pro-moral, pro-American" (according to *Listen, America!* the book Falwell wrote in 1980 that described the Moral Majority's basic agenda). The organization's stated purposes were registration, information, and mobilization. With registration drives (one report said that eight million evangelicals were not registered to vote at the time of the Moral Majority's inception), information "scorecards" that helped readers to assess the stands of candidates on key evangelical issues (often distributed through churches), and the mobilization of evangelicals through his TV show, direct mail campaigns, and networking with local churches, Falwell's group quickly became the most well-recognized voice for the Christian right. Further, as a pastor, Falwell was able to take away the stigma of political action seeming "unspiritual" for rank-and-file Christians.

In Their Own Words

"Are you in favor of your tax dollar being used to support abortion on demand? Do you agree that voluntary prayer should be banned from the public schools? Do you believe that smut peddlers should be protected by the Courts and the Congress …?"

—Questions from fund-raising letters sent out by the Moral Majority, quoted in *With God on Our Side* by William Martin

At its height, the Moral Majority played a major role in partisan politics. Along with other newly-strong evangelical political operatives, the organization was a key part of the mobilization of evangelicals in the 1980 election, which many credit as being the key to Ronald Reagan's victory.

In 1986, Falwell announced that the Moral Majority would be enfolded into The Liberty Federation. Public opinion polls showed that the Moral Majority was being viewed increasingly more negatively by many who thought (in the words of a popular bumper sticker) that "The Moral Majority is Neither." Further, Falwell's activities had resulted in large declines of giving toward *The Old Time Gospel Hour* and Liberty University, the college he had started. After being the clear leader in the initial mobilization of the new religious right, Falwell stepped back, making room for a new rising star.

The Christian Coalition

Pat Robertson grew up as the son of A. Willis Robertson, who served in the United States senate for 34 years. Politics is, quite literally, in Pat's blood.

After graduating from Yale University Law School in 1955, he experienced a religious conversion. As a result, he shifted gears from the pursuit of a law career, choosing instead to enroll in New York Theological Seminary, from which he graduated in 1959. In 1960, he started the Christian Broadcasting Network in Virginia Beach, Virginia, by purchasing one UHF station in the area. A natural businessman, by the early 1980s Pat had parlayed that and other media purchases into a thriving religious broadcasting network, anchored by his *700 Club* talk show. Because of his high profile, he was connected into much of the evangelical political network in the late 1970s and the 1980s. In September of 1986, he announced that he was running for the presidential nomination of the Republican party.

Robertson surprised everyone by coming in ahead of then Vice President George Bush in the Iowa caucuses. However, as the primary season wore on, his finishes were weaker and weaker, and he eventually dropped out of the race. However, he and his organization had learned some crucial lessons about the inner workings of political machinery.

Taking advantage of those lessons and the momentum of his campaign among evangelicals, Robertson started the Christian Coalition in 1989. He chose 29 year-old Ralph Reed as its president. The organization, realizing that the Bush White House would not carry the evangelical agenda forward as the Regan White House had, decided to focus their efforts on grass roots politicking.

It was very successful in its early years, and by the fall of 1991, the Christian Coalition had more than 82,000 members. Its primary focus in those days was on grassroots campaigning for conservative candidates, and lobbying for conservative causes. At its height, the coalition received estimated contributions of $26.5 million (1996). It distributed over 70 million voter guides (helping voters to get a fast understanding of candidate's positions on key religious issues) in the 2000 elections, and 30 million voter guides during the 2004 elections.

More recently, the organization has struggled to maintain its influence and financial base (according to some estimates, recent annual contributions are in the $3 million range). Reed left the Christian Coalition in 1997, later becoming the Southeast Regional chairman for the Bush-Cheney campaign, based in Atlanta, and then running for Lieutenant Governor of Georgia. In 2000, Roberta Combs became President of the Christian Coalition, and has focused on bringing a more spiritual focus to the organization. The organization's current goals include voter education, advocacy, political training through its "leadership schools," and the "protest of anti-Christian bigotry." Its annual Road To Victory convention reaches a large and influential audience, involving numerous congressional representatives.

Other Christian Right Organizations

The Moral Majority and the Christian Coalition were the first, and are perhaps still the most well known, of the modern Christian right organizations. Although one is currently defunct, and the other is struggling, they played an indispensable role in mobilizing huge numbers of evangelicals to get involved—and to stay involved—in politics, and even in political careers. The impact of that is huge, and perhaps even yet incalculable.

Further, the two of them showed what can happen when Christians unite around a common cause. Neither were solely evangelical in their make-up, and the efforts of both spawned a plethora of other organizations, as others saw what could be accomplished.

Perhaps the most well known organization of the current decade is the Family Research Council, originally headed up by Gary Bauer, who had been a domestic policy advisor to Ronald Reagan (and who made his own short-lived bid for the presidency in 2000). This group was originally a spin-off from James Dobson's Focus on the Family organization, which overall, is one of the largest multifaceted evangelical parachurch groups (which we'll profile in Chapter 17). Now led by Tony Perkins, the Family Research Council has established itself as a major ongoing player at the political table, with an annual budget of around $10 million. Another key player currently is a group called Concerned Women of America, founded and headed up by Beverly LaHaye (wife of Tim LaHaye, coauthor of the massively successful *Left Behind* books). LaHaye started the organization in 1978 as a counter to the National Organization for Women, and the organization declares itself to be "the nation's largest public policy women's organization."

Culture Clash!

Christian stay-at-home moms often feel devalued by their secular, working-mom counterparts. The working moms often feel judged by the stay-at-homes. Why not break down the politics of both by sponsoring a celebration of both at your local church? Having an honest panel discussion exploring the issues both face could do wonders for opening up communication.

The Southern Baptist Convention is also a major player at the table, through its Ethics and Religious Liberty Commission. Richard Land, the current head of the effort, is one of the most sought-after evangelicals for public policy consulting.

There are literally hundreds of other political organizations aligned with the Christian right—too many to adequately cover within this book. For more information on other organizations, check out the politics area of beliefnet.com.

Key Issues of the Christian Right

The organizations we've profiled so far are all distinct in their own ways, but for the most part they are actually very similar in their primary policy agendas. From them and others, we can summarize the basic Christian Right issues over the past few decades:

- **Protection of the sanctity of life.** This includes activity such as abortion, euthanasia, and most currently, genetic issues such as stem-cell research. All of these activities are based in the evangelical belief that life is sacred, and only God is sovereign over it (see Chapter 13 for more info on this concept). Also related to this is the issue of capital punishment, which is not a consensus issue for evangelicals. Some believe that it is mandated by the Bible (Genesis 9:6) in order to respect and protect life (as a deterrent to murder); others believe that it was never God's best intention for humanity, and that the kingdom proclaimed by Jesus requires a different approach.

- **The protection of the traditional marriage and family.** This encompasses issues ranging from tax advantages for married couples, to opposition to gay marriage initiatives, to pornography legislation. These activities are based on the evangelical belief that marriage (between a man and a woman) and family are both institutions ordained by God, and thus should be protected.

◆ **Freedom of religious expression.** Though this sometimes swings into the desire for a "Christian nation," the underlying principle common to all evangelicals here is the need for government to support free religious expression.

◆ **Educational issues.** Issues here include everything from curriculum reform to sex education. In general, the Christian Right has sought to have public schools be receptive to the values of evangelicals instead of discriminating against them. An important part of these issues to evangelicals includes assuring that parents retain the ability to hold the primary authority over the development of their children—both intellectually, and in the arena of values.

Although the above represent the issues that are consistently addressed by the primary players of the Christian right, other issues come up frequently (though not as consistently), in their ranks. Their scope ranges from law and order issues (the Christian right is usually quite hawkish here), to fiscal conservatism (again, usually quite conservative, based on the biblical stewardship ideal), to policies regarding Israel and the Middle East (very often in support of Israel; often based on the various end-of-the-age theologies of different groups, who see a responsibility to protect God's chosen people).

Overall, the agenda of the Christian right is consistently based on their interpretation of biblical principles, and how those principles translate across specific policy lines.

A Bridge to the Future

Of particular interest, because it represents a clear bridge between the past and the future, is the political arm of the National Association of Evangelicals. In 2004, the group's Board of Directors unanimously adopted a "principled framework for evangelical public engagement" contained in a document called, "For the Health of the Nation: An Evangelical Call To Civic Responsibility." The document represents quite a different tone from the more confrontational leanings of some of the other organizations we've mentioned. For example, it states:

> We will differ with other Christians and with non-Christians over the best [governmental] policies. Thus we must practice humility and cooperation to achieve modest and attainable goals for the good of society. We must take care to employ the language of civility and to avoid denigrating those with whom we disagree.

This approach is certainly different, for example, from the Falwell fundraising letters quoted earlier in this chapter. As the NAE's document essentially lays out the political agenda for the organization in the coming years, it lists the following issues under the heading of "Principles of Christian Political Engagement":

- The protection of religious liberty and freedom of conscience

- The nurturing of family life and the protection of the unborn

- The protection of the sanctity of human life (includes euthanasia and bioethics issues)

- Justice and compassion for the poor and vulnerable

- The protection of human rights (politically, economically, and socially)

- Seeking peace and restraining violence

- The protection of God's creation (environmentalism)

In Their Own Words

"Evangelicals may not always agree about policy, but we realize that we have many callings and commitments in common: commitments to the protection and well-being of families and children, of the poor, the sick, the disabled, and the unborn, of the persecuted and oppressed, and of the rest of the created order."

—From the Preamble to the NAE's policy document titled "For the Health of the Nation: An Evangelical Call To Civic Responsibility"

Engaging in a much broader political agenda, the NAE is evidence of a growing concern within Evangelicalism for what in the past few decades have not been evangelical hot buttons. These kinds of issues seem to be the growing edge of evangelical political involvement, and are congruent with many of the values of the "emerging church" movement (which we'll profile in Chapters 19 and 20).

The times, they are a-changin'.

The Least You Need to Know

◆ Many evangelicals believe that the principles of scripture contain a very clear calling from God to political participation, in order to encourage the living out of biblical principles in our society.

◆ Although the Moral Majority is defunct and the Christian Coalition is not as strong as it once was, historically both organizations played extremely important roles in mobilizing an ongoing evangelical presence in politics.

◆ Key evangelical issues for the past few decades have revolved around the sanctity of life, marriage and family, education, and religious liberty.

◆ In recent years, many evangelicals have become less associated with the Christian right, and are increasingly broadening their political agenda.

16

Spreading the Word: Evangelical Media

In This Chapter

◆ Some surprising history about evangelical media

◆ An overview of modern Christian media

◆ Is all this really necessary?

◆ The unique challenges that face leading-edge evangelical creatives

Hello. My name's Vernon Billings, and I'm pastor of the New Hope Village Church of Mount Prospect, Illinois. As you watch this tape, I can only imagine the fear and the despair that you face. For this is being recorded for viewing only after the disappearance of God's people from the earth. The fact that you are watching indicates that you have been left behind.

Thus begins a videotape, that according to its ending credit, has an important purpose: "Every Christian needs to keep a copy of this video accessible in his or her home for those left behind." The video, called, *Have You Been Left Behind?*, is part of the evangelical publishing juggernaut spawned by the *Left Behind* books, a series of fictional works that depict the end of the age, using biblical prophecy as a guide. Written as supernatural thrillers, the books have spawned a cottage industry including everything from the video quoted previously, to greeting cards, calendars, a children's version of the series (which on its own has sold ten million copies), a worship CD, and even a video game.

Although Vernon Billings is fictional, as is his New Hope Village Church of Mount Prospect, the fact that people actually do keep a copy of this 20-minute video in their home so that someone could find it after Christians are raptured (check out the online discussion boards about the video for proof) is evidence of the power of the *Left Behind* books. And crossing as many media genres as it has, the series shows both the power and the reach of evangelical media. In this chapter we'll take a look at the sometimes strange, sometimes sophisticated, and often conflicted inner world of evangelical media enterprises.

Selling for the Soul

It wasn't that long ago that Christian-themed items, from books to household decorative plaques, were sold alongside other normal household goods. However, as modernization took firm hold of the cultural ethos in post-war America, most of these things disappeared from the shelves of department stores. This created a niche that was first filled by Mom and Pop "Christian bookstores," but that soon became much more than that. As the "Jesus people" cultural wave made Evangelicalism more hip in the late 60s and early 70s, baby boomers began looking for connection to their new-found faith in the most American of ways: consumerism.

From denim-covered Bibles to the burgeoning Christian rock industry, sales soared. Between 1975 and 1985 (as the tide of popular Evangelicalism was rising in the United States), the number of Christian bookstores in the country nearly tripled. As the wave caught on, by the early 1990s sales at Christian bookstores exceeded $3 billion; by 2000, they had reached $4 billion. Evangelical Christians had become an identifiable target market, and as such, they began to make their mark on the evangelical communication industries that catered to their wants and needs.

Although not all of the current Christian media should be classified as evangelical, evangelicals are a driving force behind a substantial portion of it. Let's take a brief look at some representative pieces from the history of various Christian media, in order to get a handle on the enormous scope of all of this.

Books and Magazines

Christianity has a long history of innovation in the creation of books. The Guttenberg Bible, as a matter of fact, was the very first book printed in movable type (in 1450), and is credited by many as the beginning of mass communications in the Western world. Even today, over a half a millennium later, the Bible (in all its various translations) is by far the best selling book year after year. This heritage of printed mass communications has been a foundational part of evangelical history, from the printing of tracts during the Great Awakenings, to the massive numbers of Christian book sales in more modern history.

For instance, as Evangelicalism was spreading its wings in the early 1980s, you might be surprised to know that Francis Schaeffer's *A Christian Manifesto* outsold *Jane Fonda's Workout Book* (a huge seller in its day) at a ratio of two to one. An earlier cousin of the *Left Behind* series, Hal Lindsey's 1970 nonfiction work on prophecy, *The Late Great Planet Earth*, has sold over 28 million copies. The *New York Times* called the book, "the number one nonfiction best-seller of the decade."

In more recent times, Rick Warren's *The Purpose Driven Life* sold over 25 million copies in the first three years of its publication, selling more copies in a single year than any other nonfiction book in history.

And then there's the *Left Behind* series. As of 2006, the twelve books in the series had sold a combined total of a mind-boggling 62 million copies. (To give you some perspective, John Grisham's 17 books have sold a total of about 60 million.) One of the books in the series was the first Christian novel to ever hit #1 on the *New York Times* bestseller list.

Add to this the plethora of specialty Christian magazines (*Christianity Today* alone boasts a circulation of 2.5 million through its 11 Christian specialty magazines) and you have a publishing empire (although certainly not under one magnate) that would make Rupert Murdoch blush.

Radio

From the early days of radio, evangelicals have been in the forefront of this media. As mentioned in Chapter 3, one example was Charles Fuller, whose *Old Fashioned Revival Hour* reached a base of 20 million listeners in the 1930s. At its peak, it was the most popular radio program of its day, with a higher listenership than Amos 'n' Andy,

Charlie McCarthy, and even Bob Hope. Featuring a gospel choir, Fuller's wife Grace reading letters from readers, and Fuller preaching to his congregation on the air, the show serves as a template for similar evangelical radio shows even today.

> ### The Gospel Truth
>
> According to Arbitron (which measures radio listenership), the number of listeners to Christian radio now rivals their secular counterparts. According to one Arbitron report, "Ratings-concious advertisers and ad agencies are now being forced to seriously consider these stations as a part of their media mix."

In recent years, however, more and more Christian radio stations have adopted the familiar "drive time" and music format of other stations, building a steadily growing audience in the process. Through a variety of formats, the growth in Christian radio is impressive. In 1972, there were about 399 Christian radio stations in the country. By 1995, that number had more than tripled to 1,328. By 2005, the number had nearly doubled yet again to over 2,000. Estimates are that Christian radio currently reaches tens of millions of people each week.

Television and Video

The Trinity Broadcasting Network, founded in 1973 by Paul and Jan Crouch, is the nation's most watched Christian broadcasting of its kind. Its holdings include twelve full power and 300 low power stations nationwide, and its 5,000 cable outlets make it accessible to over 70 million households. Its programming includes religious talk shows, original movies, news, music, and special programming for teens and kids. It also broadcasts the services of some of America's largest churches.

Another huge player is CBN, Pat Robertson's empire. It is available in 71 languages in over 200 countries, anchored by Robertson's *700 Club*, which is available through various outlets to over 90 million homes and claims an average daily viewership of over 1 million people.

Perhaps even more ubiquitous are the numerous straight-to-video productions created by and for Christian viewers. A series for kids called *BibleMan* features Willie Aames (from *Eight is Enough* and *Charles in Charge)* as a scripture-quoting superhero. Focus on the Family's *McGee and Me* is a live action and animated show about the trials and tribulations of an eleven-year-old Christian boy. With its solid Christian messages, it has sold well over 15 million copies.

Perhaps the most popular current offering in this genre is *VeggieTales*, a highly creative computer-animated series starring talking vegetables. Its creators have chosen to widen their audience by making *VeggieTales* not as specifically Christian as others in the field (usually using Old Testament stories as the basis for each 30-minute episode), and have thus been able to widen their market appeal. Retail stores such as Target and K-Mart regularly stock the *VeggieTales* titles, as do mainstream toy stores (*VeggieTales* characters have been licensed to Fisher-Price). In 2002, *VeggieTales* produced a feature film, *Jonah*, that received wide theatrical release. When the DVD of the film came out a year later, it sold 1 million copies in three weeks.

Movies

Billy Graham's World Wide Pictures has been producing movies for evangelism since the early 1950s. The company's catalogue includes 56 films. Some of them have been released through major studios and gained wide appeal, such as *The Hiding Place*, which earned a Golden Globe nomination when it was released in 1975. Most of World Wide's releases are meant to be shown in churches, and most carry a very specific evangelistic appeal. The Graham association estimates that over 2 million "decisions for Christ" have been recorded as a result of their films across the years.

Perhaps the most well-known film of this genre during the past few decades is *The Cross and the Switchblade* (1970). Chronicling the story of a gang leader's journey to conversion, the true story starred Erik Estrada as Nicky Cruz (the gang leader), and Pat Boone as Reverend David Wilkerson. Taking more chances than other Christian films of its day, it included scenes of drug use, and even some mild profanity in its depiction of gang life. It is considered a Christian classic, having been translated into over 25 languages, and shown in churches, camps, and other Christian venues across the world.

In modern days, the success of Mel Gibson's *The Passion of the Christ* has shown Hollywood that evangelicals are not only a large potential audience, but a potent marketing force. *Passion* was preceded by a massive grass roots marketing campaign, with special preshowings to evangelical leaders and pastors across the country. This was followed up with extensive church marketing, with the producers of the film sending out invitation cards, door hangers, and posters for church members to hand out in their community to promote the film. Seeing the success of that effort, *The Polar Express* (a film loosely about belief, but with no

> **The Gospel Truth**
>
> While many evangelicals found *The Passion of the Christ* to be a powerful witness, many others found the violence extreme and refused to see the film.

specific Christian message) sent out preview DVDs to churches prior to its 2004 release, along with special study guides that enabled churches to use the film clips in sermons and other venues, and create follow-up discussions in their church.

The Chronicles of Narnia (2005) followed on the heels of these grassroots efforts by expanding them even further, sponsoring special regional gatherings of pastors prior to the movie's release. In addition to handing out posters, invitation cards, and study guides, the film's marketers went ingeniously indigenous: they created extensive pastor-to-pastor marketing, recruiting very typical (i.e., not megachurch) pastors in communities across the country to run local meetings with other church leaders. At these meetings, these pastors discussed full-on multiweek church campaigns and sermons based on the film, inviting their peers to join them in creating these kinds of campaigns and in taking their entire churches to the theater to see the film. The producers of *Narnia* even sponsored a sermon contest on a popular Christian website that offered the winner a free trip to C. S. Lewis's homeland of England.

In late 2006, Twentieth Century Fox launched what is being seen by many as the full maturation of the development of Christian cinema when it unveiled "FoxFaith." FoxFaith is a new branded distribution label from Twentieth Century Fox, created, according to Fox, "to house and distribute its growing portfolio of morally-driven, family-friendly programming." In addition to selling such content through a FoxFaith website (including films such as the recent *Cheaper By the Dozen*, *Garfield*, and *Home Alone 2*, complete with study guides to be used in churches), the studio plans to produce as many as a dozen full-production value films a year with specifically Christian content. These films will have wide releases and marketing budgets to match. These resources, combined with FoxFaith's growing partnerships with key evangelical media players (such as the Dove Foundation) could make FoxFaith the most important player in the future of Christian movies and DVDs.

By far, however, the largest evangelical film effort as of yet in modern years has been the *Jesus* film, sponsored by Campus Crusade for Christ. Based on the gospel of Luke (the filmmakers took great pains to make sure the film was a word-for-word depiction), the film was originally released in 1979 to a limited theater distribution. However, the purpose was much larger than simply a theatrical release. From the beginning, the producers of the film had a much larger strategy in mind to use the film to spread the gospel literally all over the world. Typical of Campus Crusades's business acumen, they put great organization into making sure it happened. Since its release, the *Jesus* film has become a separate missionary ministry that takes the film everywhere from house parties in suburban U.S. cities to the deepest jungles of Africa, where people had never even seen a movie before. It has been translated into an astounding 962 languages, and currently has a staff of 4,600 showing the film in over 100 countries. The makers of the film estimate that it has had 6 *billion* viewings since its release.

CCM–The Contemporary Christian Music Explosion

From its roots in the late 1960s and early 1970s, contemporary Christian music has seen a meteoric rise in popularity. But it is also the place where there has been perhaps the most internal conflict within the evangelical media world.

From its beginning, Christian rock had to struggle with being considered too worldly for the church, and too churchy for the world. After years of fighting this battle, it is now virtually universally accepted in Evangelicalism, with its form even being a part of the vast majority of weekly services in evangelical churches (many of whom use soft-rock praise choruses as their main form of musical worship).

It has also gained the respect of the mainstream. Currently, Christian rock in all of its various forms (pop, alternative, heavy metal, reggae, hip-hop, etc.) commands a very impressive six percent of overall music sales in the United States. At nearly 50 million units a year, that's more than the total sales of classical and jazz combined. Christian artists regularly outsell secular artists, and fill stadiums and arenas on their tours. Most of the early Christian labels have been purchased by mega-media conglomerates, such as CBS or Sony. Gone are the days when Mom and Pop record companies produced the artists and sold the product at church gatherings.

> **In Their Own Words**
>
> "Well, my brothers criticize me
> Say I'm just too strange to believe
> And the others just avoid me
> Say my faith is so naïve;
> I'm too sacred for the sinners
> And the saints wish I would leave."
>
> —From the song "Stuck In the Middle" (1981) by Christian artist Mark Heard

Leaders of the movement include diverse personalities. There is Larry Norman, generally considered to be the father of Christian rock, who opened for artists like The Greatful Dead, The Doors, and Janis Joplin, remaining straight ahead in his faith in the midst of the secular rock culture. Then there's Amy Grant, the pop cross-over whose recordings have sold over twenty million copies, and whose 1991 hit *Baby, Baby* (completely devoid of evangelical or religious content) eventually became the number-one record in America—an achievement that *Contemporary Christian Magazine* (the flagship evangelical publication in this realm) called "the most significant event in the history of contemporary Christian music." In the eighties, there were heavy metal bands like Stryper, whose glam-rock look was quite controversial in its day; as well as Michael W. Smith, who was once named to *People* magazine's "Most Beautiful People" list.

Today, there is more of an emphasis on praise and worship music in the CCM charts, with artists like David Crowder and Third Day leading the way. There is also a new breed of Christian bands who are dropping the Christian label altogether, hoping to make a creative and spiritual impact as artists in the wider musical and public arena. The band Switchfoot is perhaps the best current example.

Bands like Switchfoot show that as Christian music has grown more diverse and sophisticated, the artists have continued to wrestle with their identity. Many have crossed over to the mainstream arena, taking their Christian fan base with them, and tempering their message accordingly. Others have stayed squarely within the evangelical fold, creating music that is specifically targeted to the already convinced. But regardless of their target, Christian rock is here to stay.

Harnessing the Internet

One of the most intriguing areas of evangelical media is the growing online presence of Evangelicalism.

According to the *Pew Internet & American Life Project* (2004), 64 percent of wired Americans have used the internet for spiritual or religious purposes. With over one million "God sites" online, every major religion (and quite a few that are, shall we say, out of the mainstream) are represented. For the most part, the study found that the most common religious use of the internet is as a means of seeking out individual spiritual growth. Interestingly enough, online religious searching tends to increase activity of the individuals with organized religion. In other words, the internet is a portal to the church.

The percentage of evangelicals using the web for spiritual purposes is even higher than the general population, reported at 69 percent. Currently, key internet sites for evangelicals include gospelcom.net, which bills itself as an "alliance of over 300 online Christian ministries"; beliefnet.com, which features interviews, links to numerous other Christian sites, daily devotionals, and articles by popular Christian writers; and Christianitytoday.com, which includes all of the content from the publisher's magazines, as well as a host of just about every other kind of information relevant to Evangelicalism (including everything from Christian school directories to Christian chat rooms).

As with all things in cyberspace, the internet presence of Evangelicalism is a moving target because it is growing and changing so fast. A growing edge for evangelicals, for instance, is using the web as a resource for ministry training and church curriculum distribution. Overall, as a means of spreading the word, the web is full of more possibilities than have yet been imagined. At the same time it raises some interesting questions about virtual community and the consistency of the evangelical message.

One important early leader in actualizing the possibilities of the Internet in this arena is theooze.com, whose postmodern focus is quite congruent with its Internet form. It features articles, blogging, links, message boards, media reviews, sign-ups for conferences that it sponsors, and, of course, a store. At this writing, it is probably the best evangelically oriented example of a community space for interactive information sharing, and likely represents (with many other similar websites) the next-gen form of Christian media assimilation.

In addition to internet sites, most churches now have websites of their own, which at this point tend to mainly look like electronic brochures online. Some, however, are taking a more interactive approach including blogging and message boards, and many churches have taken advantage of podcasting as a means of distributing weekly sermons.

> **In Their Own Words**
>
> "A church without walls where the sky is the limit."
> —The slogan of Godfocus Internet Church, a church that exists solely on the internet (www. godfocus.net)

Why Is All of This Necessary?

The massive amount of Christian media that is available begs the question of what all of it is used for. Indeed, it is possible for evangelicals to surround themselves with Christian books, music, DVDs, movies, and internet sites to the point that they literally live inside of a cultural bubble. But isn't that contrary to their core passion and calling of reaching out to the world around them?

To understand the typical evangelical sensibility in all of this, it is helpful to identify five major uses of Christian media for the evangelical. Within these purposes, the historic populism of Evangelicalism comes together with the characteristic spiritual pragmatism of the movement:

◆ **Evangelism.** Much of the media, as we have seen, is specifically designed to reach out to others with the message of Jesus. This can be either overtly, as in the early Billy Graham movies, or more gently, as in the songs of bands like Switchfoot that raise important life questions and thus plant a seed that will cause people to think about their spiritual need. Many of these more "gentle" message spreaders (including Switchfoot) would eschew the evangelism tag altogether, saying that they are simply artists making music for any audience (see the last bullet below).

◆ **Spiritual growth.** Some of the media is designed specifically for evangelicals as a means of helping them to gain more knowledge of how to grow in their faith. Podcasts of sermons, certain types of books and magazines, and worship music CDs often fall into this category. (Although many would argue here as well, saying that worship CDs can also be important evangelistic tools to be given to those who are not followers of Christ.)

◆ **Information.** Most evangelicals believe that the general media of our culture is obviously biased to the left; news programs like *The 700 Club* offer a different perspective.

◆ **Wholesome entertainment.** Christian music, kids' videos, or even fiction are often simply a way for evangelicals to unwind. It's tough these days to find good entertainment that doesn't in some way collide with Christian values. Evangelicals appreciate what *VeggieTales*, for example, calls, "Sunday morning values, Saturday morning fun."

◆ **Artistry.** Here (finally!) is where pragmatism takes a back seat. There is a growing number of evangelical artists who see that art is simply good and valuable in and of itself. Believing that God's basic nature is creative, they understand that human creativity is a key part of the expression of God's image in humanity. For them, and for other evangelicals who share their views, creating media forms that aspire to free the aesthetic imagination needs no justification. Further, grounded as they are in the perspective of spiritual truth, these artists see that they have a unique opportunity to develop the highest levels of creative communication.

The Media Is the Message

Of course, coupling "evangelical" with "the highest levels of creative communication" aesthetics may seem like a glaring oxymoron. To be honest, much of what passes for creativity in evangelical media is second-rate (again, my gift for understatement coming through). Indeed, if the media is the message, then the message of evangelicals is often lame. This raises some important questions for evangelical media if its purveyors intend it to live up to the importance of its message, and if they intend the media they are producing to have lasting impact. This is a conversation that is very current in Evangelicalism, and below are some issues that evangelical creatives wrestle with in this regard:

◆ **Creativity in a closed culture.** By definition, creativity needs a wide palette to draw from. Many evangelicals, because of their theology and their lifestyle, are quite separatist in their daily lives from artistic influences that could help them grow. Critical engagement with the wider culture is an important learned skill that needs to be developed among many evangelical media creators. Artistic depth needs to be a developmental value; quite frankly, people are tired of *Jesus junk*.

def•i•ni•tion

Jesus junk is a name often used for the plethora of tacky products (Christian knick-knacks, t-shirts, etc.) that are sold primarily in Christian bookstores.

Culture Clash!

Speaking of creativity … Looking for a gift for your evangelical friend? Try Virtuous Woman perfume (according to its maker, when people ask what your friend is wearing, it opens the door for her to share her faith). Or, for a man or a woman, how about Follow the Son flip-flops? They feature patterned soles that leave the message "Follow Jesus" in the sand.

◆ **The counter-intuitive power of the "outsider" voice.** Christian media creators often lose their distinctive voice by imitating the established media around them, instead of blazing new trails. Frequently, the power of art is that it speaks with an outside (often irritating) perspective. Christians do have an outside perspective, and they have a unique opportunity through it to speak prophetically into the culture. It is one of their most important artistic gifts to the world at large.

◆ **Learning to communicate in intriguing subtlety.** Jesus spoke in parables. Perhaps that is because spiritual truth cannot always be understood in literal terms. There is power in mystery and questions. Evangelicals often feel a compulsion to "close the loop" and tie everything up with a nice bow. It doesn't always work that way in real life, and people (especially those who are new in genuinely seeking God) will appreciate Christian media that doesn't claim to have all the answers.

◆ **Balancing artist identity with economic reality.** This is a perennial problem for artists of all stripes; evangelicals have an added layer of issues here (particularly in the music world), due to the tension of working for media distributors who often pressure them to change not only their creative content, but their spiritual message, in order to reach a wider audience.

◆ **An honest perspective about who is listening.** Often, evangelical media claims to speak to "unbelievers" but in actuality is preaching to the choir. Honestly recognizing this is desperately necessary for many evangelicals, as a first step for them in learning how to actually (and effectively) share their perspective with others.

There is an expanding number of evangelicals who are working through these and a myriad of other questions that face the fast-changing environment of media engagement. And if history proves anything, it is that evangelicals are strong communication innovators who *can* learn to speak to the culture—if they will first listen to it.

The Least You Need to Know

◆ Evangelical media of all types regularly outsells its secular counterparts.

◆ Evangelicals see various media as useful for sharing their faith with others, as well as for growing in their own faith.

◆ A growing number of evangelical media creators see themselves first and foremost as artists, and are working hard to drop the "Christian" label.

◆ Creativity in evangelical media faces a more complex road than it does in other, more secular contexts, due to the spiritual beliefs of the media creators, the distributors, and the end users.

Chapter 17

Lending a Helping Hand:
The Parachurch

In This Chapter

- ◆ What is a "parachurch" organization?
- ◆ How have these organizations increased the impact of Evangelicalism?
- ◆ Are churches and parachurches in competition?
- ◆ What challenges do parachurch groups face in the future?

"Are you still breathing? Then be encouraged, and get busy!"

Thus wrote the founder of one of the largest parachurch organizations in the world—himself dependent on oxygen—just four days before his death.

On July 20, 2001, Dr. Bill Bright, founder of Campus Crusade for Christ, drew his last breath. In a letter written on July 16, and posted online the day after his death by *Christianity Today*, Bright's characteristic energy and passion showed through in the above quote. Its three-point message is a perfect picture of a man who literally lived and breathed his mission, who was an incredible encourager of others, and whose busyness produced more than most can hope to accomplish in several lifetimes. At the time of his death, Dr. Bright's ministry had grown from a dream to reach college students that he and his wife shared in 1951, to a ministry with 26,000 staff in over 100 countries and a budget of a half billion dollars.

The quote is also a good summary of the work of parachurch organizations (para is roughly translated from a Greek word meaning *alongside*) throughout the land. They are definitely alive, with more than 100,000 of them in operation through a one hundred-fold expansion in the last century. By definition, they are encouragers, coming alongside established churches to accomplish specific tasks around the Christian mission. And they are most definitely busy—as a matter of fact, sometimes much busier than churches (which is where a bit of controversy enters the story).

In this chapter, we'll take a look at the phenomenon that perhaps more than any other single force has shaped and created an overall evangelical "movement" across the United States: the parachurch.

Defining the Parachurch

Like defining Evangelicalism itself, the diversity of *parachurch* organizations makes defining them somewhat complex. *The Dictionary of American Christianity* gives us this: "Voluntary, not-for-profit associations of Christians working outside denominational control to achieve some specific ministry or social service."

def•i•ni•tion

Parachurch literally means, "alongside" the church. As defined in Chapter 4, it denotes a plethora of organizations that have a Christian mission, but are not a church.

Another way to define them is to survey their wide range of services. Here are a few of the activities of just a few of the wide-ranging parachurch organizations currently in existence:

- *Re-enactors for Jesus Christ* reprints religious tracts from the Civil War era and distributes them to people participating in Civil War reenactments. Since 1984, they claim that over 900 people have made decisions for Christ through their ministry, which includes holding Sunday Services at many of the Civil War battle reenactments held across the country.

- *The Eden Conservancy* was founded in 1993, and is partnered with a group of other organizations known as Target Earth. The Eden Conservancy buys up thousands of acres of at-risk rainforest land, saving it for the benefit of the earth and humanity. In the name of being good stewards of God's creation, they are representative of a plethora of other Christian environmental parachurch organizations.

◆ *The Missionary Computer Fellowship* in Orlando, Florida collects computers, upgrades them, and then gives them away, or sells them at radical discounts (up to 75 percent) to Christian workers.

◆ *Athletes in Action* (a ministry of Campus Crusade for Christ) sends out high-level, former college basketball players to play against varsity teams. At half-time, the Athletes in Action players share their faith with those who have come to watch and play. In addition, each year the group sponsors a Super Bowl Breakfast—an NFL-sanctioned event in which marquee NFL celebrities share their faith. The group also sponsors sports camps and clinics, and creates high-quality DVDs that share the testimonies of sports stars.

◆ *Christians in the Visual Arts* exists to encourage those in the field of fine arts who are believers to develop to their highest artistic potential, and to establish a Christian presence in the secular art world. Towards that end, the group sponsors exhibits, conferences, travel tours with artistic educational missions, and online and live auctions, among a host of other opportunities.

From the Civil War reenactors, to rainforest activists, to computer nerds and sports jocks and fine artists—this list only scratches the surface of the amazing diversity of parachurch organizations that shape the face of Evangelicalism today.

In *The Prospering Parachurch*, authors Wesley Willmer, J. David Schmidt, and Martyn Smith list what they call a "taxonomy" of parachurches. As a result of their extensive research, the authors list sixteen general categories of parachurch organizations, from health care organizations to "constituency-based ministries" (ministries that work with a specific demographic, e.g., youth, prisoners, business people). Within the broader categories, they list up to 24 specific subcategories of ministries, each of which represents hundreds or even thousands of even more specific ministries.

The fact is, if you can think of a need or an interest, there is no doubt a parachurch organization out there to partner with. And although the organizations profiled in the bulleted list above are fairly small, there are many parachurches whose staff and budgets rival those of some of the largest corporations in America.

A Very Short History of the Parachurch

Although its modern form carries unique distinctives, parachurch organizations have been around throughout the history of the United States. From Catholic orders that settled much of the American West as missions to voluntary associations such as the Young Men's Christian Association of America, they are part and parcel of the history of our country.

In the early nineteenth century the organizational form that eventually morphed into the typical modern parachurch structure began to emerge. There were missionary organizations, independent educational groups, moral reform groups, and even Bible tract societies (like the ones who printed tracts during the Civil War, mentioned above). As the twentieth century dawned and the industrial revolution began making its mark, the form of the societies changed with the times, evidencing more business-like structures and becoming more able to reach more people.

Today, the most successful parachurch groups have organizational structures, flow charts, mission statements, and strategic planning mechanisms that would give any for-profit group a run for its money. For example, in the case of both Campus Crusade and the Willow Creek Association (both of which are profiled in this chapter and the next), the ministries' current presidents are Harvard MBAs. Both wrote case studies about their ministries as a part of their time at Harvard. This kind of business acumen is characteristic of many of the larger evangelical parachurches, which have had to learn the business of ministry in order to grow to their current levels of impact.

> **In Their Own Words**
>
> "Customer service, Growth management, Marketing strategy, Service management, Social enterprise, Strategic planning."
>
> —Description of the subjects covered in a Harvard Business School case study of Willow Creek Community Church, as listed in the Harvard Business Online catalogue

It is fair to say, however, that the business is only in the service of the ministry. Parachurches—large and small—generally owe their existence to a primarily spiritual vision (or visionary). Their focus is a need that must be met—a mission to be accomplished in the service of Christ.

Three Modern Parachurches

The idea of a mission is clearly seen in several of the largest and most obviously evangelical parachurches, three of which we'll profile in the coming sections.

Focus On the Family

In the late 1960s, the sexual revolution was in full swing. And California was leading the way, with the Summer of Love in 1967 in San Francisco, and the southern California seed-bed of music, movies, and the beach culture.

At least one Southern Californian was not happy with what he saw. Finishing up a Ph.D. in the field of child development in 1967, James Dobson was a pediatrician in Los Angeles who felt that the trajectory of the culture was headed in an unhealthy direction. In 1970, he published a book called *Dare to Discipline*, containing a no-nonsense approach to child rearing that advocated strong parental authority and traditional values—both seemingly out of step with the times. But Dobson's approach struck a chord. The book sold over three million copies, and became the foundation of a new ministry for the young physician.

Dobson began to lead weekend seminars based on the principles in his book, and eventually took a year-long leave of absence from his job in pediatrics at the Children's Hospital of Los Angeles. After seventeen years on the hospital staff, and fourteen years teaching as an Associate Clinical Professor of Pediatrics at the USC School of Medicine, in 1976 he left both to pursue his growing ministry. His seminars became a series of films that could be used by local churches, and he began a weekly radio broadcast. Thus, the ministry of Focus on the Family was born.

> ### In Their Own Words
>
> "Lest I be misunderstood … I am not recommending that your home be harsh and oppressive …. I am recommending a simple principle: when you are defiantly challenged [by your child], win decisively ….When the child asks, 'Who's in charge?' tell him. When he mutters, 'Who loves me?' take him into your arms and surround him with affection."
>
> —James Dobson in *Dare to Discipline*

Because of the wide range of issues affecting the family, Focus on the Family has become an organization with a wide reach. It has been one of the most important players politically in the religious right. Dr. Dobson served on Jimmy Carter's White House Conference on Families in 1980, was appointed by President Reagan to several high-level commissions, and has advised both Bush White Houses. Along the way, Focus on the Family launched a purely political organization, the Family Research Council, to be a lobbying force for family issues on Capitol Hill. In 1992, Family Research Council became a self-sustaining entity, and is today one of the most important religious right political organizations.

Besides its political activities, Focus on the Family has become a Christian media giant, producing one of the best-selling Christian video series of all time (*McGee and Me*), in addition to retaining a huge ongoing radio listenership. Dr. Dobson has written 35 books subsequent to *Dare to Discipline* (which has now sold over 4.5 million copies), in addition to creating five other film series. Approximately 2.3 million people subscribe to the organization's ten specialty magazines, which include titles targeted to adolescent boys and girls, parenting, and legislative issues.

Today, the ministry has a budget in excess of $120 million, 1,300 employees, and a 47-acre campus. It is affiliated with 36 state groups, and has 74 different international ministries. It has created ministries for Christian attorneys, teachers, and doctors, among others. It continues to produce a wide variety of Christian media, and it is estimated that Dobson's radio audience is over 200 million people a day, through over 9,000 radio facilities across the world, in 116 countries and 15 languages.

World Vision

According to an article published in *Christianity Today*, Bob Pierce was "an extreme version of post-WWII Evangelicalism: entrepreneurial, energetic, independent, and out to evangelize the world." Although his zeal for his mission ultimately consumed his personal life, Bob Pierce did reach the world through founding perhaps the largest parachurch organization in history: World Vision.

It all started as Bob, as a Youth for Christ worker, saw the extreme needs of children orphaned by the Korean War. Bob created a way that individuals or families in the United States could sponsor a child from South Korea, providing for the child's food, education and health care with a modest monthly donation. The plan worked, and soon World Vision expanded its ministry beyond Korea. Seeing the underlying needs that were creating the poverty of people, the organization soon expanded into larger and more multifaceted relief and development efforts, and today is involved in everything from micro-finance loans to help the poor develop their own businesses, to HIV/AIDS relief work and advocacy.

In 1967, Bob Pierce resigned from World Vision. The organization continued to grow under the leadership of men like Stan Mooneyham, and later Ted Engstrom. During the 1960s, the organization continued its expansion by beginning its global relief efforts. In the '70s the organization began to provide vocational and agricultural training to its sponsored families and communities, which eventually evolved into World Vision's current community development work. The 1980s and 1990s saw continued expansion, as World Vision became a major international player during the famine in Ethiopia and moved into international advocacy for child welfare and justice, as well as AIDS relief. In the current decade World Vision's expansion continues, providing multiple kinds of assistance to victims of the 2004 tsunami, as well as taking a lead role providing relief for the African famine.

Culture Clash!

Evangelicals are often accused of not caring for the real needs of the world. World Vision stands as a $300 million a year refutation.

Perhaps one of the most interesting aspects of World Vision's operations is its governance. Seeing the need for indigenous leadership in the areas it served, World Vision created a unique system. The organization operates through an interdependent partnership of national offices in various countries, bound together by a common mission statement and shared core values. Each national office has its own board of directors, and an international board oversees the overall World Vision partnership. In all of this, World Vision's goal is to keep decision-making as close to the ground as possible, while maintaining the overall partnership in a healthy way.

Today, World Vision has a budget of approximately $1 billion, with over 23,000 staff serving in 100 countries. About 80 percent of its funding comes from private sources, the rest coming from governments, multilateral agencies, and in-kind donations. Its primary focus continues to be on children through community development, disaster relief, and global advocacy on issues such as child exploitation, AIDS, and education.

Campus Crusade for Christ

In 1951, Bill Bright had a vision. With the post-war boom in America drawing thousands to college, Bright, who at the time was running a gourmet foods business, saw a market opportunity: no one was actively reaching out to college students—the leaders of tomorrow. Inspired by a very specific vision from God (that included a personal, dramatic experience of receiving a calling from God which he was always reticent to talk about publicly), Bright dropped out of Fuller Seminary and started Campus Crusade for Christ on the UCLA campus. A combination of building relationships with students, evangelistic zeal, and a unique ability to develop training processes and materials brought Bright and his wife more staff and more students in the years to come. By 1959, Campus Crusade was active on over 40 campuses and in three countries.

In 1965, sensing the need for a tool that would make it easy for people to share their faith, Bright wrote a gospel tract that he called, *Have You Heard of the Four Spiritual*

Laws? The tract presented a concise, four-step explanation of how to become a Christian. Eventually, it would become likely the most widely distributed religious booklet in history, with over 2.5 billion printed by 2006. Further, the booklet had an inestimable influence on the message of twentieth century Evangelicalism, effectively becoming the core message of Christianity for a generation of rising baby-boomer evangelicals.

In 1972, at the height of the Jesus Movement, Campus Crusade sponsored *Explo '72*— a gathering of over 80,000 college students in Dallas that featured celebrity guests and in-depth "discipleship" training, and which created a cultural impact far beyond those in attendance. The conference was expanded and taken international in 1974, when *Explo '74* trained over 300,000 in evangelism in Seoul, Korea.

In 1976, Campus Crusade created its most far-reaching experience yet, going beyond college campuses with the "I Found It!" campaign, an evangelistic campaign geared to reach entire cities. By 1979, the campaign had gone international, and Campus Crusade estimates that 3.5 million people made decisions for Christ as a result. Further, in 1979, the organization launched its *Jesus* film project (see Chapter 16), arguably its most far-reaching evangelism initiative ever.

Throughout the 1980s and the 1990s the organization continued to grow, building its core campus ministries as it expanded into all kinds of other territory. By 1996, when Bill Bright was awarded the prestigious Templeton Prize for Progress in Religion, Campus Crusade had a plethora of specialized ministries, reaching everyone from American corporate executives to some of the remotest villages in undeveloped areas around the world.

Reflecting Bright's business abilities, Campus Crusade has been called the most efficient religious ministry in the United States (*Money Magazine*) and the top religious charity in the nation (*U.S. News and World Report; Chronicle of Philanthropy*). Today, the ministry has over 26,000 employees involved in over 60 separate ministries, and is led by Steve Douglass, who was chosen by Bright as his successor in 2001.

Key Parachurch Characteristics

While the diversity of parachurch organizations is almost unimaginably wide, the stories above show that there are some prevailing characteristics common to many of them. Together, they help to fill in the picture of why these organizations have had such a huge impact on Evangelicalism.

First, most parachurch organizations tend to operate with a strong entrepreneurial ethos. This is also a key characteristic of Evangelicalism as a whole, and much of that impetus has come from parachurch activity. Parachurch groups usually start because of a willingness to try new things, to break out of the box, to do things differently—all key entrepreneurial characteristics. Further, they also tend to be much faster moving; in particular, they are able to respond faster to cultural shifts than a traditional church or denomination. As a matter of fact, many start precisely because of shifts in the culture or the overall environment (social, political, etc.) that are not being met by existing churches or institutions.

> **In Their Own Words**
>
> *Come Help Change the World* is the title of one of Bill Bright's early books; the "small" goal suggested by the title clearly reflects the visionary, entrepreneurial spirit of many parachurch organizations.

A second key trait of parachurch organizations is that they move beyond traditional church or denominational structures. In other words, they transcend them. Finding common ground by moving to higher ground, parachurches are often more tactically successful in their missions than traditional Christian bodies because they have a higher level of freedom. The Billy Graham Evangelistic Association is a good example of this, as Graham toned down fundamentalism, welcomed Pentecostalism, and cooperated with Catholicism in the context of his city-wide crusades. In a traditional church or denominational environment, much of that transcendence would have been impossible.

This transcendence also creates a lack of connection to any one church authority, as well as enabling a more business-like model that is typically too hard to implement in the much more "political" environment of a local church or denomination.

A third characteristic common to many parachurch groups is the presence of a strong, passionate, dynamic leader, especially at the organization's inception. James Dobson, Bob Pierce, Bill Bright, Billy Graham—all of these were men of unusual personal vision and passion. In each of these cases, and in many beyond, the leaders claimed a very specific supernatural calling from God to engage in their work. Often, the organization exists as a working out of that vision in the reality of the culture. Regardless of what you believe about the validity of these types of callings, it is obvious that a common characteristic of these groups is a clear and personal sense of divine mission on the part of their founders. If you tend to be less skeptical, you might even see evidence of God's hand in the quite amazing growth of some of these groups, not to mention their personal impact on the people involved with them.

Related to that is a fourth characteristic, which is that successful parachurches tend to be focused on a specific purpose. As they grow, many have tended to diversify, but even in their vast numbers, Focus on the Family is still focused on family issues, World Vision is still about giving practical help to those in need around the world, and Campus Crusade is still primarily about crusading on campus. The specific focus of a parachurch group (especially at its beginning) often allows it a degree of intensity that is missing in a church or denominational environment. Often, the parachurch is meeting a specific need that the church is not addressing effectively, providing alternative solutions that can be implemented due to a higher degree of freedom or a lower degree of attachment to tradition.

Finally, parachurch groups tend to be more culturally sensitive to their environment. Churches and denominations can by their nature become disconnected with cultural changes. Parachurches operate much closer to the ground, again, often having their impetus in a cultural shift that creates a disconnect between the traditional church and the world around it. Not only does this happen on a social or political level, it can also happen on a technological level. Parachurches are often way out in front of more traditional ministries with regard to their assimilation and use of new technology.

The Impact of the Parachurch

It is almost impossible to overstate the impact of the parachurch on Evangelicalism. It may well be accurate to say that parachurch organizations actually *created* Evangelicalism as a movement—that without them we might have a lot of churches with similar beliefs, but nowhere near the modern evangelical network and ethos that exists today. The incredible impact of parachurch organizations can be summarized within several key observations:

- ◆ **Parachurches are often the pioneers of new ministry trends.** Their entrepreneurial characteristics make them incubators for new ideas in ministry—some that succeed and some that fail. The successful ideas pioneered by parachurches are often picked up, extended, and given ongoing life by churches or denominations, who are often unable to experiment freely, but who can and usually do pick up ideas that have gained a track record.

- ◆ **Parachurch organizations create communication lines between traditional ministries.** For example, at a typical Promise Keepers rally (see Chapter 12), men from nearly every denomination rub shoulders, creating friendships and cross-pollinating ideas. This is multiplied thousands of times as various parachurch groups transcend denominational lines and bring church leaders together. Further, through big events, publications, and other media outlets, parachurch organizations create a common culture among evangelicals that has resulted in the sense of an "evangelical movement" in our culture at large.

♦ **Parachurch organizations train evangelical leaders.** Campus Crusade recruits thousands of students onto their staff who later move into both parachurch and church ministry settings, both as professional pastors and lay leaders. Again, this is but the tip of the iceberg of the kind of training impact parachurch groups have in developing long-term ministry leaders in the church and in the culture at large. Further, the parachurch provides opportunities for full-time ministry work to talented leaders who are not interested in a more traditional ministry ordination track.

♦ **Parachurch groups provide a day-to-day presence that enhances evangelical identity in everyday life.** From James Dobson's radio broadcast that beams into millions of households daily, to the World Vision project engineer on site at a water treatment plant, parachurch organizations provide an immediate, ongoing presence of Evangelicalism that churches are often unable to provide. This presence both cements the connection of many evangelicals to their faith on a daily basis, and reaches into the lives of nonevangelicals who would never darken the door of a church.

Challenges for the Parachurch

As parachurch organizations enter a new era, they face several important challenges.

First, they face the continuing challenge of resource development and (dare I say it) competition with churches. Indeed, according to the latest statistics, giving to parachurch groups outpaces giving to churches ($100 billion to $94 billion). Can this trend continue without damaging the churches that parachurch groups exist to serve? The answer lies in a spirit of cooperation—not competition—between the two. Some excellent models of this kind of symbiotic relationship are already evident; many are currently building.

A second challenge is the culture shift of a postmodern world that in terms of spiritual endeavors values a business model less and less. Most of the large parachurch groups came of age in the baby boomer era, where their business-like efficiency and energy was a breath of fresh air to a generation moving away from what they saw as a lethargic traditional church. However, a new generation is arising that is skeptical of how business models and efficiency translate into authentic spirituality. Further, in a post-modern world that values diversity, most parachurches are extremely homogeneous.

Finally, many of the most successful parachurches have been founded in the last 50 years or so. As such, many have (as is typical of all organizations) become addicted to their own paradigms. Perhaps the most important challenge for them in the future will be to continue to innovate in the context of a more complex—and slow moving—maturing institutional environment. In short, many parachurches are in danger from their own success.

In Their Own Words

"Old pictures of parachurch staff look remarkably similar. They feature a group of white men sitting around a large table or standing in front of a new building."

—Wesley Willmer, J. David Schmidt, and Martyn Smith in *The Prospering Parachurch*

And yet, the future is full of possibilities. One particularly interesting one is a trend that is developing where the parachurch paradigm is turned on its head: churches themselves are beginning to spin off parachurches. This is happening most frequently among a group of churches that may well be the most identifiable symbols of Evangelicalism in America, and to which our attention turns in the next chapter: the mega church.

The Least You Need to Know

- Parachurch organizations are groups that work on a Christian mission, but are not a church.

- Parachurch groups are a very important reason that Evangelicalism has been able to coalesce as an identifiable movement in the modern world.

- The diversity of parachurch groups is astounding.

- As they move into the future, parachurch groups and churches will need to focus on cooperation, not competition.

18

Meet the Megachurch

In This Chapter

- ◆ What is a megachurch?
- ◆ The story of two of the most influential megachurches
- ◆ Common traits that describe megachurches
- ◆ Criticisms of the megachurch phenomenon

It was a moment that no one who was there would ever forget.

It happened in the United Center in Chicago, home of the Chicago Bulls basketball team, with 20,000 people packed into the seats. But the people weren't there for basketball.

This was the twentieth anniversary celebration of Willow Creek Community Church, which when this event took place (1995) was the largest church in North America. In order to accommodate the crowds, the church had to rent out the arena. Quite a far jump from the 1975 group of barely-out-of-their-teens kids who started a new kind of church, with no experience and no idea of what to expect. One thing that they did know, however, which became a rallying cry through the years for the church: people matter to God.

The evening had been filled with celebration, music, and tears of joy. The incredible history of this church, which had started a worldwide movement of "seeker churches," had been recounted. There was even a videotaped greeting from then President Bill Clinton. But the moment that topped every other that evening was a simple one that brought the rallying cry of the church to the center. At one point in the service, all the lights were turned out, and everyone who had become a Christian through the ministry of the church was asked to turn on a small, candlelike penlight. As each small light came on across the auditorium—thousands upon thousands—the impact was overwhelming. Scarcely an eye was dry throughout the arena. The message was clear. People mattered to this church, too.

Here was the megachurch at its best.

In this chapter, we'll take a look at the impact and the controversy surrounding these churches, unique in all of the history of Christianity, that are so much a part of the evangelical experience.

What Is a Megachurch?

Most scholars define the megachurch as a church with a sustained attendance of 2,000 or more. Until very recently, only a handful of them existed. Indeed, according to recent studies by the Hartford Institute for Religious Research and the Leadership Network (from which all of the statistics in this section come), at the beginning of the twentieth century, there were maybe a half a dozen megachurches. By the 1960s, there were no more than 16, the largest with a weekly attendance just shy of 6,000. But through the 1970s, and particularly in the 1980s, there was an explosion. By 1990 there were 350 of these churches; by 2000, the number had doubled to 600; and by 2006, the number had more than doubled yet again. As of this writing, there are a little over 1,200 megachurches in the United States.

The size of these churches ranges from 2,000 to approximately 30,000. Averaging the attendance figures, the typical megachurch sees about 3,000–4,000 people a week come through its doors (only 16 percent have over 5,000 in attendance). Still, added together, that means that well over 4 million people a week are a part of this. Studies show that the typical megachurch attendee is college educated, usually young and married with kids. These folks not only attend the churches, they support them—the average megachurch budget is around $6 million per year.

That budget supports a typical staff of 20–25 pastors (in addition to the Senior Pastor), and anywhere from 30–50 additional administrative and program staff (some of the largest megachurches have staff that number into the hundreds). Most megachurches meet in facilities that are too small to hold all their people at once, so typically 3–4 services are held over the course of a weekend. Sometimes, multiple services are held simultaneously on the same campus (stylistically targeted to different demographics), and some churches even broadcast parts of their services (usually the pastor's message) to satellite sites up to an hour's driving time from the central location. At these satellite campuses, live music and other worship elements are experienced in addition to the video feed.

> **The Gospel Truth**
>
> Even though megachurches have large budgets, according to a study by the Hartford Institute for Religious Studies, there is not a heavy emphasis on fund-raising in most of them. The comprehensive study shows that, contrary to popular belief, raising money is "often a low priority" most of the time at most megachurches.

But it's certainly not all about the worship service for these churches. The plethora of programs they offer, from recovery groups to outdoors clubs, from kids to singles to senior citizen's ministries, make them seven-day-a-week operations. Indeed, one could spend all week at many and never do the same thing twice. The diversity of their programming is often likened to a spiritual shopping mall—a one-stop place for all your spiritual needs. This consumer mentality, of course, does not sit well with everyone, and megachurches receive quite a bit of criticism from both within Christianity and from without.

However you see them, these are indisputably the largest churches in the history of Christendom, and they defy categories. Part church, part parachurch, part social service agency, and even part denomination, they play a vital role in Evangelicalism.

Where Did All These Churches Come From?

Let's take a look at the societal and religious trends that have come together in the last few decades to create this phenomenon.

The Church Growth Movement

In 1954, Donald McGavran, former missionary and soon-to-be first Dean of Fuller Theological Seminary's School of World Missions, published *The Bridges of God*, launching a revolution in the way Christian missionaries reached out to new cultures.

In 1970 (while at Fuller), McGavran followed up with a book called *Understanding Church Growth*, which became a classic in the field of study that is now generally called church growth. The insights of the church growth field, combining theology with sociology to forge a much more pragmatic approach to reaching out with the gospel, are the roots of the megachurch movement. (See Chapter 4 for more details on both the church growth movement and its other leaders in addition to McGavran.)

In particular, the "homogeneous unit" principle that McGavran popularized, stating that individuals of similar culture were most likely to respond to the gospel when they did not have to cross culture barriers to do so, was the foundational academic backing. For young church leaders in the 1960s and 1970s, there was an obvious disconnect between the culture of a typical Christian church and the culture of the person who was not a Christian. McGavran's thinking freed many to explore developing the type of church that would be faithful to the gospel in the context of the modern world, but that would not require someone to "cross cultures" into the culture of the existing church.

> **In Their Own Words**
>
> "It takes no great acumen to see that ... unbelievers understand the gospel better when expounded by their own kind of people."
>
> —Donald McGavran in *Understanding Church Growth*

This new mind-set came together with the growing insights of modern management (also a key part of the overall academic milieu of the era) to create a philosophy of ministry that was crucial to the development of the megachurch. In addition to target marketing applications (very similar to McGavran's "homogeneous unit" principle), the church growth movement assimilated a modern pragmatic emphasis that included specific measurements (e.g., numbers of people in church), and the application of further modern business-type techniques.

All of this added up in general to a new way of looking at the possibilities of a church. And as this type of thinking began to be disseminated in seminaries and pastors' conferences across the land, it created a context that showed many that a megachurch was not simply the result of the unusual gifts of a specific pastor. Church leaders everywhere began to believe that they too, could develop a megachurch.

The Modern Worldview

All of this theological and academic thinking converged with a time of huge cultural change, creating a synergy that was quite unique (the less skeptical might even say divinely planned). A new generation of church leaders was ready to take on a new generation of spiritual seekers, whose characteristics were tailor made for a new kind of church. Some of the key characteristics of the rising baby boomer population in this regard included …

- A desire to "change the world"—to connect with a cause that was greater than themselves.

- A high value on choice—rising boomers were used to having options.

- A demand for relevancy—these people had little patience for anything that was unconnected to their real lives.

- A growing sophistication in communication—from TV to movies to music, the generation that had come of age with The Beatles and *The Graduate* demanded a higher level of creativity from those to whom they gave their attention.

The list could go on and on—this is quite likely the generation that will eventually go down in history as the very first postmodernists. Their approach to life was quite different from the generation behind them, and they required a new form of church if they were to be captured by the unchanging dream of the gospel.

Into this milieu stepped a rising generation of church leaders who responded with new forms of church. Often quite by accident, those new forms—and the vibrant spirit behind them—created the megachurch.

Two Modern Megachurches

Before we parse the characteristics of these churches, let's take a look at the stories of two of them (likely the most influential of the megachurches in the past several decades) that will provide the context for critique.

The Story of Willow Creek Community Church

In 1975, after experiencing unusual growth in a youth ministry that had focused on being a culturally relevant expression of Christianity, Bill Hybels and a team of young enthusiasts started a small church in a rented movie theater in Palatine, Illinois.

The young leaders began by doing a door-to-door survey in their community, asking people who didn't attend church why they did not. According to Lynne Hybels (Bill's wife), in her history of Willow Creek titled *Rediscovering Church*, the surveyors discovered four basic reasons that people avoided church.

◆ **The church was irrelevant to daily life.** Over and over again, people said that when they went to church, they heard nothing that was really of value to their everyday experiences; instead they heard a bunch of doctrine that really didn't mean anything to them.

◆ **The church services were lifeless and boring.** A sense of predictability was so prevalent, that many felt they didn't even need to go anymore—they knew what would happen anyway.

◆ **The preaching was judgmental and harsh.** People said that they got beaten up enough during the week; they didn't need to come to church for the same thing.

◆ **Churches were always asking for money.** 'Nuff said.

Based on these answers, leaders of the Willow Creek Community Church (named after the movie theater where their first meetings took place) set out to create a church that would correct the above, while remaining faithful to a strong, life-changing (and theologically conservative) message of Christ. With a clear goal in mind, an unusually talented group of young leaders, and a commitment to living out an authentic biblical community, the church grew faster than anyone had ever imagined.

Part of the reason was that Willow Creek pioneered what is now known as the "seeker service"—focusing their weekly gatherings on communicating with people who were not followers of Christ. The idea was the opposite of the way most church services were (and are) put together—focusing on the needs of the already convinced. The services included contemporary music (a new idea at the time), live drama (an even more radical idea), and down-to-earth messages that focused on day-to-day needs. Recognizing that many people who were not yet Christians wanted the space to be "anonymous" as they checked things out, the services were designed with a minimum of interaction. Primarily, they were an hour-long presentation of the gospel through various communication vehicles tied around an everyday theme (how to build a strong family, how to be more successful at work, etc.).

> **In Their Own Words**
>
> "Seeker services merely apply Jesus' methods to our generation. While he told parables, we use drama. While he built upon the common knowledge of his day, we tap into current events. While he addressed crowds from a mountainside or boat, we enhance our communication through twentieth-century technology."
>
> —Bill Hybels in *Rediscovering Church* (1995)

By 1977, attendance had reached 2,000. By 1983, attendance was about 5,000. By 1987, it had reached 9,000. By 1995, attendance had reached 15,000. Today, the church is home to approximately 21,000 attendees every weekend.

But according to Willow Creek, the attendance at the weekend services is not the real story. Its leaders say that it never set out to be a big church, just to "be the church to each other and the community." From a pragmatic perspective, one way this has happened over the years is the focus on small groups that form the core of the relationships in the church. These groups, typically of 10–12 people who meet in homes throughout the community, usually operate as a combination Bible study/prayer group/friendship developer. For many, they are the first step into Christian living after making a commitment to Christ in a "seeker service." For others, they function as a primary spiritual growth accountability group. According to Willow Creek, they are a "safe place" to really get to know others, and to be known yourself.

Further, the proliferation of other ministries at Willow Creek provides opportunities for every age group and nearly every interest one can imagine. The church has more than 100 different ministries, from financial counseling to massive helping ministries (food, clothing) for those in need. Examples of the far-ranging ministries include a ministry that fixes up old cars and donates them to people in need, and a ministry called Van Gough's Family, that serves families in whom a member has a debilitating mental health issue. Overall, one could even say that many of these ministries function as parachurches within a church.

In an intriguing turnaround, Willow Creek has started a parachurch organization outside of its church called the Willow Creek Association. As more and more churches began to seek out help from Willow Creek because of its success, the staff of the church began to find it difficult to respond. The WCA was formed in 1992 to help other churches become more able to fulfill their missions. The organization provides training conferences, curriculum and multimedia, and a host of other resources to churches, seeking to network innovative churches together. Currently, there are 11,700 member churches from 90 denominations and 45 countries.

Within Evangelicalism, Willow Creek literally birthed a movement. The term "seeker church" by which many (if not the majority) of megachurches now describe themselves, came directly from Willow Creek. Willow's seeker service model, and much of their seven-step strategic pathway for helping people become "fully devoted followers of Christ," has been essentially copied as the strategic plan and infrastructure for numerous churches. Further, through their conferences (in 2005 attended by almost 100,000 people in North America alone) and the wide reach of the Willow

Creek Association, the church has become one of the most important opinion leaders in all of Evangelicalism. Their history serves as an example of many of the key characteristics of megachurches (as we'll see a little later on).

The Story of Saddleback Church

The only megachurch that has had an influence perhaps greater than Willow Creek in the past few decades is Saddleback Church in Orange County, California.

Once again, the story begins with a visionary. According to his best-selling book, *The Purpose Driven Church*, Rick Warren's journey to eventual megachurch pastor began in 1974, when he first encountered the writings of Donald McGavran. They in turn prompted him to do his own study of the 100 largest churches in America, to determine the underlying principles of their success.

While still in seminary in 1979 (with plans to plant a church upon graduation), Warren wrote to each of the 100 churches personally, including a list of questions he believed would reveal common principles of their success. As he received answers, he also began another quest: to find the fastest growing areas of the United States, where he reasoned there would be a need for new churches. While doing demographic research in a local library, he came upon Saddleback Valley in Orange County—the fastest growing area of the fastest growing county in the United States in the 1970s. Warren had an epiphany. In his own words:

> As I sat there in the dusty, dimly lit basement of that university library, I heard God clearly speak to me: "That's where I want you to plant a church!" My whole body began to tingle with excitement, and tears welled up in my eyes. I had heard from God. It didn't matter that I had no money, no members, and had never even seen the place .... God had shown me where he was going to make some waves, and I was going to have the ride of a lifetime.

The Gospel Truth

The story of Rick Warren and his U-Haul was told over and over again at the seminary I graduated from. Typically, it brought great inspiration to the seminarians—and great nervousness to their spouses!

In late 1979 Warren graduated from seminary, packed all of his belongings into a U-Haul, and with no actual ministry (and no means of financial support) awaiting them, he and his wife and their four-month-old baby headed out from Texas to Southern California.

Wanting to begin the church with a core of people who were not yet believers in Christ, Warren spent

12 weeks going door-to-door talking to people, to find out what they thought about church. At the same time, he started a small Bible Study in his home, which grew to about 15 people or so as he continued to plan for the start of this new kind of church.

Putting together what he heard from his face-to-face interviews, Warren sent out a mass mailing to the community (about 15,000 letters), describing the reasons people did not go to church, and inviting them to a new church designed for "those who have given up on traditional church services."

A little over 200 people showed up for the first Easter Sunday service in 1980. In fifteen years, following a steady path of phenomenal growth, the church grew to over 10,000. According to Warren, during that time Saddleback also saw over 7,000 people come into a relationship with Christ as new Christians.

Although Saddleback was and is very similar to Willow Creek in its contemporary format, it is different in two significant ways. First of all, Saddleback would describe itself from the beginning not as "seeker driven" but as "purpose driven." Practically, this means that the services at Saddleback were always designed to be welcoming to the non-Christian, but unlike Willow Creek, were not designed *primarily* for the unconvinced. The sense at Saddleback was that truth is truth, and if it is presented in an accessible way to both Christians and non-Christians, both will respond. As a result, Saddleback included more congregational singing (soft-rock praise choruses), and other more specifically church-like elements in their services than did Willow Creek.

Secondly, Saddleback's purpose driven model became over the years much more structurally reproducible than Willow Creek's seven-step strategy. Although neither church designed their strategy and infrastructures for the purpose of being copied, over the years, Warren's infrastructure, based on an ingeniously clear model, has proven to be eminently reproducible. As explained in his best-selling *Purpose Driven Church* book (which preceded his *Purpose Driven Life* book), Warren identified five major purposes of the church, and tied clear programming objectives to each of the purposes. Since its publication in 1995, the book (along with numerous conferences and other resources—see later in this chapter), has resulted in literally thousands of churches adopting its simple, yet powerful methods.

Currently, Saddleback Church has an average attendance of 22,000 people a week. In addition, it boasts the vast array of subministries (over 300 by some counts) and small groups that are common to most every megachurch. But significantly, Saddleback, like Willow Creek, has also started its own parachurch organization. Purpose Driven Ministries conducts conferences, provides resources, and has reached over

400,000 church leaders, counting member churches in 162 countries. Twenty-seven thousand churches have gone through the 40 Days of Purpose campaign—an on-site revitalization program that helps them invigorate their church with new vision for outreach and new lay leadership development. Recently, Warren has also launched a major new AIDS initiative, along with an even more far-reaching plan called P.E.A.C.E., the aim of which is to mobilize 1 billion Christians to "Plant churches, Equip servant leaders, Assist the poor, Care for the sick and Educate the next generation." This new focus on caring for those in need seems to be the next incarnation of Saddleback's on-going legacy.

> **Culture Clash!**
>
> Despite their sincerity, much of Saddleback's AIDS initiative is being viewed with skepticism, especially in the gay community. As Kay Warren, who heads the initiative, says, the church will have to "earn our stripes."

Although it is currently not the largest megachurch in the United States (as of this writing, that distinction belongs to a Lakewood Church in Houston, Texas, with a reported 30,000 weekly attendees), Saddleback Church will likely go down in history as the most influential church of its era. In a recent survey, Warren himself was named as second only to Billy Graham (and by less than ten percentage points) in his influence over church leaders. This is a fascinating development—perhaps evidencing that the megachurch is overtaking the parachurch in its overall influence in Evangelicalism.

Key Characteristics of the Megachurch

As the preceding stories show, each megachurch has its own unique characteristics based on its own unique story. However, megachurches as a group do share some important distinctions that are key in understanding why and how the megachurch phenomenon has arisen in modern society. Listed below are a few of the major common characteristics:

- ◆ **Conservative theology.** Nearly all of the current megachurches hold to a conservative theology. The overwhelming majority would classify themselves as evangelical in their beliefs.

- ◆ **High commitment.** Contrary to what many think, the average megachurch calls for—and gets—a generally higher level of both personal spiritual commitment and commitment to the church, than do other churches.

◆ **A strong sense of spiritual vitality.** Perhaps this goes hand-in-hand with high commitment, in a symbiotic relationship. Studies show that a primary reason megachurches grow to their size is because there is a tangible sense of vital spiritual growth happening through the church.

◆ **A strong philosophy of ministry and ministry infrastructure.** From Willow's seven-step strategy to Saddleback's purpose driven model, most megachurches have developed a strong philosophy of ministry that enables strong organizational development. While it may be the Sunday service that draws people to a megachurch, it is the infrastructure of relationships and ministries that keeps them there. Most often, this philosophy includes a bias toward innovation.

◆ **Choice.** The size and scope of the ministries of megachurches are a common denominator to all of them.

◆ **A visionary leader.** As is obvious in the stories of both Willow Creek and Saddleback, megachurches have strong, visionary leaders at the helm. In most cases, the leaders are the founding pastors of the church, but as time passes, the megachurches begun during the baby boomer era are beginning to pass the leadership torch to the next generation. Time will tell if they can do that successfully or not.

Criticisms of the Megachurch

From both inside and outside of Evangelicalism, megachurches receive a mega-share of criticism. Those outside the church criticize the drain on community resources (roads, traffic, etc.) created by megachurches, who don't contribute to the tax base that pays for them. Further, many are suspect of the motives of megachurches, believing them to be all about money and power.

From the inside of Evangelicalism, megachurches are often criticized on several fronts:

◆ **A "soft-sell" of the gospel.** Many see in the "seeker-orientation" of many megachurches a watering down of the message of Christianity. Most studies, however, have shown this criticism to be unwarranted.

◆ **A pragmatic emphasis.** Some evangelicals take issue with the pragmatism that is a part of many megachurch philosophies. From numerical growth targets to modern management methods, some have expressed great fear that the megachurch gains the world but loses its soul.

◆ **A consumer mentality.** This criticism is especially prevalent in the more postmodern-leaning evangelical circles. The emphasis on variety and choice within megachurches have made many wonder whether or not the megachurch form, in and of itself, encourages a consumer mentality with regards to spirituality. "Shouldn't churches be focusing people on personal sacrifice and service, instead of a self-actualizing spiritual experience?" many ask. This is sometimes broadened into a criticism that because of the many choices available at a megachurch, the form encourages individualism instead of communal growth.

Whatever your opinion, one thing is for sure: megachurches are not going away as the baby boomer generation that birthed them ages. According to the most recent studies, the number of megachurches continues to rise in the United States, even among an upcoming, younger, and more postmodern generation.

However, it remains to be seen whether or not the megachurch will become the form of choice for the innovators of this new generation of evangelicals. One could make the argument that megachurches represent the epitome of the modern church. Thus, despite the huge impact megachurches have had on Evangelicalism, they may simply become the "traditional church" that the rising postmodern generation comes out of to create its own new forms.

That generation and the forms that are already starting to emerge will be the focus of our next two chapters.

The Least You Need to Know

◆ Megachurches are usually defined as churches that have 2,000 or more in regular attendance.

◆ The number of megachurches has exploded in the last few decades, and continues to grow.

◆ Among other reasons, megachurches become "mega" sized because they evidence a strong spiritual vitality.

◆ Megachurches provide a wide assortment of ministry choices to their attendees, and these "subministries" are the relational glue that holds the churches together.

◆ Megachurches have been criticized for their pragmatism and sometimes for their theology.

Part 5

The Future of Evangelicalism: The "Emergent" Church

Nothing less than a seismic shift is occurring as the *modern* era of Evangelicalism comes to a close. The passing of the current generation of leadership is giving way to an entirely new expression of Evangelicalism, based on a commitment to relevance in a *post*modern world. This new and growing expression of faith is very different from its predecessor—as different as boomer-based Evangelicalism was to its mainline denominational predecessors. In this section we'll survey the growing influence of what is being called "emergent" or "postmodern" Christianity.

In addition, we'll look at the challenges ahead for both evangelicals and nonevangelicals as our culture moves into the 21st century and beyond.

Chapter **19**

Postmodern Theology Remix

In This Chapter

- What is "postmodernism"?
- A brief description of the "emerging church" movement
- Some questions that the new postmodern movement is generating among modern evangelicals
- Is there a "third way" beyond (not between) conservatism and liberalism?

I sat in a circle with about 25 other people from around the country at an unusual gathering. It had been called together by a group known as Synagogue 3000—a network of Jewish leaders committed to exploring ways to empower Jewish congregations to become even more vital in their faith and in their communities.

I was there as the guest of one of the leaders in a similar Christian network, known as Emergent. This group is committed to exploring new directions for Christian churches in a postmodern world. The Synagogue 3000 folks had invited their Christian counterparts together for several days of discussion, to learn from one another as they both worked on innovating in their respective spiritual communities.

At one point near the end of the retreat, someone asked the Christian Emergent leaders a question about their connection to the evangelical movement. Tony Jones, the National Coordinator for Emergent, answered: "We have a deep *ambivalence* about being called evangelicals," he said. "We have great appreciation for the heritage of which we are a part, but we just don't agree with everything that happens in the evangelical world."

Tony's response is a great snapshot of the emerging, postmodern church movement in its as-yet undefined connection with Evangelicalism as a whole. Whether or not the movement continues to be part of the "evangelical fold" is yet to be seen. However, just as Evangelicalism arose out of fundamentalism in the 1930s and 1940s, creating a seismic shift, so postmodern churches who are blazing their own trails in the early twenty-first century are intimately connected to their evangelical forbearers. Regardless of whether or not they eventually become a completely separate movement, these churches are having a definite impact throughout Evangelicalism today.

Goodbye to Modernism

Step into a postmodern church service, and you will immediately see the practical differences that result from an underlying new philosophy of "doing church." Instead of the brightly lit, religiously neutral setting of a typical "seeker church," you have a darkened room, filled with religious symbols and even perhaps incense and candles. Instead of a speaker on a platform "performing" for an "audience" you are likely to see a person seated on a stool in the middle of a group of worshipers as he or she teaches. Instead of a PowerPoint presentation on a main screen, you are likely to encounter liquid, moving video images all around the room. And instead of focusing on letting people anonymously spectate as they "seek," you are likely to be invited to join in a walk through several interactive "prayer stations," or to join in the creation of a painting that is being made by the whole congregation as the congregation sings. All of these things reflect the needs of a postmodern culture, that is in some ways as different from the baby boomers as the baby boomers who built modern Evangelicalism were from their predecessors.

> **In Their Own Words**
>
> "Remember the point is not just to look cool but to do anything that helps convey the fact that Christianity is a nonmodern religion."
>
> —Dan Kimball, explaining the physical setup of a postmodern church gathering in *The Emerging Church*

Hundreds, if not thousands, of churches of this type are springing up all over the United States. The movement (and calling it a "movement" is fraught with the same difficulties of divergence that are there in calling Evangelicalism a movement) is very young, and thus getting an accurate "count" (or even a clear definition of what to count) is difficult. But the movement—or "the conversation," as it is often called among the leaders—is strong, and it is growing.

By most accounts, the early emerging/postmodern churches began to arise in the late 1980s, typically coming out of established evangelical churches. The young leaders who started them had an intuitive feel that something different was needed—that the typical evangelical experience was not working for their peers. In addition to starting new churches, several prominent evangelical churches (Willow Creek among them) began new ministries to reach twenty-somethings in the early to mid-1990s, also realizing that a different kind of approach was needed. These early churches and "church-within-a-church" ministries blazed the way, and through conferences, conversations, and more experimentation, some common characteristics began to emerge.

What Is "Postmodern"?

The key common characteristic among the emerging churches was and is a consensus that our culture has moved from being "modern" to "postmodern." Understanding that distinction is foundational to understanding the differences between the typical evangelical church that most of this book has been concerned with, and these newer expressions of faith.

The concept of postmodernism is a wide one indeed, and many others have written verbosely and more academically on the subject than I will here. (For a good overview written by a Christian academic, I suggest *A Primer on Postmodernism* by Stanley J. Grenz.) The term began in the arts and in academia (primarily referring to philosophical schools of thought), and eventually made its way to pop culture. It has now spread to everyday usage. For the purposes of our discussion here, we'll focus on its cultural significance with regard to spirituality and the various expressions of church in our culture.

A good starting point is to say that *postmodernism* essentially means "after modernism." Modernism is an overall designation often used to refer to the culture of the past several hundred years that had its roots in the Enlightenment. Modernism is thus

def•i•ni•tion

Postmodernism is a complex term that describes a rising mindset in our culture that questions many of the tenets of modernism, such as a universal worldview, confidence in human progress, and the ability to discern absolute truth.

characterized by a confidence in human knowledge and progress, and the general acceptance of authority that is based on these things. "I think, therefore I am," said Descartes, in a classic expression of the modern point of view.

Postmodernism represents a loss of confidence in these things, and a corresponding search for a new way of thinking and living. It is a rejection of many of the values and beliefs of modernism. The sense is that the "Enlightenment project" has failed. Modern man's confidence in rationalism has produced two world wars, a Holocaust, and the very possible nuclear annihilation of the planet (among other things), say postmodernists. There must be a better way.

The result of this changing philosophy (most scholars say that we are not really fully postmodern yet, but are in a "transition zone" as a culture) are some important characteristics that have worked themselves into the everyday thinking of many people in our culture. Below are a few of the most important characteristics that influence the postmodern expression of faith.

Postmoderns Are Skeptical of Certainty

Because every point of view is simply a view from a point, postmoderns live with the mindset that all claims to absolute truth are suspect. This doesn't mean they don't believe that absolute truth exists, but they doubt that any one person can understand and express it an absolutely true way. There is no such thing as an objective point of view, according to this mindset. This means that Evangelicalism's traditional appeals to the certainty of the over-arching story of God in the Bible (known as a meta-narrative in philosophical circles) are immediately suspect to postmodern non-Christians. They are simply power plays by a particular group of people who want to make sure that their version of reality is the one that wins out.

Postmoderns Are Committed to Pluralism

Because no one can have an absolute handle on things like truth, there is protection in plurality, according to the postmodern mind-set. Thus, there is a commitment to pluralism in all kinds of different expressions, from racial and national pluralism to religious pluralism to sexual pluralism. An example of this is the way this value runs up against the "white-maleness" of the evangelical movement, particularly in its leadership. Such realities in modern Evangelicalism are a cause for extreme skepticism in those of a postmodern bent.

Postmoderns Are Highly Experiential

Since knowledge is relative, only experience is real. Thus, for many postmoderns the primarily cognitive/knowledge-based Christianity of Evangelicalism is not only suspect, it is also highly irrelevant (and uninteresting). Our culture is rapidly moving toward the experiential in everything. From theme restaurants like the Rainforest Café to TV shows like American Idol—where viewers participate in the entertainment experience by voting for the eventual winner—people in our culture want to engage, rather than watch. When even TV—the refuge of the "coach potato"— becomes experiential, then it's obvious something new is afoot across our culture. Leaders of emerging churches have recognized this trend, and are responding.

Postmoderns Value Community

The most real experience of all is the intensity of authentic connectedness. As the world becomes more fragmented, and as absolutes become less and less of an anchor, postmoderns seek out the security of deep and lasting relationships. Indeed, the value of community is much higher for them, particularly for a rising generation who have grown up in households that experienced the highest numbers of divorce in history.

Although modern Evangelicalism has valued community, it has often done so on a *functional* basis—as when a church forms small groups for the purpose of building a structure so the church can continue to grow. Postmodern church leaders see a need for a new kind of emphasis on authentic community. Many of them for that reason are critical of the pseudo-community they often see present in the megachurch model.

 Culture Clash!

According to Dan Kimball in *The Emerging Church*, if, "I think, therefore I am" (Descartes) is the theme of modernism, then, "If it makes you happy, it can't be that bad" (Sheryl Crow) is the theme of postmodernism.

There are certainly many other characteristics of the postmodern mindset that we could explore—deconstructionism, post-structuralism, the impact of the Internet, artistic expression—just to name a few. But these will serve us for now. One further illustration will help to put it all together and set the stage to talk about postmodernism's impact on how evangelicals "do church."

It's a Small World

I remember the first time I went to Disneyland (a modernist playground if there ever was one!). I got on a "ride" called "The Carousel of Progress." As I sat in my theater seat, the round building rotated about every five minutes, each time revealing a new stage on which animatronic people acted out the evolution of the American family over the past hundred years or so. The same robotic family would be updated for each era, and the "actors" would run through a short script that focused on the technology each member of the family used in their everyday lives. "Now is the time, now is the best time, now is the best time of our lives!" went the little "It's-a-Small-World" type ditty—the theme song playing each time the building rotated to reveal a new stage, and a new era. The basic idea behind the exhibit was that as time marches on and technology gets more and more advanced, our lives become better and better through the ingeniousness of human ability. The modern message at its best.

Several years later, I returned to Disneyland. The ride had been replaced. In the same building was a new attraction with a similar theme—modern technological progress— but the delivery was quite different. The new attraction was called "Innoventions" (it is still there as of this writing). Instead of a ride where everyone sits through the same experience, this version is a walk-through where everyone chooses their own experience by going through various rooms at random within the building. Instead of one voice proclaiming the gospel of progress, there were many tour guides, all of whom encouraged interaction with the various exhibits. Instead of quietly, individually sitting through a presentation on your ride, you walk through various areas with other people—the physical space encouraging people to talk about things and try them together as they go through the exhibit.

Now I realize that it's quite a stretch to imagine Disneyland as postmodern, but the fact that "Innoventions" replaced "The Carousel of Progress" is a clear picture of the postmodern mind-set working its way into our culture—even into a part of our culture that is arguably the absolute epitome of modernism. "Innoventions" is about not one story, but many, thus exhibiting both the pluralism and the skepticism of "one voice" that are characteristic of postmodernism. It is also extremely experiential— the level of choosing and interacting with your own experience stands in stark contrast to the rest of the rides in the park that are religiously "programmed" to insure consistency. And it is communal, encouraging interaction in a way that Space Mountain will never be able to do.

A New Kind of Theology

All of this begins to open up a window as to why the emerging churches are emerging. Just like the "Carousel of Progress" found itself out of date, a new expression of church is needed for a new cultural mind-set. It needs to be interactive, communal, and more like a guide for a journey than an authority that sits you down, tells you what to think, and even defines where you will go and when you will go there. Before we describe the details of these new emerging expressions of church (which we'll do in Chapter 20), we first need to spend the rest of this chapter working through the theological shifts that underlie much of the newer practices of postmodern churches.

A bit of a warning here—there is some dense territory in the next few pages. However, the density is necessary to understand how and why the emerging church is different from its predecessors.

Beyond Conservative or Liberal

The foundational shift for emerging theology is, ironically, a shift away from foundationalism. This has to do with how we come to know what we know, or what academics call *epistemology*. (Use that word at a party to impress your friends—if your friends are nerds.) Basically, a foundationalist epistemology asserts that we know what we know by virtue of building new knowledge onto foundational facts that are unassailably true. (If $2 \times 2 = 4$ is true, then $2 \times 4 = 8$ is also true.) Think of it like a building—first you lay the foundation, and then you build the rest of the building on top of it, each part relying on the ones beneath it for its structural integrity.

def•i•ni•tion

Epistemology is (in layman's terms) the study of how we come to know what we know.

In the modern world, nearly all theology was done this way. In very general terms, for conservative theologians the foundation was the Bible, and for liberal theologians the foundation was experience. Postmodern theologians, both conservative and liberal, are less likely to believe that foundationalism is reliable. They would say that foundationalism is a rationalistic basis for epistemology (try that phrase out on some folks to *really* impress them), and that it is thus only one starting place for theology, not the *only* starting place.

A more attractive starting point for most postmoderns is to think of how we know what we know in terms of a web. In nature, a spider holds its web together by virtue of the fact that each strand is connected to and holds up other strands. In terms of knowledge then, a web-based model asserts that our facts are deemed true not by any single foundation, but by virtue of their consistency as they support each other. This is often called "holism." As theologian Nancy Murphy puts it in her book, *Beyond Foundationalism:*

> [H]olism means that each belief is supported by its ties to its neighboring beliefs, and ultimately, to the whole. Justification consists in showing that problematic beliefs are closely tied to beliefs that we have no good reason to call into question. So the coherence of the web is crucial for justification.

This idea of a web of knowledge instead of an unassailable foundation for knowledge is much more in line with the postmodern mindset. In addition to evidencing an appropriate humility with regard to human rationality, it connects with the reality in which most postmoderns live. Indeed, one of the ways postmoderns have been defined by Stanley Grenz in his *Primer on Postmodernism* is as people in whom there exists "an integration of all the dimensions of personal life," and further, as those who recognize "a consciousness of the indelible and delicate connection to what lies beyond [themselves], in which … personal existence is embedded and from which it is nurtured."

In other words, all of life is a web for postmodern people. The experience of surfing a website and clicking on a variety of options in a nonlinear fashion is not only a common occurrence for postmoderns, it is characteristic to their personality.

All of this represents a third-path approach to theology—beyond both modern liberalism and conservatism. It also results in many postmoderns drawing their theology from a much wider array of sources, even as they remain committed to the fidelity, finality, and inspiration of scripture—as befits their evangelical heritage. As this way of thinking develops, in emerging churches it is often being referred to as a "generous orthodoxy."

Let's take a look at how this approach works itself out in the context of three key areas of theology for the postmodern church: the gospel, the Bible, and the church.

A New Look at the Gospel

A web-based paradigm of thinking about theology can lead to a new, more comprehensive way of understanding the gospel. Instead of viewing the essence of the faith as "the four spiritual laws," a less propositional and more web-like approach is possible. Not only is this more consistent with a postmodern mindset, it is also (and more importantly) closer to the biblical representation of the gospel that Jesus taught.

Throughout the gospels, we see Jesus taking a variety of approaches to invite people into the kingdom. From the rich young ruler, who was authoritatively told by Jesus to "sell everything you have and give it to the poor," to the woman at the well who was gently invited by Jesus to take a drink of "living water," there is much more nuance and fullness in Jesus' approach than has often been communicated by modern methods that tend to reduce the gospel to "four spiritual laws" in order to have it make sense to a hurried-up world. Indeed, postmoderns would say that if we look at the way Jesus talked about salvation and the kingdom of God, we come to see that a prepackaged gospel may not actually be an accurate one.

> **The Gospel Truth**
>
> The phrases, "accept Jesus into your heart" and "accept Jesus as your personal Savior"—both of which are so prevalent in modern Evangelicalism—never actually appear in the Bible.

Nancy Murphy takes this idea a step further, stating in *Beyond Foundationalism* that, "The whole of Scripture can be read as a complex identity narrative, telling who God is by recounting his deeds—his promises and fulfillment of those promises in history." Seen in this light, the gospel that comes to us through Scripture becomes less a collection of propositions, and more of a narrative—a story. The web of the gospel comes together like the characters and plot lines of a grand narrative, each leading us through a different approach to the center—God's identity and activity. Further, in this light, spiritual formation for postmoderns is often referred to in the language of "journey"—the story of the individual being intertwined with God's big story of which everyone is a part.

Thus, for the emerging church, the gospel itself—the center of Christianity—is more holistic and expansive than the typical gospel communicated by the modern evangelical movement. As we will see in Chapter 20, this has lots of implications as the emerging church widens its focus beyond individual salvation after death, emphasizing as well the idea of the redemption of all creation, both now and in the future.

Rereading the Bible

This more "narrative" approach to theology brings us to a second key shift that is taking place in the theological underpinnings of the emerging church: a slightly different approach to the Bible.

In modern Evangelicalism, the key issue regarding the Bible was its trustworthiness based on its inerrancy or infallibility. Many postmoderns would say that the doctrines of both inerrancy and infallibility (see Chapter 5) are based on a logical inference about the scriptures that does not come from the Bible itself. The logical inference goes something like this: since the Bible is the word of God, and God is perfect, therefore the Bible must be perfect as well. Anything less is not consistent with God's character.

However, according to many postmoderns, the logical inference part of this argument comes from a typically modern, foundationalistic frame of reference. In other words, inerrancy and infallibility may be more modern doctrines than biblical doctrines. Put another way, they may claim something for the Bible that the Bible never claims for itself. And even more distressing, postmoderns might say that this approach puts a modern filter between the Bible and its reader that actually distorts and blurs the real message of scripture.

Instead of seeing the Bible through the filter of its being a set of propositional truths, postmoderns are moving toward reading the Bible through the lens of it being an ongoing narrative of God's relationship with his creation. On a very practical level, the power of this for postmoderns is that a story can teach truth in a wider and more expansive way than a propositional approach, which can be narrowly focused, and thus reductionistic. A more narrative approach to scripture is therefore preferred by most in the emerging church movement.

In addition to a more narrative approach to scripture, postmodern evangelicals seem also to be finding the authority of scripture in different places than their predecessors did. For them, the Bible's authority is not completely based on its logical consistency and perfection (i.e., inerrancy), it is instead based on its obvious inherent power. The doctrine of infallibility is not being thrown out by postmoderns, but added to it is conversation about the fact that in reading the Bible, its power speaks for itself. It is indeed the very word of God—it renews our minds, convicts us, encourages us, and energizes us for mission. These ideas, for postmoderns, are just as important with regards to the Bible's authority as are ideas like inerrancy and infallibility.

Rethinking the Church

A new understanding of the church is growing within postmodern evangelicals as well. Much of it is in reaction to the consumer mentality seen among many typical evangelical churches, which have become, in the oft-repeated words of many postmodern leaders, "dispensers of religious goods and services."

This may be the most biting critique of the postmoderns toward the modern church, because there is an undeniable element of truth in it. As evangelical church programs have proliferated—with something for nearly every age, interest, and spiritual maturity level—the unintended consequence has sometimes been a tendency of evangelicals to "shop" for a church that "meets my needs." Although evangelical church leaders are quick to note that this has never been their intent, they will also admit that this has indeed happened.

Part of this is connected to a "church as a place where" mentality, instead of a "church as a people who" mentality. Many leaders in the emerging church movement note in their writings that modern language usage about the church betrays a mind-set that is inconsistent with a New Testament definition of the body of Christ.

> **In Their Own Words**
>
> "Churches are called to be bodies of people sent on a mission rather than storefronts for vendors of religious goods and services …"
>
> —George Hunsberger, in *Missional Church*

"I am going to church" we say, instead of "I am the church." Thus, the primary way we think about church is as a place where things happen, instead of a people through whom things happen.

This mentality is being challenged by postmoderns both theologically and practically. On a theological level, the importance of community in both spiritual formation and mission are being rediscovered. On a practical level, lots of experimentation is being done with regards to church forms; in particular the burgeoning "house church" movement (which we'll talk about more in the next chapter) is a picture of this kind of theology that is blooming into practice.

Finally, a new theological conversation is emerging with regard to the future of the church—and the future of those who are not a part of the church. Significant new thought is going into the doctrine of heaven and hell within postmodern theology, and as yet the jury is still out as to whether the prevalent theology of current postmodern evangelicals will, in the long run, remain closer to the traditional evangelical position, or become more pluralistic in its approach.

Questions and Controversy

Of course, all of this has raised questions both inside and outside of the evangelical community. Among other things, there are questions about the emerging movement's understanding of the gospel. Does it emphasize individual conversion enough? There are questions about the emerging theology of the Bible. Is it faithful to the highest levels of respect that evangelicals have traditionally given to the scriptures? There are questions about the church—in particular the future of the church and the future of those who are not Christians. Is universalism creeping into postmodern/evangelical theology?

It's possible that the emerging movement may simply be a next-generation version of what happened with evangelicals in the earlier part of this century. Evangelicals came out of Fundamentalism with a fresh approach, more culturally relevant than the past, and with a few new theological distinctions. Although there seems to be more of an emphasis on theological issues with the postmodern movement, there are striking historical parallels. On the other hand, some are concerned that the emerging movement is a repeat of another historical precedent—more conservative Christianity turning leftward, as in the case of the liberal/conservative split even earlier in this century.

Given the great concern that the emerging church leadership (e.g., author Brian McLaren, Emergent head Tony Jones, Emergent founder Doug Pagitt, etc.) consistently exhibits for theological integrity, it seems more that the first scenario is happening than the second. But in actuality, it is perhaps unfair to draw any parallel at all. This is a new movement for a new era, and it will blaze its own trail.

In Luke 5:36-38, Jesus says:

> No one tears a patch from a new garment and sews it on an old one. If he does, he will have torn the new garment, and the patch from the new will not match the old. And no one pours new wine into old wineskins. If he does, the new wine will burst the skins, the wine will run out and the wineskins will be ruined. No, new wine must be poured into new wineskins.

According to many postmodernists, the Evangelicalism that is prevalent in today's culture is a child of modernity. At its best, the theology of the emerging, postmodern church movement can be likened to "new wine" for a new culture. In the next chapter, we'll take a look at the new wineskins—some of the more practical form changes that this movement is creating for the church of the twenty-first century.

The Least You Need to Know

♦ Postmodernism is a complex term describing a rising mindset in our culture that questions many of the tenants of modernism.

♦ People of a postmodern mindset are (among other things) skeptical of certainty, highly experiential, and interested in authentic community.

♦ The emerging/postmodern church movement is coming primarily out of Evangelicalism, and is addressing the needs listed above (among others).

♦ The emerging/postmodern church movement is not without controversy; many modern evangelicals are concerned about its approach to key evangelical doctrines.

Chapter 20

A New Kind of Church

In This Chapter

- ◆ Is postmodernism all bad?
- ◆ A profile of several key postmodern churches
- ◆ Common characteristics that describe the form of these newer churches
- ◆ An old old ritual with a new new meaning

At one of our Sunday Gatherings not long ago, I asked the people of the church I serve an interesting question.

Back in the '90s, the band R.E.M. had a huge hit with the song, "Losing My Religion." Playing off of that idea, I took out a flip chart, stood in front of the gathered church, and asked, "What about religion would you like to lose?"

As the answers came back, I listed them on the flip chart: judgementalism, meanness, sexism, guilt, a sense that "we've got all the answers, and everyone else is wrong," lack of authenticity, anger. The list went on, and could have gone on longer had I not stopped the group in order to move on with the message I was sharing that morning. What struck me about the list was its consistency. The people of the church were clearly focused on what are often seen as the downsides of evangelical Christianity. They are looking for a new kind of church.

Having briefly traced some of the underlying theology and philosophy of ministry in postmodern churches in Chapter 19, in this chapter we'll take a look at some of the nuts and bolts of this "new kind of church."

The Opportunity of Postmodernism

A lot of the emerging church movement's uniqueness as compared to their evangelical forbearers comes from the fact that they see lots of opportunities in the postmodern mindset for the advancing of the kingdom of God. Many traditional evangelicals simply complain about postmodernism, sort of like the kid with his finger in the dike trying to hold back the flood. But the truth is, the flood is already here. The emerging churches that are successfully reaching our culture are taking advantage of the upsides of the postmodern mindset, including facts such as the following:

♦ **Postmodern people are open to the spiritual.** In past generations, to be "spiritual" was often seen as backwards or uneducated. In today's culture, spirituality is universally accepted—even hip—creating an openness to Christianity that has not been evident for some time in our culture.

♦ **Postmodern people are willing to listen.** Because they are skeptical of any one truth, postmoderns tend to be open to listening to differing perspectives from their own. This creates quite an opportunity for culturally sensitive Christian ministries.

♦ **Postmodern people are impressed by authenticity.** The church—really being the church—*is* impressive. This concept alone could revolutionize the internal workings as well as the external outreach of Christianity. To use an older evangelical term, postmodernism itself could very well be an impetus to true "revival."

♦ **Postmodernism can widen Christian expression.** Modernism as a mindset has constrained evangelical Christianity. For instance, much of its focus in the past few decades has been on "out-logic-ing" the world with regards to the truths of Christianity. Postmodernism provides a bit of a course correction, as it draws out the more experiential side of Christianity. For example, most postmodern churches maintain a higher value on practical service to their community than did their evangelical forbearers.

◆ **Postmodernism restores a Christ-like gentleness to the faith.** The humility characteristic of the postmodern mindset seems to be playing itself out in a more generous and gracious expression of Christianity, in contrast to some of the harder edges of Evangelicalism that have been seen in recent years.

Again, the list could go on. In general, it is important to see that postmodernism, as with any cultural meta-trend, has both downsides and upsides. Successful emerging churches are aware of this, and are responding appropriately.

> **In Their Own Words**
>
> "Q: What do we Christians often call our evangelistic initiatives?
>
> A: Crusades.
>
> Q: How do many Christians describe their social activism?
>
> A: Culture wars, 'taking' America for Christ, etc."
>
> —Brian McLaren, describing the need for a more gentle and culturally sensitive approach in *The Church on the Other Side*

Three Emerging Churches

Below are brief profiles of three emerging churches, each representing one of several different forms that are taking shape in the early years of this movement.

Solomon's Porch—Minneapolis, MN

Identifying itself as a "Holistic, Missional, Christian, Community" Solomon's Porch, near Minneapolis, is a clear example of an emerging church.

The leader of the church is Doug Pagitt. Pagitt previously worked for an influential evangelical parachurch organization known as the Leadership Network, and in the late 1990s he set up several national conferences that gathered together some younger leaders (mainly from larger churches) in postmodern-focused ministries. From those gatherings, Emergent—a network of postmodern leaders which is now perhaps the most visible entity in the postmodern ministry movement—eventually emerged. Pagitt is still involved with the leadership of Emergent.

In 1999, Pagitt formed the community of Solomon's Porch in order to live out biblical values in a way consistent with a postmodern ethos. The church's name comes from a place in the Jerusalem temple where people in Jesus' day would come to discuss spiritual issues. It was also a place of ministry for the early church.

Although the format of the weekly gatherings at Solomon's Porch is obviously different—Pagitt speaks from a stool in the midst of a circle of couches—the real difference in the church is in its intentionality around community. The church's focus is on *being* a community of good news, not just being a church that tells good news.

As Pagitt says in a recent article in Christianity Today's *Leadership Journal*:

> [W]e need to begin by asking some important questions. Why are students transformed by one mission trip? Why does one week with Habitat for Humanity impact an adult's soul in a way 50 sermons never do? Every experience counts for spiritual formation, not just the ones we have in the church building.

The infrastructure of Solomon's Porch is quite different from the kind of evangelical form represented by, for instance, the typical evangelical purpose driven model. Whereas the purpose driven model is very linear in its structure (each step of involvement is clearly defined as to its aim, and based on a sequentially experienced developmental pathway), Solomon's Porch is more fluid in its structure. According to a book about the church written by Pagitt and other participants in the church called *Reimagining Spiritual Formation*, a Sunday worship gathering is often followed during the week by activities such as:

- A Monday yoga class

- A Tuesday Bible discussion group that helps form Paggit's upcoming Sunday message

- A weekly community dinner at someone's home on Wednesday evening

- A "Life Development Forum" (an adult study time on various topics) on Thursday

- A creative team (i.e., visual arts, music, etc.) gathering on Friday

- A community service event on Saturday

This form of spiritual formation, quite different from the more standardized approaches in modern evangelical churches, comes both from the church's value of seeing ministry arise naturally from the needs and gifts of its people, and from a stated corporate value that "God's Spirit takes precedence over structures and systems." As Solomon's Porch continues to live out "missional community," it serves as a prime example of how the values of these new kinds of churches define their forms.

Vintage Faith Church—Santa Cruz, CA

In Santa Cruz, California, a different sort of missional church is growing fast.

Vintage Faith Church, led by Dan Kimball, grew out of the "church-within-a-church" model that was (and is) being practiced in several modern evangelical megachurches. In this case, the church that birthed intage Faith was Santa Cruz Bible Church, a conservative evangelical church of several thousand. According to Kimball, it was felt that to truly be missional in the predominantly liberal and obviously postmodern college town, a new church, not a "church-within-another-church," would be needed.

Birthed in early 2004, Vintage Faith grew in a little over two years to an attendance of about 400. The church's philosophy of ministry is seen through some of the information on its website:

> **In Their Own Words**
>
> According to Dan Kimball, "vintage" faith has a positive connotation in today's culture. It describes a way of "simply looking at what was vintage Christianity. Going back to the beginning and looking at the teachings of Jesus with fresh eyes and hearts and minds."
>
> —From the Vintage Faith website (www.vintagefaith.com)

> We hope to see those who are disillusioned with their evangelical church experience drawn to this type of a church. We hope to see families who resonate with a family-based approach to ministry attracted to this type of Christian community. We hope to see the younger emerging generations who are getting their very first exposure to Christianity drawn to Jesus by being part of this community of faith. We also hope to see those who feel like they could never "fit in" to most churches drawn to the distinctive culture and heart of Vintage Faith Church.

Positioning itself as both an alternative to evangelical churches, and as a place for people to investigate church for the first time, Vintage Faith clearly shows the ethos of many of the newer postmodern churches.

Vintage Faith's approach to infrastructure is clearly more standardized than that of Solomon's Porch. Its primary focus in this regard is on what it calls *Community Groups,* which are virtually the same in structure as most modern evangelical churches' *small groups.* In addition, other Vintage Faith ministry areas for involvement include kids' ministries, youth ministries, compassion ministries, prayer ministries, and media ministries. Although each of these might be found in a more traditional evangelical church, each has a distinctive postmodern flavor that separates it from a more traditional evangelical approach.

For example, the website of Vintage Faith has the following to say about its children's and youth ministries:

> We plan to develop a holistic family ministry at Vintage Faith Church. Approaching the family holistically means that we will have a very strong children's ministry, yet we will not departmentalize ministry to the extent where families never worship together, or have church schedules which separate and cause conflicts in how a family functions in a Christian community. Our youth ministry will also be designed in a very unique way, using a different approach as well. We are extremely passionate about youth since three of our core leaders, Dan, Josh and Rob, have a strong background in youth ministry. Youth ministry is undergoing a transformation right now in America, and we see Vintage Faith Church at the forefront of this new movement for how teenagers can be part of church community.

Further, the church lists a group of ministries it desires to start (many of which may be in action by the time this book is published). The list includes a call for volunteer leaders to be involved in activities such as personal mentoring and spiritual direction, arts-oriented outreaches in the community (such as poetry slams, theater, or visual arts exhibitions), and an Internet team that will develop the utilization of the web as a tool for interaction, discipleship, and outreach.

Vintage Faith is passionate about creating a culture of people "being the church" throughout the week instead of just "going to church" on a Sunday. According to Kimball, they try to break down the traditional status level commonly experienced in churches between those who are the paid "pastors" and the average person in the church. A lot of emphasis is placed on the importance of volunteer leaders being trained to be the "pastors" and leaders of others in the church—not just those with the formal title. The resulting need for training and systems in order to accomplish this goal is a key reason, according to Kimball, that Vintage Faith may not seem quite as free-flowing and unstructured as some other postmodern churches may be.

Overall, Vintage Faith seems to be a leading example of a postmodern church whose organization is more intentionally structured by its leadership.

Mosaic—Los Angeles, CA

If Solomon's Porch represents a more fully postmodern church environment in its structure, and Vintage Faith represents a postmodern church with a more modern structure, Mosaic (in Los Angeles) could perhaps be seen as a bridge from the modern to the postmodern church in Evangelicalism. Incorporating clear elements of modern Evangelicalism, but also exhibiting some postmodern characteristics, the church is an interesting hybrid.

The church is large by most postmodern church standards, with a combined attendance of about 2,000 from its three locations. Although it is a "multisite" church (it meets in Beverly Hills, Pasadena, and downtown L.A.), the Lead Pastor, Erwin McManus, typically teaches in person at all three sites on a given Sunday. McManus, a native of El Salvador, is a visionary leader, similar in many ways to other evangelical megachurch leaders in his entrepreneurial gifts, but different in many of his values and his postmodern-tinged outlook.

> **The Gospel Truth**
>
> Many modern evangelical churches have multisite ministries. As a matter of fact, there are enough of them to have periodic conferences, websites, and a plethora of other resources specifically dedicated to their needs.

For instance, based on a specific vision of McManus's, Mosaic church is very intentionally multiethnic. According to the church's website:

> We are a community of followers of Jesus Christ, committed to live by faith, to be known by love, and to be a voice of hope. The name of our community comes from the diversity of our members and from the symbolism of a broken and fragmented humanity which can become a work of beauty under the artful hands of God. We welcome people from all walks of life, regardless of where they are in their spiritual journey. Come to Mosaic, and discover how all the pieces can fit together!

In addition to its value of diversity, the church further evidences a postmodern mindset in the high value it places on the arts and creativity. According to McManus, in his book *An Unstoppable Force*, the traditional church has in general been "heavy on reason and weak on romance." He states:

> The image we've produced of a biblical congregation has been one in which the teacher taught and the congregants were students in the Bible school of God, but the arts were absent … If the church is to be an expression of an apostolic ethos, then the fingerprint of God's creative hand should be all around us.

Mosaic lives out their value in this regard not only through their regular worship services which include music, dance, and other creative elements, but also in a periodic forum they call Velocity. This purely artistic gathering (i.e., not a worship service) includes the opportunity for artists to sing, dance, show short films, and even do comedy. By providing the opportunity and venue for artists to develop in the context of the church, Mosaic is an example of the desires of many postmodern churches that long for the day when, as McManus puts it his book, "the Steven Spielbergs and the Quentin Tarantinos will be forced to visit churches to keep up with the newest innovations and the most creative artistry."

Mosaic is not a "new" church—it is 60 years old, and has reinvented itself several times. Interestingly, it does not see itself as a part of a specific postmodern movement in evangelical churches. According to one Mosaic staffer, "We wouldn't describe ourselves as emergent, emerging, gen-X, or postmodern. We like to consider ourselves a church with a high view of God, a high view of people, and a high view of Scriptures. We do what we do and how we do it because we are in Los Angeles trying to reach our friends and family. We are a sixty year-old church that has seen part of our calling as creating the future to affect our city and our world. We believe mission is why the church exists and love is the context of mission."

Moving from Modern to Postmodern

There are lots of other churches that could be profiled; there are even postmodern megachurches out there (although some would say that's an oxymoron). Mars Hill Bible Church in Grand Rapids Michigan, for example, currently has an attendance of over 10,000 people per week, and its pastor, Rob Bell, is a best-selling author who defines the best of a postmodern preaching style. He has also created a series of completely unique high-quality, creative, short films that are widely used in teaching in churches and small groups (check them out at www.nooma.com). On the other end of the spectrum, there are also networks of house churches that meet in homes and intentionally stay small, multiplying through new groups starting in more and more homes. This movement is also clearly a trend of the future in postmodern church life.

But even in their variety, some important common characteristics of postmodern-oriented churches can be identified. Below are several of these characteristics that I'll explain by contrasting them to some key modern evangelical church characteristics.

From Pragmatic to Organic

The modern evangelical church, particularly the modern evangelical megachurch, is a model of pragmatism. From the community surveys that are a part of the story of the beginnings of many modern megachurches (see Chapter 18), to target-marketing specific demographics and even psychographics (i.e., Rick Warren's "Saddleback Sam" as described in *The Purpose Driven Church*) as an approach to church growth, the modern pragmatic impulse is part of the DNA of these churches. This has been very helpful in bringing in more learned and sophisticated models to church development, but many postmoderns would say that it is time to reevaluate these kinds of methods in light of a culture that has changed.

A more organic approach, evidenced in many of the emerging churches, places a higher value on naturally occurring ministry that spontaneously arises from the gifts and passions of those involved in the church. These churches focus more on creating environments in which ministry can erupt than on trying to "place" people in already-existing (and sometimes rigid) ministry structures. Further, emerging church leaders would say that organic ministry is naturally generative—it multiplies itself into more ministry through the natural excitement generated by the passion of those involved. Although it presents definite challenges with regard to sustainability (that's a whole other chapter!), an organic approach to ministry is seen by many postmoderns as an antidote to a less soulful "management by objective" approach.

From Rational to Experiential

Rationalism has its roots in the Enlightenment ideals of reason ("I think, therefore I am") and shows up in modern churches in both message and method. As discussed earlier, the modern church's evangelism is focused on a rational, propositionally based gospel. Spiritual formation has been similarly structured, with much of the focus on information-based learning. Further, rationalism shows up in the pragmatic structures of modern evangelical churches, as discussed in the section above.

Culture Clash!

The "experiential" in church seems to be a flash-word for trouble in some evangelical circles. But its tradition goes back a long way—incense was around in Catholicism way before it became a staple of flower-children!

Emerging churches are rethinking rationalism. As a result, they are moving toward a more overall experientially based ethos. This shows up most obviously in the worship services, where experiential interactivity replaces the anonymous spectating valued by many seeker-oriented churches of modern Evangelicalism. Interestingly, the experiential focus often comes into play by resurrecting or reinventing high-church liturgy. In a remix culture, postmoderns are moving Evangelicalism from a focus on the contemporary to a focus on the eclectic.

The experiential value is also obvious in the emphasis placed on creativity throughout the life of the church. Mosaic's Velocity gatherings, for example, are an opportunity not only for the artists, but for the entire church in this regard. Additionally, the experiential focus is evident in the variety of interactive spiritual formation activities prevalent in postmodern churches, such as those that Solomon's Porch makes the centerpiece of its day-to-day church life.

Recognizing that we are immersed in an experience-based culture, a key characteristic that separates emerging churches from their more modern counterparts is this heavy emphasis on creating opportunities for people to engage in highly experiential ways.

From Individual to Communal

Although mostly unintended, modern Evangelicalism leans toward individualism, with its vast variety of ministry choices and its emphasis in its core message on a "personal relationship with Christ." This concept too, is being rethought in the postmodern church.

One clear example is Doug Pagitt's practice of developing his weekly sermon through the process of working through a scripture passage together with his community. (The church also speaks back into the message in a response time during the services after the message has been given—see Pagitt's book *Reimagining Preaching* for more details.) Here, what is normally the most individual of all practices in the life of the church—the preparation and delivery of a sermon—becomes a community event.

Additionally, many emerging churches are becoming more intentional regarding "doing" spiritual growth in community. Newer theological reflections in emerging church writings, for example, are very much oriented toward the idea that spiritual growth happens as much to a community as it does to an individual. In other words, spiritual growth as self-actualization (again, an unintended but often clear message of modern Evangelicalism) is out.

Even conversion is becoming more communal. In a typical modern evangelical church, a person must make a commitment to follow Christ (i.e., have and clearly express a conversion experience) before they would be invited into official church membership. Recognizing that postmoderns want to belong *before* they are likely to believe (because of their high value on community), emerging churches are changing the norms regarding "membership" in churches. Many are dropping the concept altogether, instead opting for an invitation to all to join in some sort of a *covenant* (an in-depth biblical term for promise) of growth together.

From Evangelical to Missional

Overall, much of the difference in the modern and postmodern approach can be summed up in the idea of moving from *evangelical* to *missional*.

An evangelical church typically focuses on bringing a message to the community. A missional church focuses on *being* the message in the community. Leslie Newbigin, a key theologian for postmoderns, puts it this way in his book *The Gospel in a Pluralistic Culture*:

> I am suggesting that the only answer, the only hermeneutic of the gospel, is a congregation of men and women who believe it and live by it. I am, of course, not denying the importance of the many activities by which we seek to challenge public life with the gospel—evangelistic campaigns, distribution of Bibles and Christian literature, conferences, and even books such as this one. But I am saying that these are all secondary, that they have power to accomplish their purpose only as they are rooted in and lead back to a believing community.

In other words, the church—being the church—*is* the primary evangelistic *method* for postmoderns. Everything the church does—from the spiritual deepening of the already convinced, to the practical serving of the community, to verbally sharing their faith with others—is *missional*. The mission is thus a holistic pursuit of *all* of the purposes of God for *all* people and *all* creation. (This is why, for instance, you find many postmodern evangelicals lining up with the political left on issues instead of with the traditional evangelical right.

The Gospel Truth

It may be that the evangelical left (actually more of a centrist position) is currently growing much faster than the evangelical right in today's political arena. Jim Wallis' book *God's Politics* spent many weeks on the *New York Times* best-seller list, and was read and praised by liberals, conservatives, Christians, and non-Christians alike.

See Jim Wallis' book, *God's Politics*, for more details here.) In general, this is a broader perspective than has often been lived out by many modern evangelicals.

Everything Old Is New Again

Key characteristics of emerging churches, then, can be described as organic, experiential, and communal (among others). The movement of these characteristics away from the pragmatic, rational, and individual tendencies of the modern church can be summed up by saying that postmodern strategy and structure is overall a movement from the *evangelical* ethos to a *missional* ethos. And the organic, experiential, and communal characteristics of the missional ethos can be tied directly back to both the Scriptures and church history through a practice described in Scripture and rehearsed through the ages (Matthew 26:26-29):

> While they were eating, Jesus took bread, gave thanks and broke it, and gave it to his disciples, saying, "Take and eat; this is my body." Then he took the cup, gave thanks and offered it to them, saying, "Drink from it, all of you. This is my blood of the covenant, which is poured out for many for the forgiveness of sins. I tell you, I will not drink of this fruit of the vine from now on until that day when I drink it anew with you in my Father's kingdom."

The sacrament of communion is simultaneously organic, experiential, communal, and missional: arising out of life as naturally as a daily meal, extraordinarily experiential in the drama of the body and blood, obviously communal in its implementation, and with a *raison d'etre* of mission.

Here then, is the "new" paradigm for the postmodern church.

The Least You Need to Know

- Postmodernism provides some exciting new opportunities for culturally sensitive Christian ministries.

- Postmodern churches are emerging in many forms, from house churches to megachurches to everything in between.

- A few of the common characteristics that distinguish postmodern churches are that they are moving from pragmatic to organic, from rational to experiential, and from individual to communal in their emphases.

- Overall, a good way to summarize postmodern churches is to say that they are moving from evangelical to missional.

Chapter 21

Looking Ahead ...

In This Chapter

- ◆ A very important final question
- ◆ Four issues that confront Evangelicalism as it faces the future
- ◆ A paradigm for looking ahead
- ◆ An important challenge for nonevangelicals

So—we come to the end of our journey.

We have looked at the history of Evangelicalism, the core beliefs of the movement, how those beliefs translate into both the personal lives of evangelicals and the public life of our culture; we've even looked at the up and coming trends within the movement that may significantly change it in the future. And now it's time for the final question:

So what?

If you've read this far, it's likely you've invested hours in understanding all of this. But when you put this book down and go on with whatever your next activity will be, what will your investment have produced?

Remember that in the "Dear Reader" letter at the beginning of this book, I expressed three goals for the book: (1) A hope that the book would help those of you who are not evangelicals get a grip on the *real* beliefs and practices of Evangelicalism. (2) For evangelicals, my hope has been that reading the book will provide a deeper understanding of your faith community. (3) And for everyone, my hope is that the book creates the opportunity for real, substantive, and gracious conversation.

The first two of those goals, I trust, have been met (at least to some degree) as you've read. But having been around quite a while now in the evangelical mix, I know just how hard the last goal can be. But I'm hopeful. So in order to give you one last push to get involved in the conversation, I'm going to close out the book by giving everyone a few more things to talk about.

As we look ahead, what are some challenges that Evangelicalism faces, and what challenge do I have for those who are not evangelicals?

We begin with four challenges for the already convinced.

Globalization

The first key challenge for evangelicals (that can provide lots of fodder for conversation) is globalization. This book has been focused on American Evangelicalism, but the reality is that American Evangelicalism is only one small part of a vast world-wide movement. Although America has arguably been the center of gravity of that movement over the past century or so, that is changing fast—which is a cause for celebration. So just as globalization is affecting every other area of life through the standardization of mass media, the lowering of trade barriers, the instant world-wide, person-to-person communication of the Internet, and numerous other trends, American Evangelicalism faces the challenge and the opportunity of a new global age. Already, there are obvious signs of globalization's impact on Evangelicalism. Below are just a few.

> **In Their Own Words**
>
> "If the first era of globalization shrank the world from a size 'large' to a size 'medium,' this era of globalization is shrinking the world from a size 'medium' to a size 'small.'"
>
> —Thomas Friedman, in *The Lexus and the Olive Tree*

The Alpha Course

Time magazine said it was "coming to the rescue" of the Christian church in Europe and throughout the world. The *New York Times* said that it is "a novel approach to Christian education that has been catching on nationwide." *Christianity Today* said that it "has succeeded in many cases in turning faithful churchgoers from an inward focus on church work to an outward focus on evangelistic outreach ..."

All of this praise is going towards a course in basic Christianity that has been experienced now by over 7 million people worldwide, and has sparked a revival in Europe that extended to the United States. It is called the Alpha Course, and it began in one Anglican parish in Britain called Holy Trinity Brompton.

Starting off as a course in basic Christianity for prospective members, the course took on new life as one of the associate pastors of the church, Nicky Gumbel, saw its evangelistic potential. The course now consists of about a three-month-long series of weekly meetings, where people first have dinner together, then watch a video of Gumbel describing the basics of Christianity, then have coffee and dessert while they discuss the video in small groups.

The simple approach is creating huge waves across Evangelicalism. Alpha courses are popping up in churches large and small across the world, including the United States, as well as in workplace formats, groups on college campuses, prisons, and in special courses that have been modified for younger students. It has had a marked impact on American Evangelicalism, with thousands of churches crediting it with revitalizing their congregations. This British export is one of the clearest examples of how globalization has affected mainstream American Evangelicalism.

The Korean Megachurch

America may be the home of the super-sized everything, but even the largest megachurch in America is dwarfed by the Yoido Full Gospel Church in Seoul, Korea. Dr. Paul Yonggi Cho founded the church, and still serves at the head of its massive 800,000 membership (yes, you read that right).

Since its founding in 1958, the church has pioneered the development of "cell groups" as a way for a church to continue to grow smaller and larger at the same time. What Cho learned about this method has been a help to both the practical and theological foundations of the growth of the small group movement in American churches (remember, nearly every megachurch relies on some version of this method for creating community among its large numbers). Cho's writings and conferences continue to have an impact on American Evangelicalism, particularly the Pentecostal churches (Cho's church is Pentecostal in its theology). The church, generally believed to be the largest in the world (and listed as such in the Guinness Book of World Records), is the mother-of-all-megachurches.

South America and Latin America

By 2025, scholars tell us that Africa and Latin America will be the center of gravity of worldwide Christianity. Indeed, in his book, *The Coming Christendom*, scholar Philip Jenkins says that, "If we want to visualize a 'typical' contemporary Christian, we should think of a woman living in Nigeria or in a Brazilian *favela*." While evangelical Christianity has been struggling in Europe and growing in the United States, it has absolutely exploded in South America and Latin America; currently there are more Christians in these areas of the world than in the United States and Europe combined.

The impact of this explosion on Evangelicalism is already being seen. In the recent controversies, for example, in the worldwide Anglican church regarding the ordination of gays and lesbians, contingencies from the Southern hemisphere have been leading the conservative charge; evangelical Anglicans in the United States have been much less at the forefront. This is a harbinger of a coming trend across Evangelicalism—the "third church" as it is sometimes called, is fast becoming the first. Indeed, even now, these countries are beginning to send missionaries to the United States, turning the stereotypical idea of global missions (i.e., the white man going into the jungles of Africa) on its head.

> ### The Gospel Truth
>
> Although the United States still sends more missionaries abroad than any other country, other countries are catching up. From Russia to Africa, countries all over the world are now sending missionaries to North America, seeing it as perhaps the largest mission field on the planet.

Obviously, all of this presents great opportunities for Christian Evangelicalism. Church leaders in the United States are generally overjoyed at these developments, representing as they do the forward movement of the biblical mandate to go to "all nations" with the gospel.

The question for American evangelicals is whether or not they will be willing and able to take a back seat when necessary and transfer leadership. Americans tend to be quite ethnocentric, especially the predominantly white male leadership that characterizes modern Evangelicalism. In addition, institutional evangelical churches (and increasingly, some of the larger parachurches) are typically about a generation behind cultural changes. How will they react to globalization? Will Evangelicalism be able to shift with the obvious tide of world culture?

It's a great question for conversation.

Incarnation

A second question for conversation brings us back closer to home—both physically and metaphorically.

The American evangelical enterprise—both in its church and parachurch forms—has over the last century primarily utilized a "come and see" approach to fulfilling its mission. In the postmodern world, this will have to change. Evangelicalism will need to move its emphasis from "attractional" models of ministry to "incarnational" models.

What does this mean? It means that the postmodern culture—even more so than its predecessors—doesn't care what you say until you prove that you care. Incarnational ministry (ministry "in the flesh") focuses on *being* the gospel as the foundation for telling the gospel. This has important and far-reaching implications, especially for the evangelical church.

Returning to the Center

First of all, it means that the "mission" of the church will need to be redefined.

Ask a dozen evangelical church leaders, and you are likely to get two main (and different) answers to the question, "What is the *primary* mission of the church?" Typically, about half will say it's evangelism (i.e., helping others to become followers of Christ), and half will say it's discipleship (i.e., deepening the spiritual lives of those in the church). Of course, those who talk about evangelism as the primary mission will say that discipleship must take place alongside it, and those who identify discipleship as the center will say that deeper Christians will automatically become people who reach out to others. The trouble is, historically, neither one of those statements are automatically true.

To provoke conversation, let me suggest a third way.

What if we took away the false dichotomy between evangelism and discipleship, and instead made *spiritual formation* the center point? For those who are not yet Christians, spiritual growth is a positive idea in our culture today. For those who are Christians, spiritual growth is a huge felt need. Instead of an artificial distinction between believer and nonbeliever in our churches, why not speak to everyone as human beings with the vision and language of being spiritually formed to become the kinds of people Jesus described in the Sermon on the Mount?

Why not position the church as an alternative community that is seeking to live in the way of Jesus? And why not structure our churches around this very thing? One thing this will require is a brand new emphasis on the importance of "doing life together" as a community. No doubt, this will be hard in a culture where everyone is way too busy, but isn't the vision of being an authentic alternative to the craziness of our culture worth it?

As an alternative community within our culture, *the church* then becomes the expression of the gospel. As we serve, as we worship, as we live differently, and as we invite others to join us in this pursuit in our homes, neighborhoods, and workplaces, the alternative nature of our pursuits (if we are indeed pursuing them seriously) will speak volumes to the people around us.

Surprising Evangelism

Here's an interesting anecdote in regard to this "incarnational" model of doing church. Not long ago, the church where I serve took over a local (non-Christian) meals delivery nonprofit organization for a day. We helped gather the food from local vendors, helped cook the food with the help of the staff of the nonprofit, and then spread out all over the community to deliver the meals to folks who needed them.

In the process, we discovered something very important: it wasn't just the people we served who were helped. Of course, it was us too, but I'm talking about something different from even that. As we engaged in this incarnational helping activity, non-Christians from around our community joined in to help. In other words, they were evangelized *by serving*.

> **Culture Clash!**
>
> Instead of arguing about theology, evangelicals and non-evangelicals who try serving together find that the space that separates them is nowhere near as large as they thought …

As we planned the event, our thoughts were running more along the lines of evangelization happening for the people we served. That may have happened as well, but it was the not-yet-Christian people we served *with* who were possibly the most impacted. As they saw an alternative community giving up their time to serve, and as they joined with us in that effort, they encountered the gospel. They were drawn into the life of the kingdom, drawn closer to a group of people seeking to live it, and in the context of ongoing relationships that were forged that day that would never have been created through "normal" church activities, these people are encountering the gospel over and over again. I have no doubt that through their ongoing connection with our body, some of these folks will eventually "hear" the message of Jesus in a way that finally makes sense to them, and they will make personal professions of faith. But it was incarnational living that opened the door.

Now *that's* worth talking more about.

Leadership Transformation

Dan Kimball, in his book *The Emerging Church*, quotes a book by Os Guinness called *Dining With The Devil*, in which Os reports a Japanese businessman saying, "Whenever I meet a Buddhist leader, I meet a holy man. Whenever I meet a Christian leader, I meet a manager."

This brings up a third topic of conversation that I believe is key to the future of Evangelicalism: leadership transformation.

The comment above strikes close to home for me, especially as one who came out of the business world to vocational church work. Often, my bias is towards "getting things done"—and I know that is a bias often shared by many of my colleagues.

Much has been written about this, but in the coming era, there is a great need for pastors and Christian leaders to regain the respect of the culture, not just through their accomplishments, but through their personhood. To a culture that has grown up on Presidential sex scandals, Enron-type corporate scandals, and is turning from Wal-Mart to iTunes to buy their music—power and "bigness" can be suspect.

As we look to the future, this raises an important question: is *all* CEO-type leadership bad in the ministry world? Is *all* holy man–type leadership good for all organizations at all times?

> **In Their Own Words**
>
> "The church of the twenty-first century needs missional thinkers and apostolic leadership."
> —Dr. Eddie Gibbs, in *LeadershipNext*

This is a fascinating—and important— conversation to enter into. For instance, there are many in Evangelicalism today who need to learn to lead in a way that continually restores their soul (and, by extension, the souls of those they lead). Yet there are certainly biblical calls to ambition—Jesus' call to take the gospel to the world is a prime example. Where are the leadership models that balance these issues?

It's a great conversation to have ...

Further, how do shepherd/entrepreneurial leaders learn the skills of what is perhaps the most important leadership trend of recent years—team leadership? Evangelicals, because of their core value of community, have a unique opportunity to show the rest of the world—business, nonprofit, and government alike—what team leadership really looks like.

But again, it all depends on starting the conversation.

Redefinition and Revolution

By definition, evangelicals are out to change the world. So ultimately, how does that "revolution" take place?

Thinking out of the box? Embracing constant change? Driving forward with undaunted entrepreneurial spirit? Spending countless hours in prayer?

Overall, if they are going to be effective for the next millennium, evangelical/emergent expressions of Christianity are going to have to be redefined and/or revolutionized for a new, changed culture. Maybe an old story will help provide some guidance.

It is the story of a university that was building a new campus. As the last blueprints and proposed campus maps were being reviewed, the university president noticed a key omission: no sidewalks had been planned for the school. So the president made an unusual decision—instead of redrawing all of the plans, he simply let the school be built without sidewalks.

After the school was completed, and the students made their way through the campus, the president watched where they walked. Before long, paths began to appear, as the natural flow of the students wore down the grass in certain areas of the campus. After a year, the president ordered the sidewalks put in—along the pathways that the students had already created.

Perhaps this is a picture of how Evangelicalism can operate as it moves ahead—watching where God is laying down pathways through people and culture, and partnering with him by laying down ministries, strategies, and structures that compliment what is afoot. This, of course, requires listening to both God and culture.

And listening, as we all know, is the foundation of good conversation.

A Final Challenge

Finally, a word to the nonevangelicals who have stuck with me this far into this chapter (sorry if you've felt left out of the conversation so far). I have a final challenge for you that concerns another story.

It's a rather odd story of a very wealthy and no doubt cultured man who lived during Jesus' time, and who did something quite strange in order to see what all the fuss about Jesus was.

He climbed a tree.

Zacchaeus was not the kind of guy who was wanting for much. As a tax collector, he had all the material possessions he needed. He was the kind of guy who in our day could buy front row seats to see the Rolling Stones—from a scalper—and not bat an eye.

But this whole Jesus thing was different. Wealth and privilege get you nowhere in the middle of a jostling street crowd. And Zacchaeus was short. So, when this Jesus came to his town, undoubtedly because Zacchaeus had heard so much about him, he decided to get a bird's-eye view to try to understand what all this was about. So he climbed a tree.

In a sense, if you've read through this book, that's exactly what you've done. You've gotten a bird's eye look at this whole thing. From above the fray, you've been able to get a view of what creates all this fuss in our culture. But, like Zacchaeus, there's one more step to take.

When Jesus passed by Zacchaeus, according to Luke 19:5, here's what happened:

> When Jesus reached the spot, he looked up and said to him, "Zacchaeus, come down immediately. I must stay at your house today." So he came down at once and welcomed him gladly.

Jesus' invitation to Zacchaeus was simple: let's have a conversation. And Zacchaeus's response was equally simple: he welcomed the invitation.

Zacchaeus went from an overview to an interview.

Perhaps it's time for you to do the same.

If you've invested enough time and energy to "climb the tree" of this book, it's certainly worth your while to take the next step of connecting with someone personally about it. Find a friend who is of firm belief, and talk to them about what you've read. Take them your hardest questions—talk to them about things that intrigued you (or angered you) as you read—or use the opportunity to ask them about some other spiritual issue that you've wondered about for years.

In other words, let the conversation begin.

May God bless you on your journey.

A

In Their Own Words

In this section are five stories of people who display a wide spectrum of lifestyles and ages. All are evangelicals.

Their stories may well be the most important thing in this book, because through them you can experience evangelicalism in its most authentic form: in the actual lives of the everyday people who live it.

The Politico

John (not his real name) has been active at the highest levels of politics, as you will see from his story below. His description of his own faith and his desires for seeing that faith lived out in the "public square" are both a clear expression of the mind-set of many evangelicals with regards to politics, and—in the process—a stereotype-breaking picture.

It was a scene not uncommon to the American "Public Square."

On the steps of the state capitol behind a nondescript podium with chipped veneer, one speaker after another took turns addressing a modest crowd of "pro-family" activists. A bill that would have granted homosexuals minority class status in the state's labor law was before the legislature and the heat was on to find enough votes to block its passage.

Some of the speakers were conservative Republican politicians, some were from social conservative organizations, some were preachers, but the most prominent was a Presbyterian minister who ran a statewide organization dedicated to stopping the advancement of the homosexual agenda.

I was there that day. As a recent college grad, I was fulfilling my heart's calling and working for a conservative policy organization with strong ties to evangelicals. It was a natural fit for me. Reared in a conservative home that was centered on Christ, I was fortunate to accept Jesus as my savior as a child. I have not known life without him.

My love for politics (my parents report that I kicked and screamed when ordered to bed before Gerald Ford's acceptance speech at the 1976 GOP Convention—I was 8—not normal) and my desire to follow Christ undoubtedly shaped my early career and passions to enter politics. Although I was never completely comfortable with the efforts of the Moral Majority or the Christian Coalition, I certainly worked with activists from those organizations.

So back to the rally on the capitol steps.

I stood there that day off to the side, watching the drama. My organization wasn't participating. It wasn't quite our style but we did share the event sponsor's goal of defeating the legislation.

About 100 yards from the rally, behind a line of portable barriers and a smattering of watchful state troopers, were about 30 gay activists. They were worked up into a bit of frenzy themselves. They were trying to shout down the speakers and were waving handmade signs, mostly with slogans supporting the contentious legislation.

And then I had the moment. One of the defining kind that really shapes you for life.

As my attention shifted back and forth from the fiery orations condemning the homosexual lifestyle to the activists behind the police line, one of the handmade signs held by a gay activist caught my eye.

"Why do you hate me?" it read.

I looked back to the minister. Veins bulging in his neck. Shouting his words in the name of God in angry tones. Fist pumping.

"Ya' know," I thought to myself, "if I was gay I'd think that guy hated me too." And that broke my heart. I had to fight tears.

Sixteen years later I still fight those tears. I remain convinced that my heart broke that day because Jesus' heart was broken also.

To this day, when asked to speak to Christian activists, I tell them this story and challenge them that unless they can love their foes like Christ loves them, then they're not suited to engage public debate and claim to represent a Godly perspective.

My politics remain pretty conservative. I would still oppose legislation like that one, but my epiphany that day has taught me to engage the bare-knuckled world of politics while seeing people, allies and foes, as people that Jesus loves … and so should I. He tells us as much. It shouldn't be hard to figure out, but for some it's elusive.

My life in the arena has often required me to be a political pugilist. I have been tireless and ruthless in pursuit of victory. I hate to lose.

But those are the rules of engagement in politics, and you don't put yourself on the field of play without knowing you could get hit and will have to hit back. It's the way our system is designed to work and it works pretty well.

I used to say I don't let it get personal, but that suggests indifference and conjures up a Godfather-type storyline where it's just "bidness." In fact, for me it *is* personal. I try to see people as creations of God. Loved by him, yearning for them to know Him and follow Him. Conditioned by Christ, I want to love them, too.

That's not always easy, mind you, but it's my desire and it's what I try to do. I know I often fail in the moment, but pray over time I succeed in having a real impact on people's lives by faithfully looking at them with God's eyes.

People look more frail when viewed through God's eyes. Even powerful people.

My journey has taken me into the presence of presidents, prime ministers, kings and generals. I have fielded questions from the well-coifed personalities that read you your news on network television. I have stood in offices only known to most people by how they're depicted in movies. On my wall hang pictures of me with powerful politicians, famous actors, athletes, and even rock stars.

It's been pretty cool.

Some of my colleagues I see get addicted to it. Being around power and fame tends to delude one into thinking they're important. And for fleeting moments I suppose maybe we are from time to time.

But as fun as it all is, I believe being a follower of Christ has kept me focused on life's richest experiences. My family, my friends, and my church.

It hasn't always been easy and I screw up a lot. I've never doubted my faith, but my understanding of God and who he wants me to be is an active journey. I find that following Christ is a very personal and rich experience with many ups and downs.

There are countless days I arrive home and wonder if I was truer to God or Machiavelli during my day's labor. Did I delight in someone's personal failure? Did I really need to express myself with a profanity? Did I respond in kindness? Did I respect the people I interacted with? Did I appropriate my time judiciously?

I'm not sure I've ever lived a day when I could answer all of those questions well. But I have found that God isn't interested in saddling me with guilt (others might be), but rather wants to keep shaping me, using one day after another to teach me something new.

In this personal relationship with God I find my shelter. When I feel vulnerable and weak, I am distant from him. When I am confident and strong I am near Him.

I find new ways to experience Him. Certainly through scripture, prayer, and worship, but also aesthetically, through nature and the arts. I find Him in our country's founding principles of justice and equality, which the Founders found inescapable since we are His creation.

I have found glimpses of God's character revealed to me by studying and observing other traditions. The writings of John Paul II have ministered to me. My heart has been filled with joy watching an Eastern Orthodox peasant woman fervently pray and light candles in her church. The sermons of Martin Luther King, Jr. swell my chest with a passion for justice.

I realize I'm not your stereotypical evangelical Republican. But the reality is, most of my Christian colleagues would tell you a similar story as mine. By and large we don't see the church as an institution that should be playing a significant role in politics. We're passionate about human rights and prefer principled intellectual debate over hyperbole and slogans. We wish more of our supposed leaders would be like the rock star Bono and preach the compassion of Christ for the "least of these" and, like the Irish rocker, organize us to do something about it.

We are patriots and love our nation but understand the difference between God and country. We pray for Muslims and finance Christian missionaries to the Islamic world, but support striking down those extremists who would kill innocents. Free markets make the world a better place, but greedy and corrupt CEOs deserve a long time in prison.

We don't find much use for terms like "Culture War" and would rather find ways to improve the culture rather than withdraw from it. We find self-righteous people of any ideology to be boring, and we like to be challenged to think and understand different perspectives.

Finally, I must confess I hate labels, so imagine how I feel about writing for a book about a label! Call me an evangelical if you must, but I choose to identify with the sentiment of author Donald Miller who, when once asked to "defend Christianity" on a radio broadcast, replied, "I'm not sure I know what Christianity is, but I can tell about my life being a follower of Jesus Christ."

Amen.

The Businesswoman

JoAnne's (not her real name) story, though uncommon due to her leadership in a unique marketplace-focused ministry, points out a common desire of evangelicals to make all of their lives count for God. Her honesty reveals the depth of the spiritual experience shared by most evangelicals, but that is not often portrayed in a sound-byte culture.

Sometimes we just muck it up in the church. We are all trying our best to follow Jesus, to truly live as he would have us live, but sometimes we just flat out muck it up. I was counseling a guy this past week whose church pastors are disappointed that he is spending so much time with our ministry, one that seeks to inspire business people to run their businesses and work in the marketplace according to Biblical principles.

Why in the world are his pastors upset with him? Because he is not ushering at their church as much as he used to. Instead this guy is being turned upside down for Jesus, even though he has been a churchgoer all his life. He is wrestling with what it means to really live as Jesus asked while still functioning in a secular job environment. He is more passionately alive about his relationship with Jesus than he has been in years, and his pastors want him to curb his enthusiasm and show people to their pews. Talk about mucking it up.

I have preached and taught in all shapes and sizes of churches, and this habit we have of making a mess of things and arguing about the wrong issues never ceases to amaze me. I suppose it shouldn't, since the church has been arguing about unanswerable questions for centuries and splitting into what is currently over 35,000 denominations in the United States alone.

So why am I a part of the church? I guess deep down, I still hope somehow we can change all the mess—that we can stop arguing, stop being threatened by other churches and ministries, and be more unified about what really matters—that Jesus Christ rocked the world and will rock anyone's life who is willing.

When people follow my career and my ministry, the most common question they ask is some variation of, "How in the world did you go from being a 'closet Christian' in the corporate world to a business missionary working in an international ministry to transform societies through business?"

I was not raised in a traditional evangelical home, whatever that is. Our family was religiously schizophrenic—Dad was Catholic and Mom was Protestant (Episcopalian, which honestly is about as Catholic as you can get and still be Protestant). There were tensions in our home. My Dad insisted that we kids were raised Catholic, though in the end, not only did he turn away from the Catholic Church, but so did three of the four of us kids. One of my brothers still attends a Catholic Church, but the rest of us have all become born again Christians. I wish we had another name for that since most people cringe when they hear those words.

When I was in high school, my Dad had an affair that broke up our family. It was classic—on the outside and at church, we looked like we were the perfect family, but we were rotting on the inside. None of us had really met Jesus at this time despite years of Catholic church going.

What was a dark time for any teenager got darker when you added in my parents' divorce and several other dramas including what for years I called "the incident," when a guy at the tennis club where I played raped me. Lonely, broken, dysfunctional family, abuse, you name it, stir it all up, and it was a depressing time for me.

I did what I always did when I needed comfort—I found solace in books. Because I was so miserable and broken and negative, I figured that I needed to be more positive, so I started reading a copy of a book called *The Power of Positive Thinking*. The book said to begin saying this phrase as often as you needed to say it: "I can do all things through Christ who strengthens me." Now I sort of knew who Jesus was historically, but since we never actually read our Bibles as Catholics (I know some do, but we never did), I didn't realize at first that this was from a verse in the Bible.

Since I was saying the phrase about a hundred times a day whenever I felt negative, and since the saying started to work, I figured that I needed to know who this Jesus was. So I turned to another book—the Bible. I asked God to show me who Jesus was and to show me the Truth, not the fake pack of lies I had experienced in what we called religion.

I believe God will honor that prayer with anyone. He loves that prayer. So show up he did while I started to read the Bible. He came to life in a way that was real to me. So while I was alone in a room with my two books, I asked Jesus to come into my life and lead it. For a few years, I was never really sure if I had done it correctly, said the right words, you know, so I was always going forward at churches to "learn more about Jesus," which I came to understand later were the secret code words for accepting Jesus into your life at some churches.

Some people have life-changing, whopper dramas when they begin to follow Jesus. My story is more like gradually dipping more of myself into a hot tub and eventually discovering that I am in and warm all over. Things did not magically change with my outward circumstances right away. Over the years, I went to therapy and got healing from the years of brokenness that had built up. I continued to make mistakes, including dating the wrong guys and even getting married and divorced by the time I was 23. At that time, a woman at a church Bible study meeting asked me not to come back when she found out I was divorced. Being young in my faith, I did not know that she was mucking it up and was wrong. I fumbled around in and out of learning about Jesus for some years.

There have been several big "moments," as churchy people like to call them—times when I have made a deeper commitment to Jesus, times when I have given more of myself over to God, and times when I have felt God's love and forgiveness at deeper and deeper levels. I believe these are all part of my conversion, to use another churchy word. My journey to find Truth began when I gave control of my life to Jesus with those two books watching, but has continued and deepened over the decades.

As I began a career and as my faith continued to grow, it was natural for me to wonder how to integrate both faith and work. This has led to a twenty-five-year (and counting) learning process exploring what it means to be a Christ follower at work. How does each influence and inform the other? Over nearly a decade while working full-time as an officer at a Silicon Valley company and an executive at a San Francisco start-up, I also went to seminary at night and learned even more about my faith. It became a natural process for me to blend the two worlds—business and faith.

One watershed moment came when I was on a long flight with a gay co-worker who had become a friend. For nearly a year, I had kept my faith hidden at work because I knew how hated Christians were in my part of the world. But the reading load in seminary was enormous, so on this flight I risked pulling out my Bible to catch up on my assignments. As soon as my gay friend saw it, he rolled his eyes and with disdain said, "You aren't a Christian, are you?" I confessed that I was, and asked why he spoke with such disgust. He shared stories of horrible things Christians had said and done to him in the name of Christ, and his stories brought tears to my eyes. I told him that Christians and people in church had also done painful things to me, but that is not what Jesus was about.

Following a long conversation, I agreed not to judge him but to love him even though I did not live the way he lived or believe what he believed. And I asked him to extend the same attitude to me. That conversation began a lifelong friendship and up to now our relationship includes working at three companies together, and coauthoring two books. We have covenanted to love each other even though our lives may take us in opposite directions. How ironic that it was a gay man who helped me come out of the closet with my Christian faith at work.

The journey to learn about integrating faith and work has taken me from that situation to working undercover for God in several publicly held Fortune 500 companies, to having conversations with nonbelievers about God after staff meetings, to praying with co-workers when trauma hits and more. One thing God has impressed upon me is that even though only about 2 percent of people in my area go to church, most people go to work. And almost all people are hungry for spiritual conversations. Studies also show that jobs are about more than the money. People want to make a difference and to do meaningful work, and to work alongside people they like. I also believe it is a spiritual truth that we are created with a longing to be intimate with God. Understanding these dynamics, the workplace, and not the church, becomes the venue for spiritual conversations to happen.

I am now happily married and a mom. And I now work with an organization that trains people on a business model as seen through the lens of the Bible. What is the purpose of a business according to God? How would God market your products? And how is your career part of your calling to serve God? Asking questions like these and living with the tension in some of the answers is part of the training we offer. Then we take teams of business people overseas in three nations to work with and re-purpose mid-size businesses for the kingdom of God. Pretty funny when you think about it—a skeptic like me who came at the Christian faith backwards and always questioned the type of religion that is packaged up all neat and clean. And now I am leading others to pursue a life sold out to Jesus Christ through the work that they do in their job. One thing I am certain of is that life with Christ is all about authenticity, and if you let it, is a breathtaking adventure!

The Artist

David's story is an excellent example of how someone of a more postmodern bent processes their faith journey. David currently leads a nonprofit ministry called Interfaces, Inc. that is focused on artistic endeavor and the experience of community, connected to both the North American Mission Board of the Southern Baptist Convention, and BayMarin Church in San Rafael, California.

Ten years ago I sat down in a coffee shop on Irving Street in San Francisco, tasted my coffee, looked out the window, and faced the truth. It was my first day of home-lessness. I was experiencing substantial fear, laced with an occasional feeling of excitement and adventure, but mostly fear. I had grown accustomed to certain char-acteristics that identified me, and now through a series of losses, it seemed I had none of them.

Throughout the previous two and a half years, I had consumed myself with trying to keep my design business going. I had put in almost fourteen years, and was deter-mined to keep it. In my determination, I took financial risks that, while somewhat adventurous, left me sitting in that window that day terrified by what had happened. I began to understand the phrase "What a nightmare." I'd had nightmares as a kid, and there was an emotional similarity. Not only did I have no money, but it seemed that I owed money to just about everyone. This was the crash. Now for the burn.

Fourteen years earlier I had started a business, if you can call it that, with some basic equipment: a potter's wheel, an electric kiln, some random art supplies, and $800 in the bank. I set up a small shop where I produced art projects, mostly in clay. My work sold. I became known as a sculptor and an artist. Over the years, I employed a few others, teaching them how to do the work. Eventually, I was running a 12-person shop with some very cool equipment and customers in thirty states. I had somehow found my way into the "giftware industry." There was much about the business that I deeply enjoyed, but it was also extremely hard work, and I was never able to capture the feeling of having what I truly wanted.

During the early years of the business, I met a woman who seemed to fit me well. We were both involved in artistic and creative work (aside from painting and sculpting, I was also involved in theatre). She was exploring the world of the performing arts. She could act, dance, and sing. She was also intrigued with my artwork. Almost from our first meeting, we would make time to hang out with each other and share creative ideas. I was also delighted to discover that she had a strong feeling of devotion to God.

The story she shared about how she encountered Christ moved me deeply. We got married, and both pursued our creative endeavors together.

Having been raised as a preacher's kid in an evangelical Christian family, I was accustomed to the idea that one's faith in God should permeate every area of life, not just the "religious" aspect. I was taught that good behavior pleases God, and I was determined to please him. With that perspective, I prayed regularly that God would help my work flourish and I did my part with good behavior. I was doing alright, but did not feel confident about the future, and I still didn't feel like I had what I wanted. I really didn't know what I wanted. I had assumed that all my creative endeavors would eventually produce a feeling of arrival or fulfillment. Not only did that feeling never come, but life felt flat. I was losing track of things like hope and joy.

One evening in my shop, after everyone else had gone home, I got honest with God. I prayed from the core of my being. I told God that I was tired of trying to please him, and instead, I wanted to know him. I told him that I wanted to feel alive and creative again, like when I was a kid. I wanted to be connected to him deeply and permanently. I meant it, and I knew that he knew that I meant it. I didn't know what would happen, but something was different, like after you make an important choice, but in this case, I wasn't sure what the specifics of my choice would look like.

What happened next, I would have never expected. After praying that prayer, it was as if my life began to unravel; like the proverbial downward spiral. A chain of events began to line up in a way that made me feel like I was being destroyed. One day I received some bad news: my designs were directly copied by another company, one that I hoped would soon become a customer. They employed a Chinese factory to flood the market. I had always been somewhat of an idealist, and did not expect this. By the time I was able to respond, the damage had been done. In the months that followed, I watched my own designs sell more than I had ever imagined and it was making someone else rich.

My wife and I hit a wall. I was determined to salvage what I had worked so hard for, whereas she didn't want to live with that level of stress. She felt like my work had become a mistress, something in competition with our marriage. I plugged in to my work, she plugged in to hers, and we made choices that weren't flowing from our relationship to God, but from selfish ambition. We tried counseling, but one day I found myself sitting with the counselor and my wife never showed. Soon after that, I came home one Saturday evening to a very empty house. I stood there trying to catch my emotional balance. She had moved out. Eight months later she called. She wanted me to know that she was in another relationship with a man, and that they were pregnant.

The next hit was losing my coworkers. We had developed a great work atmosphere that we all enjoyed, but as I continued to lose customers, they needed to find other work. Soon I found myself in an impossible situation, unable to pay the bills. In the end, I lost the shop, and had accumulated so much debt that I could not even afford to pay rent on a place to live. I sold my equipment and other possessions to pay some bills, closed the business, and wondered how I would face the music of debt with no car, no money, and no home.

The accumulated stress had taken a toll on me physically, and I found that I needed surgery on my stomach and esophagus. So there I was, in San Francisco General Hospital, having major surgery, paid for by public funds. I hurt physically, I hurt emotionally, and I hurt spiritually.

But, here I sit years later, looking back with the clarity of hindsight. When I think about that chapter of my life, I see the genius of God and his love for me. That is not what some people would expect me to say, I realize, but it's true. I had filled my life, not with things that flowed from who I am, but with things that were supposed to make me into someone. I was an addict. My addiction wasn't a physical substance, it was found in the props that I set up around myself to make me feel like someone. I had placed my identity in The Artist, The Actor, even The Christian. When I truly gave myself to God that day in my shop, he began to treat the addiction. He wanted to introduce me to my true self, "created in God's image," without the need of props in my life to give me a sense of value. He taught me that we are spiritual beings, and what life on Earth has to offer spiritual beings is not particularly found in the stuff, but in learning truth, and relating deeply with God and with other people. These are things we can keep forever.

It's clear to me now that God was not being mean or cruel when he allowed me to lose everything. At the time, life was extremely painful, but I learned that God is profoundly committed to helping us find our way, even when we have invested heavily in things that are not our true way. Those experiences have resulted in a deep trust in God. I know now that the spiritual journey that is marked by willingness to do anything or to give up anything to live in freedom and in the truth is totally worth whatever else may be lost in the process.

I'm now experiencing a renewal of artistic expression that is unrivaled by anything in the past. I am often sought out by other artists who are looking for a deeper spiritual life and we gather to share our work, give feedback, and so on. The resulting fulfillment and sense of freedom comes, not merely from expressing ourselves artistically, but from the interaction, the trust, and the glimpses of how amazing each person is when seen as the living spiritual story that they truly are. We have been learning that when we are honest and truthful, and create, from that mindset, we resemble God. And shared creativity results in relational and spiritual growth.

My life as a Christian and my life as an artist are, in one sense, the same thing. As an artist, it's my aim to communicate, through some creative expression, what I believe and feel inside. Given my belief that God, in some true sense, lives within me, my art will reveal (in some way or another) God's creativity. My very desire to create reveals that he works through me, and that I myself am a work in progress. My beliefs about Christ, and his passion to see humanity become healed and whole, permeates my artistic expressions, though it may not be obvious in all my work.

Unlike many Christians, I don't have a specific time when I "became one." For me, it's been a spiritual journey through which I've learned how to hear God, how to understand life, and how to find my place and identity as a person. This has all been a continual process more than a moment of conversion. Having been born into an evangelical Christian home, my own experience of coming to faith had less to do with learning evangelical Christianity, since that was already my native culture, and more to do with the discovery that God was actually aware of me, liked me, and could be known by me. His intentions for me actually make sense and fit who I am. He doesn't need me to be particularly religious. What he wants from me has less to do with specific actions, and more to do with being my true self.

The cultural experience of Christianity has a profound influence on my thinking, but ultimately, I had to find God in a way that went beyond "God, the religious icon," and into something real. As a kid in church I believed that God loved people because I was told repeatedly that "God is love." But I also believed that Santa Claus brought gifts to children all over the world at Christmas time, and that he knew who was naughty and who was nice. I was told that repeatedly as well. So when I say that I discovered that God liked me and could be known by me, it came, not from the stories about him, but from God himself. It was a discovery made outside of the cultural experience of Christianity. It was something I found to be true in regular life. I found that relating to God, not as the religious icon, but as a very normal relationship that exists all the time, resulted in a greater understanding of who I am and what I'm made for. I find that my life is a good idea, and that my identity is something God has put thought into. I believe this kind of experience of God is not unique, but available to anyone who wants it.

I still, on occasion, find myself sitting in a coffee shop, looking out the window, and thinking about that day when I spent my last dollar on that cup of coffee. That day I got down to the bottom of myself and discovered that I had indeed been telling the truth when I said I wanted to give myself to God. I would follow him into the vague future with its threats and uncertainty, and believe that he would build me back up into something new. He has.

One of my favorite things about Jesus is that he never asked anyone to do something that he himself wouldn't do. My faith in Christ is based, at least in part, on the fact that he lived a regular life, like mine, pulled it off with exquisite perfection, and now wants to teach us how it's done.

The Parachurch Pioneers

Swede and Judy were among the very first staffers of Campus Crusade for Christ (profiled in Chapter 17). As such, they were a part of some of the biggest "happenings" of the rise of evangelicalism in the 1960s and 1970s. Their personal stories give context to a social movement that is ultimately rooted in a personal faith commitment.

Swede: "We finished high school half a continent apart and then met as freshmen at the University of Colorado in 1956. Judy skied on CU's championship team. I still ski like a midwesterner. But whenever I see the Flatiron mountains behind Boulder, I think about how radically our lives were changed in those four years."

Judy relates: "During high school I changed from a private girls school to a public school. Though my background included church, I was surprised and puzzled by how some of my new friends spoke of God, describing their experience as 'having a personal relationship with Jesus Christ.'

"Two events brought me into that same experience. First was hearing a talk by a Young Life leader explaining that Christ's death on the cross was not just a remote event to atone for the sins of the world, but that it was personal to me, that He loves me and that His sacrifice was for my sin.

"Second, at midnight before leaving for my freshman year at CU, a friend and I went for one last swim at Gravelly Lake. Spring fed, no one had ever found its bottom nor recovered a drowned body from there. So our group of friends was always daring each other to swim there, especially at night!

"Sitting on the dock by myself for a while, I realized that I could go on studying and asking questions about Jesus Christ, but that I now knew enough to make a decision: would I accept Him as my personal Savior or not?

"In silent prayer I invited Him to enter my life, to forgive me. I thanked Him that the cross was for me and that He would begin to make a difference in my life. I knew I had done the right thing.

"In moments I had an assurance that was in total contrast with my previous thinking about religion. I knew that if I dove into the lake tonight and never came up, I would immediately be with the Lord in heaven forever."

Swede says: "Coming from a loving home, but one without any factual understanding of real Christianity, my interest in Christ grew gradually for a year through casual conversations with new friends at CU. But it all turned a corner in one afternoon.

"At the beginning of my sophomore year, I got together at the campus coffee shop with a guy who had just arrived to begin Campus Crusade for Christ's ministry at Colorado. Verne, a couple of years out of college, was likeable, easy to be with.

"He showed me the Four Spiritual Laws, a clear summary of the Bible's teaching about how to begin a personal relationship with God. Religion did not interest me. A personal relationship with the Creator of the universe did. Later that day, alone in my room, I invited Jesus Christ to come into my life.

"No 'religious experience' or special emotion accompanied that prayer. But Verne had explained to me that inviting Christ in might not produce that, that the crucial factor was 'Did I believe Christ would keep His Word? Is He trustworthy? Did I trust Him?'

"I did. And about a week later I found that a deep peace had settled into my heart and a confidence that finally I was linked to God.

"After a new birth, physical or spiritual, growth is normal if we are healthy. We grew spiritually by starting to incorporate 'four talks' into our lives:

"Letting God talk to us (by reading His Word).

"Talking to God (prayer).

"Talking with Christians (that is part of what the Bible calls 'fellowship').

"Talking with non-Christians about the Lord (part of being His witnesses).

"Our lives were beginning to change.

"In the summer before our senior year we each hit a crisis: Judy in Austria, where she was participating in the Experiment in International Living, I in Minnesota at a Campus Crusade conference.

"By now we were straight on the relationship between faith and works. Faith comes first. 'For by grace you have been saved through faith; and that not of yourselves, it is the gift of God; not as a result of works, that no one should boast. For we are His workmanship created in Christ Jesus for good works, which God prepared before-hand, that we should walk in them.' (Ephesians 2:8-10)

"But our commitment to Christ's leadership in our lives, His Lordship, was partial and periodic, not complete. So one day in August Judy biked to the nearby village church and was alone on her knees there for hours. Half a world away, I sat on a big rock by Lake Minnetonka.

"Both of us struggled internally as never before.

"For me, the struggle was between fear and trust. I was afraid of what God might do with me if I entrusted myself completely to Him (Romans 12:1-2). I looked for a friend from CU to listen to me and help me. He took me to Romans 5:8. 'But God demonstrates His own love toward us, in that while we were yet sinners, Christ died for us.'

"It dawned on me! If God loved me enough to give me the maximum gift of all time, His Son, couldn't I trust Him with (by comparison) the much smaller matters of my life and future?

"Back on the rock, I said to the Lord, 'Here's my body. I give it to You. From this point on it is Yours. I don't care where you take me or what it costs. I'm Yours.'"

Judy: "My breakthrough prayer came as I focused on Hebrews 13:5 and 8: 'Be content with what you have; for He Himself has said, "I will never desert you, nor will I ever forsake you."' And 'Jesus Christ, the same yesterday, today and forever.'

"I thought, 'What do I have? What makes up my life?' I thought of people, family, money, plans, dreams, school, everything. Then, holding nothing back, I gave it all to the Lord to completely change it or leave it the same, whatever He chose."

Swede: "Though our issues and our prayers were different, the result was the same. Based on His love for us and unknown to each other, we chose to unreservedly give our lives to Him. From then forward, we have trusted Him to lead us and to enable us.

"And what a life He's given us! Jesus said, 'I came that they might have life, and might have it abundantly.'

"Our relationship changed from rocky and difficult to love. He guided each of us to want to share Jesus' love and truth with collegians, so we joined Campus Crusade staff the year the number of full-time staff went over a hundred en route to its current twenty-six thousand around the globe.

"That steady growth in the movement opened all kinds of opportunities: we opened ministries at Penn, Cal-Berkeley, Washington, Texas Woman's University, Drexel, North Texas State, and more, thus getting to live in several interesting places in the United States.

"We participated in developing new strategies of evangelism and discipleship, like summer beach outreaches and EXPLO '72.

"Wired to work cross-culturally, we have lived in eight countries, three of them in Latin America, four in Europe.

"We invested fifteen years in Washington, D.C., developing outreaches to and opportunities for political, military, and diplomatic leaders. As always, our work there was nonpolitical, interdenominational, and highly personalized.

"For the last fifteen years, we have gone back overseas, working alongside staff colleagues and nonstaff to help them create and develop ministries to their countries' leaders in business, politics, and the arts, in Asia, Latin America, and Europe.

"What an adventure!

"As all this was happening, God gave us three very special children ... what joy they bring to our hearts! ... each of whom now have very special spouses and in each family three great children.

"Campus Crusade's contacts and camaraderie plus our church relationships have been great places to develop family life. We also owe so much to the faculty at the two seminaries and one university where we have had the privilege of doing graduate work.

"And with us all along have been our amazing friends and enablers: individuals, couples, and churches who love us, pray for us, provide our financial support, and have walked close to us through the trying times, for example my battle with pancreatic cancer and Judy's thyroid cancer.

"As age seventy is now in sight, I say of Judy: She is described in Proverbs 31. Read about her there! ' ... She stretches out her hands to the needy ... strength and dignity are her clothing ... the teaching of kindness is on her tongue ... her children rise up and bless her.'

"Our shared life, our love, our children, our grandchildren, our opportunities to make known the love of Christ to others, are all gifts from God. His grace grips us. His love presses in upon us.

"As Judy read that day on her knees in Austria, ' ... He Himself has said, "I will never desert you, nor will I ever forsake you."'"

The Young Dreamer

Jessica is a 19-year-old ballet dancer with a passion for God. Her story shows the youthful enthusiasm of faith that is shared by many evangelicals of her up-and-coming generation.

My name is Jessica, and here is what I would want to be *my* story. I say it in this way because it hasn't fully happened yet. You see, these are my dreams. Being an ambitious young woman I have many of these dreams. Sometimes I get carried away by all the things I would like to accomplish in my lifetime. The neatest thing is when one of my enormous dreams actually comes true. This happened to me about a year and a half ago when I signed a contract with a professional ballet company.

Yes, I am a professional dancer, and yes, I have been envisioning this day since I was a little girl. When I would dream about becoming a ballerina, it seemed so impossible at the time. That reality felt unattainable to me, but I didn't let that get in the way of my vision. I have many other aspirations besides dance. I dream about going back to school someday to become a physician, about getting married and starting a family, and about what it will be like in heaven when I die. Most importantly, however, I dream about how God will use me to demonstrate and share His love for the people of this world.

Yes, I am a professional dancer, and I am a dreamer, but above all, I am Christian. Ever since I can remember I have been aware of God. He is probably the first thing my parents taught me about. As a young child I warmly welcomed Him into my life and have never looked back since. I have never wanted to desert my faith, never desired to leave the church to explore other ideas. I always found hope, comfort, and love in the arms of my Creator and Father. I am not saying that my life has been a smooth ride. I have been faced with many challenges, and my perseverance has indeed been tested, but I have never been able to deny the amazing gift of salvation I have been given by my Jesus. I cannot deny any of the gifts He has given me.

I became a dancer because it was what I loved to do. It made me happy. As I grew older and the thought of making dance into a profession became more vivid, I began to question my validity in venturing into the world of professional dance. I asked myself if that was where I really belonged. "There sure aren't a lot of Christians out there," I would tell myself, as if the art world was some uncharted abyss. Through high school, however, as my ballet training ensued, I slowly came to realize where I stood as a Christian dancer. If I really could "make it," that is, land a job in a professional company, I had no other option *but* to be who I was, wherever I ended up. I am a follower of Jesus Christ; there's nothing more plain and simple than that.

Who cares if I am the only one in my company? What, will all the dancers stone me to death when they discover my faith? Hardly. But the questions I then began to ask myself were these: What exactly does being a Christian mean in an environment like that? How am I to go about sharing the gospel with my fellow dancers? How do I become a dancing evangelist?

When I was introduced to a saying by Marianne Williamson from her book *Return to Love*, I began to understand a new form of evangelism that I could apply to my life as a dancer. She states:

> Our deepest fear is not that we are inadequate. Our deepest fear is that we are powerful beyond measure. It is our light not our darkness that frightens us. We ask ourselves, "Who am I to be brilliant, gorgeous, talented, and fabulous?" Actually, who are you not to be? You are a child of God. Your playing small doesn't serve the world. There's nothing enlightened about shrinking, so that other people won't feel insecure around you. We were born to make manifest the glory of God that is within us. It's not just in some of us; it is in everyone. And as we let our own light shine, we unconsciously give other people permission to do the same. As we are liberated from our own fear, our presence automatically liberates others.

This light, this manifestation of God's glory that Williamson talks about, is in you and in me. When I dance having Christ in mind, I exude this glory from my body, from the very movements I execute. I believe that I can reach people when I am performing onstage, but I can also reach my colleagues when I am performing in the rehearsal studio. By allowing Christ to be represented in my artistic expression, I am able to convey His beauty and creativity without even saying a word. By allowing Christ to be represented in my daily actions and attitudes, I am also able to show the world His mighty strength in my pitiful weaknesses.

A little while ago, during my rookie year of being a professional dancer, I began to doubt whether or not I was really impacting anyone. I had joined the company excited, anticipating a wave of conversions when I arrived, but I met the contrary. I was feeling unnoticed, as if I just blended in with the rest of the crowd. Where was this "light" I was to be shining on to my colleagues? How was I to inspire others with joy when I was becoming overtaken with my own insecurity and vulnerability? Every workday became a task, a burden, something I definitely did not look forward to. I wanted to see lives being changed around me, but felt that was an impossible thought considering my life was falling apart. I was miserable, depressed, and burned out. I began to break down in tears at work, allowing my peers to see my disappointed heart and aching soul. This wasn't my vision of reaching out to God's people at all.

The Lord was still faithful, though. I didn't see it coming, but He used my struggles to touch the life of a young woman in the company. She saw my tears and identified with them. She approached me one day and shared that she too was hurting. We connected because we had something in common: our hardship. We shared with each other about our burdens and encouraged one another with hope. My hope was in the Lord; I challenged her to question where hers was.

Looking back on that experience I see now how God used me. It wasn't in the way I had expected and it wasn't easy, but He still used me to touch a precious individual. You see, this is part of my dream. I yearn to make a difference, to be real with people and to show them that when life is difficult we don't have to go at it alone. I want to reveal to the people around me our need for Jesus, why He is so vital to our existence as humans. God has given us the chance to be liberated, and I dream of expressing this reality in my dancing in such a way that when people watch me, they cannot help but be drawn to Him.

To me, dance is an expression of worship and love for my Lord. I guess if I wasn't a Christian, I would dance for myself, but oh, how disheartening that would be. I would never measure up to my standards; I would always be a failure in my mind. What would be my inspiration to keep going? On the flipside, when I come to my Father with my art, He never turns me away. He delights in my dancing, and He delights in me. I know that when everyone including myself has rejected my creative pursuits, God is still rooting me on. I can rest in knowing that all He asks from me is an honest heart. I can do that.

As dancers, we are extremely hard on ourselves. We are always striving for absolute perfection: in every inch of our bodies, in our musicality, and in our interpretation and artistry. Recognizing that it is much too easy to get discouraged and begin to doubt one's own gifts and talents, I have established the goal of being the mental, emotional, and spiritual "cheerleader" of my company. I want to shine so brightly—that is, I want Christ to shine in me—that the artists around me are inspired to shine too.

I want to help my colleagues be liberated of their fears and dance without inhibition. My dream is that when people watch me dance, I will stand out not because of my exceptional talent, but because they can identify with what is occurring inside my soul. I want my motivation for dance to be recognized, and I want others to question this motivation. I dream of empowering my colleagues, by showing them just how capable they are when they tap into the bigger and greater source of life, the Creator of life Himself.

Glossary

agnosticism A belief that it is not possible to know whether or not there is a God.

atheism A belief in the nonexistence of God.

atonement The theological word used to describe the death of Christ as the payment for the penalty of human sin.

born again Terminology used by evangelicals to describe an experience of personal conversion. Comes from John 3, where Jesus has a conversation with a religious leader (Nicodemus) and tells him that he needs to be "born again" in order to become an authentic God-follower.

camp meeting A frontier camp meeting was a several-day-long camp-out, typically with hundreds of other people, where multiple experiences of singing and preaching were designed to convert unbelievers and encourage new holiness in those who already believed. Camp meetings were an important part of the 2nd Great Awakening in the late 1700s to mid-1800s in the United States.

canon A name for the corpus of books that are accepted as a part of the Old and New Testaments.

CCM An abbreviation for Contemporary Christian Music, CCM has become the primary name used for the genre that regularly outsells many popular acts on the charts today.

charismatic A type of Evangelicalism that emphasizes the gifts of the Holy Spirit (charismata = "grace gift" in Greek). Often this type of evangelicalism is distinguished by exuberant worship including speaking in tongues, miraculous healings, and other supernatural manifestations.

church growth movement A theological perspective that gained important influence in evangelicalism, particularly in the 1970s through the 1990s. Led by Fuller professors Donald McGavran and C. Peter Wagner, the perspective included a pragmatic emphasis on growing churches through the application of sociological, demographic, and modern management techniques to church work.

complementarian Describes the belief of some evangelicals that men and women are created to have different, complimentary roles in the family, in the church, and (to some degree) in society. In this view, men have a core role of leadership, and women of support and nurture.

egalitarian Describes the perspective of some evangelicals that men and women, while distinct in their sexuality, are to share equally the authoritative roles in the family, in the church, and in society at large.

emerging churches A designation increasingly being used to describe churches with evangelical roots that are seeking a more postmodern expression of the Christian faith.

epistemology The study of how we come to know what we know.

Evangelicalism Christianity that emphasizes at least five primary tenants: (1) A focus on the centrality of Jesus' death on the cross as the substitutionary payment for the sins of humankind, and on his bodily resurrection as the confirmation of God's plan in human redemption. (2) A belief in the necessity of personal conversion, based on an understanding of the above. (3) An emphasis on a transformed life based on personal conversion. (4) A passion for social activism based on personal conversion, particularly a high priority on sharing their faith with others. (5) A confidence in the authority of the Bible in all of the above, and in all matters of faith and life.

family values Describes a combination of loosely connected evangelical and conservative beliefs regarding the nuclear family and its operation in society; it connotes support for traditional morality in general. The term has been a widely used political buzz word since the early 1980s.

First Great Awakening An interconnected series of religious events that happened during the mid-1700s in America, and that many scholars point to as the beginning of the evangelical movement in the United States. Led primarily by George Whitfield, Jonathan Edwards, and (by the extension of his methods from England) John Wesley, the Awakening consisted of multiple spontaneous revivals across New England, through which thousands of people were converted to Christianity.

The Fundamentals A twelve-volume series of scholarly theological articles, published in 1910, representing a definitive conservative religious response to theological modernism and its influence in the culture.

Fundamentalism One of the theological streams of belief from which modern Evangelicalism emerged. Fundamentalists share many beliefs of modern evangelicals (a strong emphasis on the Bible, and on personal conversion, for example), but tend to be much stricter and more separatist in their theology and practices. The evangelical movement emerged from fundamentalism in the 1930s and 1940s in the United States, with a more holistic approach to Christianity that also placed a higher value on intellectual scholarship.

incarnation From Latin, "to make flesh," the incarnation describes the Christian belief that, in Jesus, God became a human being.

inerrancy A belief that the Bible is absolutely without error in all its teachings, including those teachings that go beyond theology and have to do with areas like science and history.

infallibility The belief that the Bible is accurate in all its teachings with regard to matters of faith and practice. It is sometimes used as a synonym for inerrancy, but is distinguished by some evangelicals as being a claim for the Bible that is not related to issues in areas such as science, history, or minor internal discrepancies in the Bible.

intelligent design A scientific argument used to counter the Darwinian perspective that gives no place to divinity in the creation of the universe and humanity. Intelligent design proponents hold that evolutionary theory has major "holes" and that a theory that provides for intelligent design of the universe is more consistent with the scientific evidence.

Jesus junk A name often used for the plethora of tacky products (i.e., Christian knick-knacks, t-shirts, etc.) that are sold primarily in Christian bookstores.

kingdom of God Terminology used by Jesus that can be said to describe the realm (anytime, anyplace) in which God's will is done. The kingdom of God is a huge concept in the teachings of Jesus, and can be briefly explained as (1) A gift to receive, (2) A life to inherit, and (3) A mission to enter.

megachurch A megachurch is defined by church scholars as a church that has a weekly attendance of over 2,000 people.

The Millennium The belief held by some evangelicals that as a part of the final events in human history, Christ will set up a 1,000-year reign on the earth.

National Association of Evangelicals The NAE is an association of 45,000 churches and other organizations from over 60 denominations, that exists as a network for ministry and social action. Formed in 1942, the founding organization was a seminal moment for the emergence of modern Evangelicalism out of Fundamentalism.

original sin Refers to the doctrine, held by many evangelicals, that human beings are born into the "curse" of sin (passed down through Adam and Eve's disobedience in the Garden of Eden), and are thus bound to sin. The capacity to overcome sin is only given by God's grace, and only actualized in part in this life.

parachurch A parachurch organization is a Christian group whose mission is directly related to the Christian cause, but is not a church. The word "para" comes from a Greek preposition meaning, "to come alongside."

Pietism One of the theological streams of belief from which modern Evangelicalism emerged. As opposed to the Puritans, who focused on the propositional (i.e., precise, Bible-based theology) to develop their spiritual lives, Pietists emphasized the experiential as key. They were less concerned about the structures and scholastic doctrines of Christian living, and more focused on the individual's personal experiences with Christ. Many scholars see Pietism as the primary progenitor of the modern charismatic movement.

postmodernism A complex term, that as it relates to evangelicalism in this book, describes a rising mindset in our culture that questions many of the tenants of modernism, such as a universal worldview, confidence in human progress, and the ability to discern absolute truth.

premillenial dispensationalism A specific, systematic way of interpreting the Bible. Using a chronology drawn from scripture, it divides human history into five different ages, or "dispensations," in which God has worked with humanity in different ways. It is the theological perspective of many fundamentalist and some evangelical churches. *Premillenial* refers to a specific belief about the order of events at the end of the age of human history, and is the basis of the popular *Left Behind* book series.

Puritanism One of the theological streams of belief from which modern evangelicalism emerged. Puritanism was a reform movement originating during the English Reformation of the sixteenth century. The name came from the desire to purify the Church of England, and eventually expanded into an impulse toward radical individual purity, and the purification of the rest of society as well.

the rapture A belief held by some evangelicals that when Jesus returns, all believers will be miraculously "caught up" in the sky to meet him.

Scopes Trial John Scopes was tried in 1925 for violating a Tennessee law restricting the teaching of evolution in public school classrooms. The trial, and the media circus that surrounded it, are generally seen as a historical marker for the movement of fundamentalism out of the American cultural mainstream.

Second Great Awakening From about 1795 to the late 1840s, what historians generally call "The Second Great Awakening" took the United States by storm. It was again characterized by the conversion of thousands, but also by some different qualities than what had happened a little over a half century before during the first Awakening: (1) It was more wide-spread geographically. (2) It lasted longer. (3) It was more intentionally orchestrated (or encouraged, depending on your point of view). (4) It foresaw the beginnings of institutionalism in Evangelicalism, anticipating the massive evangelical subculture of today. The Second Great Awakening was led by people like Timothy Dwight and Lyman Beecher in the Northeast, various "camp meeting" preachers throughout the frontier, and perhaps most importantly, Charles Finney in upstate New York.

Sermon on the Mount Found in Matthew 5-7, many believe that this is Jesus' definitive teaching on what it looks like to consistently practice a lifestyle of following him, or what many would call "kingdom living."

spiritual habits Often called *spiritual disciplines*, spiritual habits are practices that place one in a position for God to grow them spiritually. Spiritual habits of abstinence are those activities (solitude, fasting, etc.) that enable one to disengage from the normal routine of life, providing space in which God can do his work in their lives. Spiritual habits of engagement are those activities that enable one to connect with God in an active way (prayer, Bible study, etc.), providing an intentional openness to hearing from God for the purpose of spiritual change.

stewardship The word comes from a Greek word that basically translates into modern parlance as "management." Throughout the Bible, God's call to humanity to be careful managers of his gifts is unmistakable. For evangelicals, this means the management of their individual gifts and callings, the management of their time, the management of their possessions, and in a broader sense, the management of God's creation in a just and proper way.

theism A belief that God exists, in some form.

tithing The practice of giving away 10 percent of your earnings.

the tribulation The belief held by some evangelicals that as a part of the final events in human history, believers in Christ will undergo dramatic persecution.

the trinity A doctrine held by Christians that God is one in essence, existing in three persons: the Father, the Son, and the Holy Spirit.

For Further Study

As you've seen, the world of Evangelicalism is large, and incredibly diverse. If you are interested in further study, below is a listing of resources organized according to the flow of this book. I've also commented on each of the books to provide a sense of how they might be helpful.

Obviously, this is a small listing of the resources available. One helpful resource on all things evangelical is the website of *Christianity Today* (christianitytoday.com). It has a very good search engine, and is a great place to start for general info on a wide range of topics regarding Evangelicalism from an evangelical point of view.

Happy reading!

Part 1

Balmer, Randall. *Encyclopedia of Evangelicalism*. Waco, TX: Baylor University Press, 2004.

Just what it says it is.

Larsen, Timothy, ed. *Biographical Dictionary of Evangelicals*. Downers Grove, IL: Iner-Varsity Press, 2003.

Ditto to the above.

Marsden, George. *Reforming Fundamentalism*. Grand Rapids, MI: William B. Eerdmans Publishing Company, 1987.

The history of Fuller Seminary. Through the story of Fuller, you get a good view into Evangelicalism as a whole.

Noll, Mark. *American Evangelical Christianity*. Maiden, MA: Blackwell Publishers, 2001.

A thoughtful and scholarly survey that is less chronological and more thematic. Includes a final section with opinions of the author on the state of Evangelicalism and how to improve it.

Noll, Mark. *The Rise of Evangelicalism*. Downers Grove, IL: InterVarsity Press, 2003.

This is part of a very good new scholarly series that is being published. If you're interested in doing in-depth research, the books in this series may just constitute the definitive history of Evangelicalism (once they are all published).

Rabey, Steve and Monte Unger. *Milestones: Fifty Events of the 20th Century That Shaped Evangelicals in America*. Nashville, TN: Broadman and Holman Publishers, 2002.

For my money, this is probably the best way to get a quick handle of evangelical history. Fun and easy to read, but thorough. By the time you're through, you'll really understand evangelical history.

Sweeney, Douglass. *The American Evangelical Story*. Grand Rapids, MI: Baker Academic, 2005.

A fairly short work; comprehensive in scope.

Part 2

Foster, Richard. *Celebration of Discipline*. San Francisco: Harper and Row, 1988.

Perhaps the most read modern book on spiritual habits. A motivational how-to guide that carries a spirit of warm devotion.

Foster, Richard and James Bryan Smith, eds. *Devotional Classics*. San Francisco: HarperSanFrancisco, 1993.

An anthology of spiritual formation literature. A wonderful introduction to the genre.

Lewis, C. S. *Mere Christianity*. San Francisco: HarperSanFrancisco, 2001.

Undisputed best of its kind. This one has stood the test of time as a very interesting and logical case for Christianity.

McLaren, Brian. *Finding Faith*. Grand Rapids, MI: Zondervan, 2000.

Perhaps my favorite book to give to postmoderns who are seeking God. An excellent resource.

Ortberg, John. *The Life You've Always Wanted*. Grand Rapids, MI: Zondervan, 2002.

A very fun, readable introduction to individual spiritual formation.

Strobel, Lee. *The Case for Faith*. Grand Rapids, MI: Zondervan, 2000.

Strobel, Lee. *The Case for Christ*. Grand Rapids, MI: Zondervan, 1998.

Both of Lee Strobel's books are excellent for someone who needs a lawyerly-like look at the reasonableness of Christianity. Excellently researched and written.

Packer, J. I. *Knowing God*. Downers Grove, IL: InterVarsity Press, 1993.

An evangelical classic. Packer lays out a comprehensive theology of God in layman's terms.

Warren, Rick. *The Purpose Driven Church*. Grand Rapids, MI: Zondervan Publishing House, 1995.

Destined to become the classic explanation of the modern evangelical church. A how-to book for pastors and church leaders.

Willard, Dallas. *The Divine Conspiracy*. San Francisco: HarperSanFrancisco, 1998.

Hands down, the best book I've ever read on spiritual formation. It's dense, however—be prepared to take some time on this one so you can think it through as you read.

Part 3

Alcorn, Randy. *Prolife Answers to Prochoice Arguments*. Sisters, OR: Multnomah Publishers, 2000.

A good overview of the major pro-life arguments.

Bilezikian, Gilbert. *Beyond Sex Roles*. Grand Rapids, MI: Baker Book House, 1985.

A good example of the egalitarian point of view.

Clapp, Rodney. *Families at the Crossroads*. Downers Grove, IL: InterVarsity Press, 1993.

More of a postmodern take on the Christian family. Well written and compelling.

Dobson, James. *The New Dare to Discipline*. Carol Stream, IL: Tyndale House Publishers, 1992.

The classic in its field.

Johnson, Phillip E. *Darwin On Trial*. Downers Grove, IL: InterVarsity Press, 1993.

A classic evangelical critique of Darwinism.

Lewis, Robert and William Hendricks. *Rocking the Roles*. Colorado Springs, CO: NavPress, 1999.

A good example of the complementarian point of view.

Schmidt, Thomas. *Straight or Narrow: Compassion and Clarity in the Homosexuality Debate*. Downers Grove, IL: InterVarsity Press, 1995.

The best book I have ever read on this subject. Comprehensive, balanced, and written with a spirit of grace.

Sheble, Jan. *School Choices: What's Best for Your Child?* Kansas City, MO: Beacon Hill Press, 2003.

Covers public school, private school, and homeschool choices from an evangelical perspective.

Part 4

Hendershot, Heather. *Shaking the World for Jesus: Media and Conservative Evangelical Culture*. Chicago: University of Chicago Press, 2004.

A good introduction to the world of Christian media.

Hybels, Lynne and Bill Hybels. *Re-discovering Church*. Grand Rapids, MI: Zondervan, 1995.

An honest and personal look inside the story of Willow Creek by the wife of its Senior Pastor. An excellent way to get a feel for the megachurch experience.

Martin, William. *With God On Our Side: The Rise of the Religious Right in America*. New York: Broadway Books, 2005.

A very interesting read from a nonevangelical perspective.

Sider, Ronald. *Completely Prolife: Building a Consistent Stance.* Downers Grove, IL: InterVarsity Press, 1987.

An evangelical classic, representing a point of view that doesn't toe the party line.

Wallis, Jim. *God's Politics.* San Francisco: HarperSanFrancisco, 2005.

Wallis is an evangelical who doesn't take the standard conservative approach. Well balanced and well written.

Wilmer, Wesley, David J. Schmidt, and Martyn Smith. *The Prospering Parachurch.* San Francisco: Jossey-Bass, 1998.

A good introduction to the incredibly large and diverse world of the parachurch.

Part 5

Clapp, Rodney. *A Peculiar People: The Church as Culture in a Post-Christian Society.* Downers Grove, IL: InterVarsity Press, 1996.

A good overview of emergent church thinking about the church.

Frost, Michael and Alan Hirsch. *The Shape of Things To Come: Innovation and Mission for the 21st Century Church.* Peabody, MA: Hendrickson Publishers, 2003.

Another influential academic work on doing church in a new way.

Gibbs, Eddie, and Ryan K. Bolger. *Emerging Churches.* Grand Rapids, MI: Baker Book House, 2005.

Possibly the most comprehensive book yet surveying the actual beliefs and practices of new emergent churches.

Guder, Darrell, ed. *Missional Church.* Grand Rapids, MI: Eerdmans, 1998.

A work that is more academic in nature; laying a theological and practical foundation for a new kind of church.

Kimball, Dan. *The Emerging Church.* El Cajon, CA: emergentYS, 2003.

Sort of a "how to" book on doing church in a new way.

McLaren, Brian. *The Church on the Other Side.* Grand Rapids, MI: Zondervan, 2005.

Sort of a "why and how-to" book on doing church in a new way.

McLaren, Brian. *A Generous Orthodoxy*. Grand Rapids, MI: Zondervan, 2004.

An excellent overview of emerging church theology and practice that can be read easily by non-professionals.

McLaren, Brian. *A New Kind of Christian*. San Francisco: Jossey-Bass, 2001.

A book that describes the wrestling that many in the emerging church go through in breaking away from modern Evangelicalism. Written in the form of the story of two friends working through the issues together. Quite compelling.

Pagitt, Doug. *Re-Imagining Spiritual Formation: A Week in the Life of An Experimental Church*. El Cajon, CA: emergentYS, 2003.

A very readable and interesting look into the day-to-day life of an emerging church.

Tomlinson, Dave. *The Post-Evangelical*. London: Triangle, 1995.

An interesting "confessional" by someone who no longer calls himself evangelical.

Wright, N. T. *The Challenge of Jesus*. Downers Grove, IL: InterVarsity Press, 1999.

An influential book in the emerging church that gives a bit of an alternate point of view on Jesus from the standard evangelical picture.

Wright, N. T. *The Last Word: Beyond the Bible Wars to a New Understanding of the Authority of Scripture*. San Francisco: HarperSanFrancisco, 2005.

A very good expression of a new, postmodern approach to taking the Bible as seriously as evangelicals always have.

Index

LET THERE BE ENLIGHTENMENT!

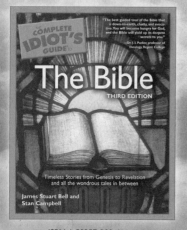

ISBN: 1-59257-389-4

ISBN: 1-59257-347-9

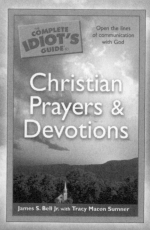

ISBN: 1-59257-582-X

ISBN: 1-59257-429-7

ISBN: 1-59257-345-2

Conversational, easy-to-understand, and fun-to-read books in all of the topics that are important to you and your faith.

ALP